SPORT PSYCHOLOGY LIBRARY:

BOWLING

THE HANDBOOK OF BOWLING PSYCHOLOGY

Praise for Bowling: The Handbook of Bowling Psychology

"Greatness comes to those who are able to combine the best of physical attributes, training, experience, and most of all, the mind. This book reveals, teaches, and inspires any and all bowlers to reach to attain their highest potential. It's an easy to read and understand, in-depth study to help bowlers at every stage, from learners to legends, profit from the psychology of the sport. The authors, aptly recognized worldwide as masters in their help to bowlers, have teamed for a tome that will give you comfort when you seek answers for questions that constantly arise. You will refer to it over and over again—and be rewarded."

—Chuck Pezzano
Noted historian, author of 13 books, and syndicated columnist; Member of 12 Halls of Fame, including PBA and USBC

"In our sport today, a strong mental game is just as important as a strong physical game. Your psychological outlook plays a tremendous part in every tournament, game, and shot. This book has all you need to know about the mental game from pre-shot routine to handling disappointments, from first frame to championship round, from competition to everyday life. It is certainly fitting for every bowler, at every level. I am confident it can take you to the next level in the sport we love."

—Parker Bohn III
PBA Hall of Fame; Twice PBA Player of the Year; 30 PBA Tour titles; 3rd all-time in career PBA earnings

"This handbook is very easy to understand and shows the best way to get to the next level of play. It effectively teaches the mental game by illustrating how various players, each in their own style, use the different techniques in competition. Readers will be able to find what they are looking for to achieve success."

—Carolyn Dorin-Ballard
Twice PWBA Bowler of the Year; 2001 Bowlers Journal International Person of the Year (first woman ever); 20 PWBA tour titles (3 majors); 7-time WIBC All-American

"An excellent book that all bowlers should read. Whatever you're level, it can lift your game. There's abundant insight and recommendations concerning the thinking of elite bowlers … [and] a wealth of information, yet the material is easy to understand. This is not so much a textbook, but real life. It deals with actual situations bowlers face and spells out realistic ways to effectively handle them … Coaches will find the entire handbook a terrific teaching tool."

—Susie Reichley
USBC Hall of Fame; PWBA titlist; Team USA coach, 1994-1999; USBC Gold Certified Coach

"The methods taught in this book have played an important role in my successes. Whether it's handling adversity, blocking out distractions, or feeling good about my game and myself, psychological skills have made a crucial difference. Wherever you are in your bowling career, you can advance to the next level and ultimately reach your potential by using the mental game techniques and principles described in these pages. Each of the authors has contributed to my development. As individuals, they're wonderful teachers and motivators, and as a team they're awesome. In *The Handbook of Bowling*

Psychology, they provide a clear, easily understood game plan for ongoing improvement."

—Michael Mullin
Three-time Collegiate All-American (St. John's); Four-time Team USA member; 1998 US National Amateur Champion & British Open Champion; Winner, 4 High Roller Red Hot Tournaments

"A very easy-to-read book and very good for bowlers at all levels, whether you're just starting out or on the pro tour. The book was immediately helpful for concentration and consistency. During tournament play in recent months, my mind has wandered to thoughts of money I might win or finances in general. Now I'm staying on an even keel, thinking frame-by-frame, and trying to make the same fluid shot every single time.

—Liz Johnson
First woman to reach a PBA Tour title match and first to win a PBA regional; Two-time member of Team USA; Twice US National Amateur Champion

"WHAT A BOOK!!!!!!! There were many times on tour that I certainly could have used it. Wonderful in-depth analysis and in-depth teaching ... world class. Beyond the instruction, the book celebrates the sport of bowling."

—Dave Davis
PBA and USBC Halls of Fame; 18 PBA Tour titles, 6 Senior Tour titles; 7 majors

"A comprehensive, easy to read, extremely well done book. The authors clearly know the sport intimately and have extensive experience in working with bowlers at all levels, especially elite level participants. The book definitely expands knowledge/practice in this sport. There is a great deal of excellent information here that will be helpful to bowlers at all skill levels."

—Michael L. Sachs, Ph.D.
Professor, Dept. of Kinesiology,
College of Education, Temple University; President, Association for the Advancement of Applied Sport Psychology (AAASP), 1991-1992

"A really excellent book . . . My confidence is going to be much better from here on out. I was very impressed by the depth and detail in dissecting the mental game. There are exact descriptions of how to do the techniques ... Part of the book said visualize something positive that happened to you. So I'll go back to winning the US Open and go back to college where I had to double in the tenth frame for us to win the title. Knowing that I came through in the clutch is what I'll focus on and see in my mind. The book gives a blueprint for what bowlers need to get to the next level. I'm going to read it again."

—Kelly Kulick
2003 Women's US Open Champion; 2000 US National Amateur Champion; Three-time Team USA member

"This is a real handbook which bowlers can refer to for problem solving related to most all competitive situations they will face. It also teaches life skills for coping with the stresses outside the center. For a coach, the book can serve as a core instructional manual about the mental game and also provide tools for their own success on the lanes and personally. Technical knowledge aside, what I've always admired about the authors is their heart—the way they believe in their athletes and fellow coaches and accept them as people. I'm glad to say that those qualities come through in this book."

—Ken Yokobosky
PBA Tour bowler; Team USA coach; Owner, Pro-Image Bowling

"The mental game is huge. I've never read anything like it. I wish I had all this information in my prime. During times of doubt and frustration, I would have found a lot in the book very helpful and achieved even more."

—Anne Marie Duggan
Women's Professional Bowling and USBC Halls of Fame; 1994 PWBA Player of the Year; 15 PWBA tour titles (three majors)

"This book is a must-read. It not only teaches how to know ourselves, it rejuvenates the competitor in all of us. This is an excellent step-by-step guide for proper mental training, being realistic about your game, and performing to your absolute best. As a bowler, I've come to recognize my physical limitations, then find and master my strengths. At any level it will make a difference—it did for me."

—Cathy Dorin-Lizzi
1992 Collegiate Champion, US AMF World Cup Champion; & Bowlers Journal International Amateur of the Year; PWBA titlist/ESPN color analyst

"Incredibly comprehensive. This handbook has fully targeted strategies for almost every conceivable situation. Yet there's no jargon and nothing complicated, the chapters flow very easily. While the focus is clearly bowling (including the many detailed examples), the methods and lessons could be applied to any sport and, for that matter, to any area of performance such as academics or the arts. What comes through as you read the book is an overall inspirational sense—that whatever the problem or goal, you can analyze it, apply specific techniques, and experience success. That powerful, hopeful message concerning the achievable is worth the price of admission."

—Andrew S. Gentile, Ph.D.
Founder & President, Empire Health Management; Expert in stress management and visualization for optimal performance

"The lessons in this handbook have already made a huge difference in my bowling and in my life. I can handle many competitive challenges which once got the best of me. I feel confident and focused and in charge of my emotions. Now I deal better with people at work, in my family, and overall. This has opened the door to the person I knew was inside. I can't imagine anyone not benefiting from the book."

—Jose Zambrano
Represented Equador in 2002 Bowling World Cup (Riga, Latvia)

"Dr. Lasser is a tireless researcher who has combined his vast knowledge, the coaching expertise of Fred Borden and Jeri Edwards, and the real life experiences of coaches and athletes from around the world. This has come together to produce possibly the most encompassing psychology book our sport has seen."

—Chris Barnes
2005 US Open Champion; Fastest PBA player to earn $1,000,000; Three-time USOC Athlete of the Year for Bowling; Four-time member, Team USA

"This is the Bible of sport psychology for bowling. Its information is invaluable for both individuals and teams. It will be an essential resource for the athletes I coach."

—Gordon Vadakin
Team USA coach & Head Coach, Wichita State University (14 national championship teams); Twice Team USA member; 1989 Amateur Bowler of the Year

SPORT PSYCHOLOGY LIBRARY:

BOWLING

THE HANDBOOK OF BOWLING PSYCHOLOGY

Dr. Eric S. Lasser

Fred Borden

Jeri Edwards

Fitness Information Technology

A Division of the International Center for Performance Excellence
262 Coliseum, WVU-PE
P.O. Box 6116
Morgantown, WV 26506-6116

The sport psychological techniques or physical activities discussed in this book are not intended as a substitute for consultation with a sport psychologist or physician. Further, because people respond differently, it cannot be guaranteed that these psychological techniques will result in an improvement in sport performance. Readers are encouraged to contact the Association for the Advancement of Applied Sport Psychology, the American Psychological Association, or the United States Olympic Committee for further information about the delivery of sport psychology services.

Library of Congress Card Catalog Number: 2005936453

ISBN: 1885693680

Production Editor: Corey Madsen
Cover Design: 40 West Studios
Typesetter: 40 West Studios
Copyeditor: Corey Madsen
Proofreader: Danielle Costello
Indexer: Corey Madsen
Printer: Sheridan Books

Cover photo © 2006, by Bill Vint, courtesy of Sleeping Dogs Communications. All rights reserved.

10 9 8 7 6 5 4 3 2 1

Fitness Information Technology
A Division of the International Center for Performance Excellence
West Virginia University
262 Coliseum, WVU-PE
PO Box 6116
Morgantown, WV 26506-6116
800.477.4348 (toll free)
304.293.6888 (phone)
304.293.6658 (fax)
Email: icpe@mail.wvu.edu
Website: www.fitinfotech.com

About the Sport Psychology Library

Bowling: The Handbook of Bowling Psychology is a strong, substantial addition to the Sport Psychology Library series. The books in this series take a new approach to the mental game of sports by combining the skills and experiences of athletes and sport psychologists to show athletes, coaches, and parents how to get the most from their sports involvement. Each book in the series focuses on a specific sport so your special questions and needs can be directly addressed.

I am delighted to bring you the most comprehensive and ambitious book yet in the series, *Bowling*. It is the work of renowned bowling coaches Fred Borden and Jeri Edwards, along with esteemed sport psychologist Dr. Eric Lasser. I have known all three for two decades, since we first worked together at the Olympic Training Center in Colorado Springs with the USA National Bowling Team. Fred is one of the most outstanding coaches in the USA—in any sport. He has a remarkable passion for teaching, and he has worked closely over the years with his two outstanding collaborators, Jeri and Eric. Their combined expertise offers you everything you need to become an outstanding and consistently successful professional bowler. Not only is this book filled with useful tips and strategies for mastering the mental game of bowling, it's also full of great stories, memorable photos and illustrations, and stimulating exercises that make it just as entertaining as it is informative. This book is a treasure trove of information and practical tools—I know you will enjoy it as much as I do!

Shane Murphy, Ph.D.
Editor-in-Chief
Sport Psychology Library

Dr. Shane Murphy is the former head of the Sport Psychology Department of the United States Olympic Committee and is currently President of Gold Medal Psychological Consultants.

To

Earl Anthony, Don Johnson, Dick Weber,
and Chris Schenkel

In skill and spirit, they graced our sport.

Table of Contents

Table of Contents

THE SPORT OF BOWLING

A True Test of Mental and Physical Skills

I have bowling, and I am lucky.
Kim Adler

There's one word to describe the scope of bowling as a worldwide sport: huge.

The stats shout out its popularity as the second largest sport in the world*: 120 million participants, 11 million in organized competition, and 200,000 competing at the elite level. In the United States, bowling is one of the very top participant sports—with 46 million adults (70 million, ages 6 and above) on the lanes at least once a year and 3.1 million sanctioned league bowlers.

Bowling is big business around the globe. There are over 12,000 venues and 250,000 bowling lanes. Bowling revenues reach $6 billion per year. For 31 consecutive years, TV broadcasts in the USA attracted the highest ratings in their time slot. The total prize money annually surpasses $2.6 billion. Bowling publications abound—some 75 in the USA and internationally.

The sport's international governing body, the Federation Internationale des Quilleurs (FIQ), was recognized by the International

* Soccer is the largest.

Olympic Committee in 1979. Today there are 122 member federations in 105 countries. Bowling is included in numerous international and regional championships including the Pan American Games, Asian Games, World Games, Central and South American Games, Caribbean Games, the South East and Far East Asian Games, and the Maccabiah Games. Bowling has been an exhibition sport in the Olympics and is anticipating permanent inclusion in the Games.

Clearly, bowling's appeal transcends national boundaries. The sport nearly transcends time as well. The game is rich in tradition—bowling is 500 years older than the Olympics. In fact, its history dates back to 5,200 B.C. in ancient Egypt. In America, the first record of bowling is dated 1611 at Jamestown, Virginia. The colonists were so involved in a game of "bowls" that a rescue ship with supplies from England went unnoticed.

As a competitive sport, bowling presents a truly demanding athletic challenge. Mental and physical precision, exceptional hand/eye coordination, unwavering muscle memory, and endurance are all required for bowling skill. Consider that in any given tournament, a bowler walks four miles; lifts, swings, and releases four tons; and must deliver every ball within four-tenths of an inch of a selected mark in order to reach a target which is 60 feet away and only one and six-tenths inches wide.*

Indeed, the challenges posed by bowling have been described as unique to all of sport. An elite bowler is confronted with a lane surface covered by a microscopic film of oil. To succeed, the athlete must correctly "read" the initial pattern through ball reaction and then continually adjust to constant changes in that surface as the oil moves (it's carried to different parts of the lane and/or absorbed by the ball covers). Due to the invisible frictional variance, the bowler must correctly choose from a wide variety of bowling balls with differing surface and balance characteristics, release every ball at an optimum angle, and make fine adjustments with respect to speed, rotation, and loft.**

In addition to the challenge it offers, bowling has special appeal as a competitive and recreational sport due to several distinctive qualities. The scoring is objective and, therefore, not dependent on potentially controversial judging. It is a gender-equal sport—women comprise 46%

---

* Metric system equivalents are 6.5 kilometers, 3.6 metric tons, one centimeter, 18.3 meters, and four centimeters.
** "Speed" is the ball's velocity down the lane; "rotation" refers to the way the ball spins; "loft" is the distance the balls travels in the air before contacting the lane surface.

of all competitive bowlers. There are no limitations with respect to height, speed, strength, or age: the number of registered youth bowlers tops one million and, in the USA, there is a senior pro tour sponsored by the Professional Bowlers Association (PBA). Also in the United States, there are national associations for blind, deaf, and wheelchair bowlers.

Bowling provides a positive outlet for youth that is safe, drug-free, and family-oriented. It is conducive to team play and other group activities and can be enjoyed by a very wide range of participants. Walk into any bowling center and you may well find a ten-year-old boy and seventy-year-old woman side-by-side on the lanes. It is a sport for a lifetime.[1]

BLUEPRINT FOR VICTORY

How Team USA Won the World Team Challenge

We played like we knew we could.
Chris Barnes

The National Bowling Stadium (NBS) in Reno, Nevada, dazzles the eye and lifts the spirit. During the day, the huge silver globe imbedded in its roof glistens in the sunlight. From the air, the effect is magnetic—drawing attention and demanding a closer look. At night, the multi-tiered stadium is quintessentially 21st century, the fringe of each layered level lit by red or pink or blue neon. The globe reflects this symphony of color while outlined itself by pinpoints of white light.

The structure is architecturally complex, its emotional effect equally so. This effect can be characterized as playful yet intense, a joy to behold, even as it inspires awe. The NBS is truly monumental. It both celebrates and symbolizes the history and current greatness of the sport, while providing a state-of-the-art home base for bowling's growth into tomorrow.

The NBS has hosted many illustrious tournaments. No event, however, was more significant or dramatic than the World Team Challenge in 1995. What unfolded there combined the timeless elements of a classic sports competition with the successful application of psychological skills. It will be your window to the psychology of bowling.

A Unique Tournament

The Brunswick World Team Challenge* was a tournament series intended to promote team bowling and present top amateurs and professional bowlers the chance to compete for a world team title. The climactic event of their ten-month journey was the Grand Championships.

Each national tournament, including the Grand Championships, combined regular team competition with the Baker Scoring System. In the Baker System, each of five players bowls two frames per game. The leadoff bowler rolls the first and sixth frames, the second bowler the second and seventh, and the pattern continues in this fashion, as the anchor bowls frames five and ten.

The Baker System is a very exciting competitive format. Fans get to see varying styles and personalities one right after the other. This type of competition creates unique challenges for the bowler. It places a premium on team communication and requires each athlete to make the most of his or her opportunities.

Team bowling is practiced by millions of bowlers throughout the country and the world. The World Team Challenge innovatively introduced this type of competition to a large television audience. (The televised tournament series was conducted by the American Bowling Congress**—bowling's governing body—and televised to over 40 million homes.)

The 1995 Grand Championships were held in the National Bowling Stadium on July 16-19. Reaching this event represented a major achievement in and of itself, a team survival of the fittest. A record of 1,265 teams had entered the Open Division events and over 100 entered the Women's Division qualifiers.

* 1993-2004
** As of January 1, 2005, The American Bowling Congress (ABC) merged with the Women's International Bowling Congress (WIBC) (overseeing women's competition), USA Bowling (the sport's National Governing Body or NGB), and the Young American Bowling Alliance (YABA) (governing youth to collegiate competition) to form the United States Bowling Congress (USBC). This new organization, as the NGB, is a voting member of the United States Olympic Committee.

These athletes were competing for more than just recognition. The Open Division prize fund was $150,000, while $50,000 was at stake in the Women's Division.

Team USA's Darkest Hour

Among the teams in the 1995 Grand Championships were the Team USA men's and women's squads. (Team USA is our national team and participates in the US Olympic Program.)

To truly appreciate the Team USA performance in the 1995 World Team Challenge, it's necessary to look back at the events of the week preceding it. The site was the same—the National Bowling Stadium— and the event, the World Championships under the auspices of the FIQ. Sixty-one nations competed in this Olympic-style competition, which awarded various individual as well as team medals.

The Americans were just plain stymied. The men's team tied for 9th (out of 60) and the women's team finished 4th (out of 39). Despite the unceasing efforts of bowlers and coaches, the team never matched-up well, never did solve these particular conditions.

There were some unquestionably bright moments, to be sure. An American woman (Liz Johnson) won a silver medal in the singles event and a Team USA bowler (Chris Barnes) earned a bronze in the televised stepladder finals of the men's Grand Masters.

Yet, more was expected from the host team. America had always dominated international events, and it was widely assumed this status quo would hold. However, the worldwide spread of bowling technique, the ready availability of top caliber coaches, and the continuity of team membership enjoyed by many foreign teams were factors which allowed the field to catch up. The result: A week of continual frustration for the US athletes and a pounding in the press.

Even before they could lick their competitive wounds, the US teams were in the midst of another full-pitched battle. The World Team Challenge Grand Championships got underway less than 24 hours after the final note of the last national anthem was sounded at the FIQs.

The Yanks are Coming

Unfortunately, the Team USA men's squad began where they had left off. If they weren't shell-shocked enough before play started, they had every right to feel that way after the first six games. At that point, our national team bowlers found themselves in 16th place out of 29 teams.

What happened next stunned the bowling world. Simply put, America's team (Barnes, John Eiss, Brian Fedrow, Patrick Healey Jr., Ed Roberts, and Mark Van Meter) fashioned an historic charge from behind. Their relentless climb—to 10th after the first Baker round then to 4th after the second—eventually led to a final qualifying match showdown with leader Ebonite International.

Trailing by 30 pins entering this position round, Team USA won both games to end 61 pins up and qualify No. 1 for the stepladder finals. In the words of TV commentator and all-time bowling great, Earl Anthony, "They moved from nowhere to first place." So, America's national team was now one match away from a remarkable and redeeming performance.

Team USA's shot at glory came in the televised two-game championship match against star-studded Turbo 2-N-1 Grips. In another gritty effort, they again stormed from behind to win 370-363. The dramatic high point came in the second game's 9th frame when Eiss' clutch conversion of the rare 3-6-8-10 split set up the win.

Amid the post-match celebration, team anchor Barnes commented, "A lot of people gave up on us last week. They didn't believe in us. They thought we weren't the best team out there. We played like we knew we could."

Head Coach Fred Borden, his eyes moist, delivered these moving words: "These guys are special, they've got heart. It's been a long battle."

In a League of Their Own

Redemption for the American women was equally emphatic, if not quite as complete. Their story was told in *USA Coach* (USA Bowling's newsletter):

> The Team USA women (officially Contour Grips/Team USA)—Lisa Bishop, Kendra Cameron, Missy Howard, Liz Johnson, Lesia Stark, and Janet Woolum—simply outclassed the field (6 teams, whittled down from 105 at the Challenge's start last September). They came out firing, setting a very high standard of play (1015) in their opening match triumph over a scrappy Vise Grips club (featuring the three Edwards sisters*). They never

* Brenda, Kathy, and Jeri

looked back, led wire-to-wire, and finished first among
qualifiers by 414 pins. In fact, the team's margin of victory understated their supremacy. At one point, their
lead was some 800 pins. Only a combination of injury
and the absence of genuine competition kept down their
final count.[2]

Although Team USA finished second best on the TV show to Contour
Power Grips (the qualifying runner-up), their impressive display of
finesse and firepower over several long days had "Number 1" written
all over it.

The Psychology of Victory

The Team USA triumph was a remarkable victory by any standards. It
was all the more noteworthy coming right on the heels of a disappointing
performance.

What enabled these 12 athletes to climb off the FIQ canvas in Rocky
Balboa style? How did they come back over the course of such long,
grinding days? What were the keys to their performing so well in clutch
situations? Through what means did they remain focused and poised
in the face of the most intense tournament pressure, in the glare of
the world media spotlight, surrounded by large crowds and endless
distractions?

A critical factor behind the Team USA success was their mental game
preparation. Maintaining optimal energy, confidence, concentration,
and self-acceptance under rugged tournament conditions required
exceptional psychological skills. Handling adversity, equipment
breakdowns, media pressure, psych-out attempts, and a barrage of
other stressors called for advanced coping abilities. In response to such
demands, the bowlers expressed emotions appropriately, effectively
analyzed their performance and conditions, adapted accordingly, and
oriented themselves towards the immediate future.

As competitive and determined as the Team USA athletes were, their
individual psychological skills by themselves didn't account for the tide-
turning resolve under fire. Team cohesion was vital. Team members
drew strength from one another and rallied as a unit in the severest of
tests. The stressful circumstances could easily have pulled the team
apart. Instead, the 12 bowlers pulled together.

The teaching of psychological skills, including the development of
team cohesion, is an integral part of the Team USA training program.

Team USA 1995: Back row (l to r)—Janet Woolum, Kendra Cameron, Liz Johnson, Missy Howard, Lesia Stark, and Lisa Bishop. Front row (l to r)—Ed Roberts, Mark Van Meter, Patrick Healey Jr., Chris Barnes, Brian Fedrow, and John Eiss.

This is the system which proved so effective:

The year's training begins with a ten-day camp at the United States Olympic Training Center in Colorado Springs. The camp combines on-lane instruction, practice, and competitions (including matches against area all-star teams) with classroom presentations by coaches, bowling consultants, and USOC* specialists. Among the topics are the physical game, lane play, equipment, strength training, and nutrition.

The mental game is taught by the team psychologist in the classroom and in one-on-one meetings. The team psychologist also provides educational consultation to the coaches with respect to the athletes and their own coping skills, lends support and offers input as sought during team events, and helps facilitate team bonding sessions. The coaching staff is highly sophisticated regarding sport psychology. This knowledge

* United States Olympic Committee

influences their teaching style and enhances their interaction with the team. They regularly reinforce the importance of psychological factors. There is an ongoing dialogue (which continues throughout the year) between the head coach and the team psychologist. Ideas are exchanged about all areas of team functioning relevant to sport psychology.

The integral role of sport psychology at the Team USA winter camp is symbolized by the team psychologist's on-lane introduction along with the bowlers and coaches prior to competitions. The high fives exchanged fittingly represent mutual respect and unity in both purpose and spirit.

This camp is followed by other training experiences and regular communication among the athletes, coaches, and team psychologist. Each competitive event provides further opportunity for the application and refinement of skills.

This book can enable you to develop the same psychological skills taught to Team USA athletes—the identical skills which enabled them to win the World Team Challenge.

Partners in Success

The coaching staff, team managers, and team psychologist shared every step of the athletes' journey at the Challenge. Their support contributed to the team effort in numerous ways: information sharing and analysis, adjustments related to physical and psychological skills, emotional bolstering, logistics, and leadership. Also, the staff modeled attributes for success through their overall rapport and interaction, their vitality and pride.

The team psychologist met formally with every athlete and then consulted one-on-one as needed; conducted group relaxation sessions; gave ongoing consultation to the coaches and team managers; offered input at official team meetings and other bonding events; and provided additional assistance.

The crucial role played by the head coach was described in *USA Coach:*

> Head Coach Fred Borden's contribution cannot possibly be overestimated. From unceasing technical insights and guidance to unwavering encouragement, enthusiasm, and bolstering, this guy delivered big time. The quintessential hands-on coach, Borden's soul is the team's soul.[3]

We all need a support team to most effectively cope with on-lane and off-lane challenges. In fact, to succeed and thrive in bowling and throughout our lives, we rely on others—such as family, friends, coach, and teammates. To derive the most from these relationships, communication skills are essential. The book covers this topic as well as provides a guide to selecting the right coach for you.

Sport Psychology's Importance to Bowling

Sport psychology services are accessed today by teams, individual athletes, coaches, and organizations on all levels of sport. The knowledge and tools of sport psychology are improving performance and enriching lives from the pro ranks down to the Little League and all that's in-between.

Psychological factors are directly relevant to how well you bowl. Think about it—to execute properly you've got to exhibit fine motor control and rapid fire decision making regarding lane play adjustments (angle, equipment, speed, rotation, and loft) in what could be called a "pressure cooker" environment. You're faced with all sorts of potential distractions (from events in your life to comments by competitors) and intense competitive challenges. To stay calm, clear-thinking, focused, and confident calls for psychological control. The mastery of psychological skills can enable you to acquire this control and boost your pinfall.

Bowling experts recognize the critically important role played by the mental game. Here's what some have said:

Palmer Fallgren, USBC gold-level coach; former Team USA head coach; PBA titlist: *Your mental game controls the whole bowling process. It's very, very important. I can't stress it enough.*

Parker Bohn III, twice PBA Player of the Year and PBA Hall of Fame member: *I hope everyone understands the importance of a strong mental game. No matter who you are, you need to be strong mentally.*

Pat Henry, head coach, Singapore national team; director of coaching, Singapore Bowling Federation: *We are teaching life skills. That is what makes people succeed at the highest levels. At this level (elite international), it's more a mental game than a physical game.*

Jeri Edwards, Team USA head coach; PWBA* titlist: *Bowling is a very mental game, especially at an elite level.*

* Professional Women's Bowling Association. This league ceased to operate in 2003. At the time of publication, a new tour was forming.

Sam Bacca, professional bowling coach/consultant: *By the time somebody is ready for the pro tour, the game is about 70 percent mental.*

Pat Rossler, Team USA coaching consultant; former head coach, San Jose State University (women's team): *Bowling is a game of emotional management.*

Bowling's Mental Game: Frame by Frame

This book is designed to teach you bowling's mental game in a sequence corresponding to the way you chronologically prepare for competition. Our aim is to maximize your competitive excellence while enhancing your life skills. The book can also be used as a trouble-shooting guide for issues of particular importance.

Part I, "The Fast Lane to Bowling Excellence," presents steps leading up to the day of an event.

Chapter 1 discusses the fundamentals of bowling skill development. The physical game, equipment, playing lanes, and conditioning, along with the mental game, are key areas identified. Two other topics are openness to learning and selecting a coach, both essential to your overall progress and optimal performance.

Chapter 2 tells you how to get the most out of practice sessions. Quality practices are necessary for steady growth and competitive sharpness.

Chapter 3 is a guide to goal setting. You will learn why goals are so important and how to go about selecting the most effective ones.

Chapter 4 considers the training key of mental practice. Ways that this technique can make you a better bowler and the specifics of what to do are covered.

Part II, "Game Face Time," teaches you how to prepare on the actual day of competition.

Chapter 5 recommends two sets of pre-game routines. These are intended to put you in the best possible frame of mind for a maximum effort. The first set consists of activities to do from the time you wake up to the time you enter the center. The second set encompasses psychological preparation inside the center before the start of competition.

Chapter 6 instructs you on what to do prior to each shot. The right pre-shot routine is essential to successful shot execution.

Part III, "Bowling Your Best," provides keys to excellence in performance.

Chapters 7, 8, and 9 present tools for developing and sustaining positive perspective, which is at the core of a strong mental game. In order, the topics covered are confidence, positive ideas, and self-acceptance.

Chapter 10 teaches you ways to better handle the frustrations of competition. The focus here is on what to do within a game in response to circumstances such as a slow start, poor shot, or an opponent's strong performance. Tips on handling success are also provided.

Chapter 11 concerns the multitude of distractions which can break your concentration and lower your pincount. Here you will learn how to better sustain focus or regain focus when encountering adversaries' comments, play stoppage, life stress, and other potentially attention-diverting occurrences.

Chapters 12, 13 and 14 cover the topic of pressure. Chapter 12 shows you how to be aware in the ways essential for managing competitive anxiety. Chapter 13 recommends relaxation techniques for mental toughness in clutch situations. Chapter 14 presents other approaches for handling competition pressure and provides a layout for fashioning an overall strategy for excelling in the clutch. Coming through at "crunch time" is a vital peak performance skill in bowling and all sports.

Chapter 15 provides a framework for coping with competitive outcomes such as the end of a tournament or league session. Completion of a game, block, and qualifying rounds are also discussed. Slump busting is among the topics covered.

Part IV, "Advanced Strategies for Tough Challenges," uses a Q & A format to present effective approaches for demanding situations.

Chapter 16 suggests strategies for adapting to general performance challenges such as low energy, testing lane conditions, dissatisfaction with your equipment, and getting in the zone.

Chapter 17 addresses challenges which involve others. Examples are match play, psych-out attempts, times when others are carrying better, and the lefty-righty controversy.

Part V, "Team and Family," conveys information about the psychology of team play and offers tips concerning specific groups of bowlers.

Chapters 18 and 19 deal with team cohesion. Whether bowling in your home center on a Tuesday evening, the Intercollegiate Bowling

Championships*, the Hoinke Classic, or the World Championships**, team cooperation and unity are vital to success. Chapter 18 focuses on information sharing with Chapter 19 addressing interpersonal support. The communication skills covered are crucial to your relationships with family and friends as well as coach and teammates.

Chapter 20 identifies special performance factors for youth, senior, and women bowlers. Coaches, parents, and teammates of those bowlers as well as the athletes themselves will find the information immediately useful. The potential of bowling to contribute to family life is highlighted.

The **Epilogue, "Glory in Havana,"** presents the account of a special sporting moment epitomizing the application of mental game skills.

Special Section

All the mental game information in this book can be usefully applied by coaches. This, of course, benefits the bowlers they instruct. Because of coaching's importance, we've included some material specifically geared towards the subject (Part V in particular). *The Coaching Corner* segments contain such coaching-related information. This is provided for athletes and parents as much as for coaches since it can help in the process of selecting the right person to guide you.

Who Should Read This Book

Bowlers at every level of development can benefit from the information contained in these pages.

New bowlers should learn the sport more quickly and enjoy success if they're appropriately energized, focused, and confident. Effective communication, the right coaching choice, and responsiveness to input are factors which can contribute to their progress.

Serious bowlers in league competition are continuing to work on essential skills and need to further develop their physical game. The previously cited psychological influences are directly relevant to performance and growth. At the same time, they must confront the challenges and frustrations of team play. Factors impacting team cohesion and adjustment to the stress of team-based competition become increasingly significant.

* As of 2006, renamed the USBC Intercollegiate Team Championships
** Beginning in 2005, divided into women's and men's tournaments, alternating yearly

Advanced bowlers (200-215 range) are seeking to refine their physical game, gain more knowledge about lane play, and increase their equipment repertoire. Entering tournament play, they're confronted with competitors possessing more advanced games. At this level, bowlers commonly worry about their own potential and how to realize it. The need for a well-developed mental game is more important than ever due to the multitude of game stressors. Methods for confidence building (including quality practices) may prove especially useful.

The top level elite bowler (215 and above)—whether a professional or elite amateur—encounters distinct financial pressures, sponsor-related issues, and varied circumstances unique to tour play and top flight tournaments. Facing the strongest of competitors, there's only the smallest margin for error. Mastery of the mental game, including an adaptable repertoire of psychological skills, is critical.

Coaches and families of bowlers contribute to the athlete's experience of the sport—both in terms of development and enjoyment. This book can help these persons facilitate the bowler's mental game mastery. Additionally, by learning lessons taught here, they may more effectively interact with the athlete, and hopefully add richness to their own lives.

In fact, all bowlers stand to gain by applying the psychological skills taught here to their larger lives. These are life lessons, lifetime skills, for all members of the bowling community.

THE FAST LANE TO BOWLING EXCELLENCE

P A R T   I

Steps to the Day of Competition

*A bowler who learns only by experience
usually knows more about what not to do
than what to do.*
Chuck Pezzano

DEVELOPING YOUR SKILLS

In bowling you're always looking to improve.
   Del Warren

Ask yourself, "Am I as committed to working on my mental game as I am to my physical game?"
   Ken Yokobosky

This book's purpose is to provide a roadmap for success. We would like to share with you what we think it takes to be successful in the sport of bowling, or for that matter, any sport. Knowledge and skill in five key areas form the foundation for performance excellence:

1. Executing proper physical movements

2. Knowing the equipment

3. Adjusting to the lane or playing surface

4. The mental game

5. Physical conditioning

Developing your skills will take a plan—a precise, exact plan. In addition to highly specific goals, you'll need to develop a monitoring and follow-through process with a checklist to ensure progress. This plan will help develop proper physical movements, understanding of equipment, understanding the playing of lanes, the mental game, and physical conditioning. We abide by a saying: "Plan your work and work your plan."

This chapter gives you an overview of a Master Plan we developed over the years:

Physical Game	Equipment	Playing Lanes	MENTAL GAME	Conditioning
Stance	Ball Make	Playing Angles	Training	Stretching
Start	Grip	Ball Choice	Outside Center	Exercise
Timing	Cover	Speed Control	Inside Center	Lifting Weights
Footwork	Balance	Loft	During Competition	Food Intake
Posture		Releases	After Competition	
Armswing				
Release				
Finish Position				

Before presenting our overview, we cover the crucial area of openness to learning. You must be open to learning—to practice and grow as a bowler. A lot of people have the wish to win and improve, yet not many have the necessary desire to prepare themselves to win. That takes some change and willingness to learn new skills, whether this involves new physical movement, the use of different equipment, the mastery of a psychological skill, or any other modification in the way you play. After the overview, we close the chapter with tips about selecting the right coach. A coach provides objectivity and guidance. Choosing a coach is very important to developing bowling skills and achieving success.

Be Open to Learning

It's been said there are three keys to real estate success—location, location, location. Likewise, there are three keys to learning—attitude, attitude, attitude. We're often not open to learning because of the time and effort it takes to achieve our goals. However, you'll never improve unless you're willing to work hard enough to successfully pursue peak performance. We firmly believe anyone can achieve their potential with the proper plan and follow-through.

Working on your game, making necessary changes, can be likened to remodeling an old home. It doesn't look bad, but it could be much better. You first select what you're going to work on. For instance, changing some doors, replacing the carpet, painting, wall-papering, etc. During the remodeling, the place looks terrible. Then the time comes to put the pieces back together. When you finally finish the job, the home is beautiful. That's exactly what could happen when you work on your game. First, make the commitment to bring about specific changes. Second, commit yourself to practice with a detailed plan. Third, commit the time required to attain a basic "feel" for these changes and then have the patience for the new part of your game to become "natural."

Openness to learning can be enhanced by asking yourself several questions:

1. Did I listen to the new idea?

2. Do I believe this could help me?

3. Do I have time to practice?

4. What is the proper sequence of steps for adopting this into my game?

5. Will I accept confusion to gain improvement?

6. Is this the correct time to make this change?

As you can see, a great deal goes into bringing about a change, whether it's learning a new release or developing a new psychological skill. Whatever the case may be, we believe the two essentials are an understanding in totality and a full commitment. If you understand exactly what the steps to mastery are, it will be vastly easier to bring about the change in question and integrate it into your game. Commitment of adequate time and energy is obviously and absolutely necessary.

Because so much is involved, we advise you to sit down by yourself and carefully consider whether any particular upgrade to your game is something you truly want. If the answer is "yes," set about creating a highly specific plan for the skill you seek to develop. That's the way to grow.

Let's start talking about our Master Plan. If you understand exactly what it is you're trying to achieve, be it a major change or simply a fine tuning, a plan will make it much easier to implement that change in your game. Once your plan is in place, committing your time and energy to the progress of your game will become a great deal more likely.

*Chris Barnes: Three-time USOC Athlete of the Year for Bowling and fastest PBA player to reach $1,000,000 in earnings**

* PBA Tour statistics are current through the 2004-2005 season.

Physical Game

There are several ways to analyze your game. The best way is to look at your delivery on video. With the help of a coach, you'll be able to see the particular parts you don't like and formulate a plan to improve. Use the checklist in the physical game area of the Master Plan and develop specific items to improve *your* physical game. Due to the fact that we're all different, you must understand what is good for you as a unique individual and develop a personalized plan accordingly.

SELF-EVALUATION: PHYSICAL GAME

1=Poor   2=Fair   3=Good   4=Excellent

1. Rate your stance: _____

2. What is the quality of your start? _____

3. Evaluate your timing: _____

4. How is your footwork? _____

5. Rate your posture: _____

6. Evaluate your armswing: _____

7. How is your release? _____

8. The quality of your finish position is _____

9. Overall, rate how well you're aligned, balanced, and synchronized: _____

Equipment

It isn't necessary to know everything a pro shop professional knows. What's important is that you be thoroughly familiar with *your* equipment—what each ball does and when to use each piece in your "arsenal." Matching equipment to the lane surface is what needs to concern you. You should know how much each ball hooks and for what lane conditions each ball is best suited.

Some equipment will skid all the way down the lane and some will hook as soon as it touches the lane. Some balls hook really hard and some hardly at all. It's your job to understand each piece of equipment. Work with your pro shop operator to develop this knowledge and understanding. You'll have to work with your pro shop professional to develop at least 1 to 6 (maybe as many as 12) bowling balls in a very systematic step-by-step progression.

SELF-EVALUATION: EQUIPMENT

1=Poor   2=Fair   3=Good   4=Excellent

1. To what degree is the make of ball suited to you? _____

2. How about grip type? _____

3. The amount of adaptability provided by your different coverings is _____

4. The amount of adaptability provided by your different balance factors is _____

5. Rate the match between your equipment and your personal game: _____

6. Overall, rate your arsenal for matching ball to lane condition: _____

Playing Lanes

"Playing lanes" is easier than people make it out to be. In lane play, you're observing and then adjusting to the length the ball travels before it changes direction and how hard it moves right to left for a right-handed player or left to right for a left-handed player.

There are several adjustments you can make to play lanes. This vital area is something that needs to be developed with your coach. Because all of us have different rotation and speed, you need to develop a plan to fit *your* style. Knowledge and experience are the keys to your success. By learning to alter your release*, speed, and/or loft, choosing the proper ball for the condition (oil pattern), and playing the angle that fits your game, you're on your way to becoming an elite bowler.

SELF-EVALUATION: PLAYING LANES

1=Poor   2=Fair   3=Good   4=Excellent

1. Rate your ability to play different angles: _____

2. Your capacity to adapt through equipment changes is _____

3. How is your speed control? _____

4. Rate your effectiveness in terms of changing loft: _____

5. What is your skill level with respect to releases? _____

6. Your ability to read lanes is _____

7. Overall, what is your adaptability to varying lane conditions? _____

---

* "Release" refers to wrist and hand position and action.

Mental Game

Now that we've talked about the physical game, equipment, and lane play, let's turn to the mental game. We feel that the blueprint we're outlining for you is crucial as a guide to optimum performance. Yogi Berra once observed that baseball is "50% physical and 90% mental." Although mathematicians might quibble, Yogi expressed an important truth in his unique style—that is, psychological factors make a critical difference in how you perform. This is as valid for bowling as it is for baseball—and all sports or for any other complex human performances that involve a learned skill (e.g., surgery, flying a plane, or acting).

In this book, we will discuss the application of psychological skills in detail to help you develop as an athlete. We want you to master essential techniques and learn where, when, and how to implement them. Our mental game Master Plan is divided into five phases:

1. **Training or "Pre-Day"** - This involves what you do leading up to the day of competition.

2. **Outside the Center** - What's covered in this first pre-game phase are activities from the time you wake up on the day of the event to the time you enter the center.

3. **Inside the Center** - In this second pre-game phase, what's involved are your actions prior to the event's start.

4. **During Competition** - This within-game phase covers all that you do in the settee area and on the lanes.

5. **After Competition** - Now we come to the post-game period including activities immediately after the event as well as long-term adjustment to your performance.

Using our blueprint, you can master the skills for optimum preparation and performance. Whether the competitive stressor you face concerns pressure, a poor start, or changing lane conditions, you'll have the psychological tools essential for meeting the challenge. Through monitoring and fine tuning, you can then hone *your* mental game. Our shorthand for the sequence of mastering, monitoring, and modifying is "M-M-M." Even if you're an elite athlete who already knows the skills required to throw strikes and make spares, you must be mentally prepared in order to succeed.

The following examples illustrate how two bowling greats benefited dramatically from timely interventions related to psychological factors.

HALL OF FAMERS BREAK THROUGH

Dave Davis, who holds 18 PBA tour titles and is a PBA and USBC Hall of Famer, struggled when he joined the PBA Senior Tour. He couldn't win. He couldn't even rely on cashing. A knee injury added to his problems. Davis was used to tremendous success. Unaccustomed to this situation, he understandably felt downhearted and considered retirement.

Davis turned things around through three days of intensive work. He used effective coaching to first make several corrections in his physical game and then benefit from confidence-building techniques. These included review of past achievements (both verbally and through viewing videotape), visualizing, encouragement, and reinforcement of character strengths. Davis regained confidence in himself and was highly positive in his outlook. The rest is bowling history, as Davis has experienced consistent success on the Senior Tour including consecutive victories in the ABC Senior Masters.* He has won a total of 7 majors.

Lucy G. Sandelin is recognized as one of amateur bowling's all-time premier players. The winner of numerous national and international titles, this Georgia native has many honors to her credit. These include induction into the Women's International Bowling Congress (WIBC) Hall of Fame and the Tampa Sports Hall of Fame, and designation as the USOC Female Bowling Athlete of the Year in two different years.

Yet Sandelin was glaringly inconsistent at the annual Team USA qualifying tournament (the US National Amateur Bowling Championships**). She had qualified in alternate years only: 1990, 1992, 1994, and 1996.

In order to become consistent in her performance, Sandelin diligently drew from a sport psychology consultation. Through discussion, she gained insight into the basis of this roller coaster pattern—namely, the pressure she was placing on herself to repeat. She then applied various psychological skill techniques so that the qualifying tournament was viewed in appropriate perspective and control gained over her emotional reactions. Mental practice, self-talk, reinforcement of bowling skills, and immediacy (a "here and now" attitude) were methods which proved highly effective. Sandelin also was responsive to encouragement to make full use of her already advanced concentration and relaxation skills.

Sandelin not only qualified for Team USA 1997 in that year's tournament, she won the televised stepladder finals to become the Women's US Amateur Champion.

The very next year, Sandelin qualified again for a record-tying sixth time. She has now been a Team USA member nine times, an unsurpassed total.***

* As of 2006, renamed the USBC Senior Masters
** As of 2006, renamed the USBC Team USA Championships
*** USBC statistics are current through January, 2006.

Top left: Dave Davis en route to second ABC Senior Masters title. Top right: Lucy Sandelin: Here, representing the US at 33rd AMF World Cup in Cairo.

SELF-EVALUATION: MENTAL GAME

1=Poor   2=Fair   3=Good   4=Excellent

1. To what extent is a systematic plan for developing your mental game in place? _____

2. Rate the quality of your practices: _____

3. How effectively do you set goals? _____

4. The amount you benefit from mental practice is _____

5. Characterize the consistency and usefulness of your pre-game preparation, including the application of psychological techniques: _____

6. The degree to which you have a pre-shot routine which incorporates various psychological methods is _____

7. Your ability to maintain confidence is _____

8. How positive is your self-talk? _____

9. Rate your level of self-acceptance: _____

10. Evaluate your handling of adversity: _____

11. How effective are you in coping with distractions? _____

(continued)

SELF-EVALUATION: MENTAL GAME (continued)

12. Your ability to identify personal anxiety factors (triggers, signs, and optimal levels) related to managing pressure situations is _____

13. Rate your mastery of relaxation techniques: _____

14. How good are you at doing what it takes to come through in the clutch? _____

15. Rate the way you deal with competitive outcomes, such as the end of a tournament or a league night: _____

16. Your ability to raise your energy level if it's low is _____

17. To what extent can you combat psych-out attempts? _____

18. Evaluate your skill in conveying information to teammates: _____

19. Characterize your understanding of what support means to a team and how to build it: _____

20. What is your familiarity with performance factors specific to youth, senior, and women bowlers and to families as a unit? _____

21. Overall, how strong is your mental game? _____

Note: The number of each item (1-20) corresponds to the chapter in which the topic is covered.

Developing a top notch mental game requires ongoing dedication to that aim. To conquer the varied challenges of high-level competition, you need a repertoire of psychological skills. This creates a versatile ability to cope. Then you can adapt to whatever the competitive moment throws your way. Reaching this goal calls for work comparable to any other area of your game. As Ken Yokobosky, PBA Tour professional and Team USA coach*, asks at the start of the chapter, are you willing to do the work? If you're serious about playing at an elite level, you'll make the necessary commitment.

Conditioning

Physical condition is a prime factor in athletic success. The list of benefits that can be derived from conditioning include increased strength, flexibility, stamina, balance, and quickness, as well as heightened alertness, reduced anxiety, improved mood, and a greater capacity to handle stress. All of these contribute to optimum bowling performance. The *right* conditioning program can help you reach your

---

* He also conducts training camps for bowlers, ranging from youth to professionals (The Borden-Yokobosky Bowling Camp under the auspices of Pro-Image Bowling).

potential and consistently bowl your best. Being fit can also reduce the risk and severity of injury and assist recovery if you're injured. Finally, conditioning can contribute to your overall health—a worthwhile result in itself, in addition to influencing how well you perform.

We use an acronym, SELF, to identify the fundamental parts of a physical conditioning program.

S is for stretching both before and after you compete or practice. Work with a trainer or other fitness specialist to develop a plan best suited for you. S also stands for sleep. Sufficient rest is vital to physical and mental functioning.

E is for exercise, both aerobic and anaerobic. If you want to play at the highest level possible, then your body must be ready. This, too, is where you need to work with a professional to help build a plan.

L is for lifting—weight lifting. If you need to be stronger or more flexible or just keep your muscles in shape, there are different programs for different needs. Again, work with a professional at a gym or health club near you.

F is for food intake. If you're overweight, underweight, tired, or tense, this can be related to your diet. What food do you eat prior to, during, and after competition? Our eating habits help control our body weight, nervous system, and ability to play at a high level. In other sports, they use nutritionists— so should we. If you're truly committed to playing your best, you can and will improve with this type of help.

SELF-EVALUATION: CONDITIONING

1=Poor   2=Fair   3=Good   4=Excellent

1. Rate your use of stretching: _____
2. The amount of sleep you get is _____
3. Evaluate your exercise program: _____
4. The extent to which you derive available benefit from lifting is _____
5. How good is your nutrition? _____
6. Overall, your current level of conditioning is _____

```
•  T H E    C O A C H I N G    C O R N E R  •
```

Choosing a Coach

In the process of selecting a coach, there are several major concerns to keep in mind. Not only is it necessary to generally respect this person, you must have faith that he or she understands the sport of bowling at a very high level. The next most important attribute is skill in communicating. One of the essential factors in this regard is your coach's capacity to listen to thoughts and feelings. It will be vital for your coach to know what your ideas and reactions are before, during, and after an event.

Speak to several people who have had the opportunity to work with this person. Find out what they think. Even if the coach and a friend of yours hit it off, be aware that you and the coach could still communicate poorly, since your personality differs in some way from that of your friend. So, first check with other bowlers and then receive a lesson before you commit to a coach. In fact, it might take two or three lessons before you decide whether or not this coach is good for you.

After the initial lesson, how will you know if this coach and you can make progress with your game? Ask yourself the following questions: "Do I feel ready to go?"; "Do I want to practice?"; "Was the information clear and precise?"; "Was the information organized and written down in an easy to understand practice plan?" If the answer to these questions is "no," this is probably not the coach for you. If you answer "yes" and are satisfied regarding the matters discussed above, you've found a coach.

Working effectively with a coach is an ongoing give and take process. As with any friendship or business association, you must continue to monitor this relationship to ensure that mutual respect, honest communication, organization, and follow-through stay a priority. You can tell if there's a genuine interest in you and your improvement.

There's an old saying about time and its value: "You can take of a person his home, car, jewels, or money and he can replace it. But if you take of his time, he will never be able to get it back." Look at the time your coach spends with you as something special. Make sure you pay his or her fee, for time is an invaluable commodity.

Exercises

1. Ask yourself, Am I genuinely open to learning? Consider whether you're willing to commit the time, energy, and emotional resources needed to grow your game.

2. State the meaning and importance of M-M-M.

3. If a coach has helped you greatly (in any sport), describe that individual and how you related to one another.

4. If you're seeking a coach, what are the qualities you'll look for? What coachable qualities will you bring to the relationship?

REVIEW

The foundation for performance excellence in bowling consists of skill in five key areas:

1. Physical movements
2. Equipment knowledge
3. Lane play adjustments
4. The mental game
5. Physical conditioning

A detailed plan is essential for attaining and implementing these skills. Our Master Plan provides a guide to help you develop a high level of competence in each area.

Openness to learning is crucial to your growth in bowling and beyond. In order to meet the goals of your plan, a wholehearted commitment is required.

A solid and versatile mental game is essential for meeting the numerous and varied challenges encountered in competitive bowling. To upgrade your mental game, it's necessary to master psychological skills, monitor their use in competition, and modify them as needed (M-M-M). A well-rounded mental game covers all phases of preparation, competing, and post-competition processing.

Selecting the right coach is vital to your success. Keys to look for are a coach's knowledge and communication skills.

Carolyn Dorin-Ballard: 2001 PWBA Player of the Year, first woman to bowl consecutive 300s in PBA competition (regional-2005)

2

THE ABCs OF QUALITY PRACTICE

Before I went on tour, every single day I'd bowl a good two hours in the daytime and two hours in the evening to try to get good enough.
Johnny Petraglia

Preparation is the launching pad for high achievement in bowling. The right preparation doesn't guarantee bowling success, but without good preparation your failure is certain.

All facets of the mental game can and should be developed and honed during your training. Descriptions of these psychological skills will be provided throughout the book. In discussing the training period over the next three chapters, special attention is devoted to these key areas: quality practice, goal setting, and mental practice.

This chapter presents the essentials for optimal practice in the training period leading up to the day of an event. Following these guidelines will help you achieve readiness to bowl your best.

Quality Practice: The Nuts and Bolts

Quality practices comprise the core of preparation during the training period. Your activities and attitude during practice sessions are crucial to your performance during competition.

Although the focus may differ from practice session to practice session, quality practice ultimately requires work on all parts of your bowling game.

Physical Game

A quality practice involves working on your physical game. The physical game is the bedrock for bowling excellence. It must be extremely consistent for your overall game to be consistent. The Master Plan identifies the eight parts of the physical game. It is necessary to systematically work on each of these eight areas. Your aim is to learn technique, become steady in its use, and then make refinements as needed.

Equipment

Increasing your knowledge of bowling equipment is an essential function of quality practice. This means learning what equipment design fits your game and gives you the maximum adaptability. The Master Plan cites four aspects of equipment with which you must be familiar. Knowledge of equipment means learning what ball can be used in what way under what circumstances. As we described, developing an equipment "arsenal" is your goal.

Playing Lanes

The key to consistent top caliber tournament performance is adaptability to varying conditions. Bowling great on house conditions is a genuine accomplishment. However, what sets professional and elite amateur bowlers apart from the rest is versatility—the ability to adjust from frame to frame, game to game, lane to lane, pattern to pattern. The factors which must be varied to successfully adjust to different, challenging (e.g., sport shot), and changing conditions are noted in the Master Plan.

MENTAL GAME

You must work on mental game skills in on-lane practice sessions just as you work on other essential bowling skills. This practice time is vital for two reasons.

- To help you master new psychological techniques and help keep sharp those skills you already know.

- To enable your use of psychological skills to become virtually automatic.

Let's look at these practice functions.

Steps to Mastery

The process of mastering a mental game skill consists of four steps.

The first step consists of gaining familiarity and ease with a new method. For instance, practicing a recommended relaxation technique (such as diaphragmatic breathing) at home. The second step involves "mental practice" in which you imagine—"visualize"—yourself using this method in competition. The third step is on-lane practice. Use of the method in competition—first league play then tournament play—is the fourth step.

This sequence permits you to use the techniques in situations of progressively greater competitive stress. That makes learning easier and more enjoyable and increases confidence.

These steps are more cumulative than strictly sequential. You continue what you've being doing as you "add on" a new step. So, when you're starting to apply a method in competition, continue to visualize and practice it. Even when you're competent and confident using it, mental practice and on-lane practice can help retain your sharpness.

The process of psychological skill mastery is ongoing. Remember the M-M-M principle. In addition to continuing, repetitive application of a technique in the steps just described, it's necessary to evaluate a method's effectiveness and to make refinements as needed. This sequence of monitoring and modifying is basic and essential to mental game excellence and your bowling success.

Make Skills Automatic

In the heat of competitive battle, the fast application of the right psychological skill method is essential. Faced with a do-or-die tenth frame, you want the most effective methods for relaxation and concentration to instantly leap to mind and be smoothly integrated into your between-shot sequence. Similarly, psychological skills which are part of your regular routine throughout the competition must be used effortlessly, without hesitation.

Whether it's learning to drive a car, use new software, or apply psychological skills when bowling, proper practice will bring you to the point where the action seems automatic. The upcoming "what to do" section tells you how to achieve this for the mental game.

Conditioning

In terms of physical preparation, treat practice sessions as you would an actual event. We strongly advise stretching before and after bowling. This is important for performance and for injury prevention. Maintain good nutrition. If you choose to have a snack or meal at the center after you bowl, select food consistent with your nutritional plan.

Johnny Petraglia: PBA Hall of Fame, 14 Tour titles (three majors) and five Senior Tour titles, three-term PBA President

What to Do in Practice

In practice use your psychological skills just as you would in competition. If your "mental game plan" calls for visualizing yourself bowling with perfect form as you wait in the settee area, do that. If your pre-shot routine at the ball return calls for a verbal cue for concentration (e.g., "Focus") and a confidence-building affirmation (e.g., "My swing is free and easy"), do these on every shot. After each shot, plan your strategy for the next shot in the way you will when the score counts.

In addition to practicing your standard between-shot routine, work on developing and honing all the psychological skills in your repertoire. As you bowl practice games, try various relaxation techniques, use skills to maintain and regain concentration, and apply methods to keep a positive frame of mind.

For instance, after a poorly executed shot, cope with your thoughts and feelings exactly as you would in an event (a topic covered in Chapter 10). If someone wants to chat and you find this distracting, use communication skills to tactfully clear the time for yourself (Chapter 19).

Through simulation you can anticipate and prepare for all competitive situations for which you must be ready. Simulation is an essential aspect of quality practice.

Two other training essentials are setting practice goals and practicing with optimum intensity, frequency, and duration ("tough fun").

Use Simulation

Simulation of various game circumstances in practice can prepare you to cope with their actual occurrence in competition. First, create the situation. Second, employ mental game tools to handle the challenge.

Any game situation can be simulated through your imagination. The following are examples of simulations:

As you bowl, imagine you're in the crucial stages of a close match. It's crunch time. To make this most realistic, create as many details in your imagination as possible. You might think of a specific event, opponent, and even a specific score. Imagine the presence of fans and teammates if this is a team event.

This simulation creates the challenge of a clutch situation. You'll want a method to stay calm and poised, such as Progressive Muscle Relaxation. If a negative thought enters your mind, "thought stopping" technique can be applied. The full range of methods to cope with game pressure is discussed in Chapters 13 and 14.

Pretend you're going to a tournament. Set a starting time and treat the situation as if you were actually expecting to compete. Bear this in mind from the time you wake up, when you drive to the center, and after you enter the center.

This simulation creates the challenge of pre-game preparation. It enables you to practice the routine you plan to use outside the center on the day of an event. It also enables you to work on the routine you intend to use inside the center before starting competition. Chapter 5 considers this type of preparation in detail.

Enlist the help of others to create potentially distracting behaviors. Someone might play the role of a teammate or competitor who loses his/her temper, plays at a slow pace, or makes a provocative comment.

This simulation creates two types of challenges. The first is maintaining concentration in the face of distractions. The second is refocusing if you become distracted. Among the methods available to you are adhering to between-shot routine and use of verbal and/or visual cues. The psychological skills needed to maintain and regain concentration are the subject of Chapter 11.

Each of these simulations produces its own challenge. Your practice aim is to apply the appropriate psychological skills to cope with the situation.

The only limit to the type of situation you can simulate is the limit of your imagination. So, use your creativity to simulate the full range of competitive circumstances you may confront:

Imagine the tenth frame is all that stands between you and a win. Imagine there's a long stoppage in play due to an equipment breakdown. Imagine you're into the tenth frame with nine strikes. Imagine you've started slowly while those around you are striking. Imagine you're hitting the pocket, yet have little to show. Imagine you're trying to concentrate and a teammate wants to talk. Imagine a family member is present and giving you unwanted advice. Imagine you've had a very tough day at work or school or a quarrel with your spouse and now must devote full attention to bowling. Imagine you have a nagging injury. Imagine you're into the championship round, in front of the cameras.

Using psychological skills to successfully handle these types of challenges in practice will represent a big step toward succeeding in competition.

Make simulations as realistic as possible. Imagine you're actually in the situation. A prime example of this is preparing to bowl on the TV show. This is a thrilling, yet stressful situation for even the world's best bowlers. Therefore, it makes sense for bowlers to mentally rehearse the experience as a way of preparing and then to simulate the situation in practice. It's possible to take the simulation of a championship round one step further. To provide a realism allowing an individual or team to optimally prepare, the use of a camera and other props in training can create the sense of being on TV.

Set Practice Goals

In order to derive the maximum benefit from a practice session, strive to achieve pre-set goals. The right goals can increase the effectiveness and efficiency of practice. They can help you improve skills, feel satisfied and confident, and make practices more interesting. If you find practices boring and/or you find concentration wavering, the solution may lie in goal setting.

Practice goals should be set for any phase of the game on which you're working. These should be consistent with your Master Plan and developed with your coach.

Examples of practice goals are as follows:

Physical Game

- To develop better timing: Work on consistent start.

- To master a minimum release for spares: Practice reduced hand rotation.

- To develop great balance at the finish of each shot: Clear my right leg and finish with my biceps by my right ear.

Equipment

- To know my equipment better: Write down the characteristics of every ball in my arsenal.

- To improve equipment decision-making: Test my different balls to see how they react in relationship to each other.

- To have the same feeling in each piece of equipment: Make sure each ball is taped similarly.

Playing Lanes

- To improve skill on my least favorite shot (perhaps the 1st arrow): Practice this shot for 10 minutes.

- To improve my 4th arrow shot: Practice this shot for 10 minutes.

- To improve my 7- and 10-pin conversions: Practice each for 5 minutes.

MENTAL GAME

- To increase the consistency of my pre-shot routine: Use the identical pre-shot routine (same thoughts, same actions, same timing) at the ball return on each shot.

- To more effectively cope with mistakes: After a missed shot, apply thought stopping to negative ideas or images and replace them with affirmations and positive images.

- To better sustain concentration: Simulate distractions and maintain my full between-shot routine.

- To readily apply process imagery between shots: In the settee area, visualize myself bowling with perfect form.

Conditioning

- To prepare muscles for exertion, accelerate their recovery after practice, and protect from injury: Stretch before and after practice.

- To cope with injury: If recovering from an injury, assess my physical status and adjust the duration of practice accordingly.

- To develop stamina: Bowl at the pace of competition with no added time between shots or games.

Bear in mind the importance of being realistic in your expectations about a practice session. Limiting the number of goals (to one or two, for instance), identifying achievable small steps towards a large goal, and designating specific amounts of practice time to work towards each goal are ways to avoid overloading yourself.

The topic of goal setting is discussed in more detail in the next chapter. There you'll learn the basic principles of establishing goals for overall development and for a specific event.

Tough Fun

Another key to quality practices is what we call "tough fun." You want to work hard, yet enjoy yourself and not become overly stressed. Some bowlers may enjoy pushing themselves to their limit all the time. However, this could lead to excessive mental and physical wear and tear and produce decreased motivation and susceptibility to injury.

Practice is a personal choice and you need to balance the amount and intensity of it. More practice with less intensity or less practice with more intensity allows you to improve. Too much practice with too much intensity creates burnout. On the PBA Tour, there are bowlers who practice a lot and those who practice very little. Two great professionals, Marshall Holman and David Ozio, had radically different practice regimens. Holman didn't like to spend a great deal of time practicing, while Ozio practiced relentlessly. Both are great champions, yet each approached practice in a way that was comfortable to him.

An important factor to consider here is how much bowling you do. If you're in three leagues each week as well as tournament play, then you want to be especially careful about overtaxing yourself. If your bowling schedule is lighter, then practice can be more prolonged and frequent.

The right amount for you to practice will be determined by your bowling schedule, your work/academic schedule, and your individual needs. Together, you and your coach can determine what practice schedule works best for you.

It's not uncommon for a professional bowler to bowl 20 or more games a day in practice when preparing for an upcoming series of tournaments. If you're preparing for a tournament on occasion, bowl more games consecutively in practice than you will in competition.

Plan your practices. This is highly important. For instance,

Marshall Holman: 1987 PBA Player of the Year, PBA Hall of Famer, won four majors, PBA color analyst 1995-2001

the following is a typical 60 minute practice plan:

- 5 minutes focusing on my start
- 5 minutes focusing on my hand position through my swing
- 5 minutes focusing on my posture
- 5 minutes focusing on my finish
- 5 minutes at each of the 1st, 2nd, 3rd, and 4th arrows
- 5 minutes practicing my 7- and 10-pins
- 5 minutes practicing refocusing technique
- 10 minutes bowling for the fun of it. Feel the motion and lock your attention on the target. Vary your practice plan based on the time you can commit on that particular day.

Keep in mind that you're striving for a high quality practice session. While it's important to get enough practice, quality must be foremost in your mind. A half-hearted, mediocre session not only wastes your time, but can lead to bad habits. So, be determined, focused, and goal-oriented. This will result in the experience of challenge and accomplishment, which creates the sense of fun in sports.

Exercises

1. List the four steps to mastering a mental game skill.

2. Circle the areas of your game which have received sufficient attention in practice:

   Physical Game   Equipment   Playing Lanes

   MENTAL GAME   Conditioning

3. Based on your self-evaluation in Chapter 1, which aspects of the mental game will you work on during practice?

4. Which other aspects of your bowling need the most work?

5. Describe three situations you will simulate in order to practice mental game skills.

6. Identify three practice goals related to these situations (this book will increase your ability to cite specific techniques).

7. Create a 60 minute practice plan, including a mental game segment.

REVIEW

Proper preparation is essential for success. Chapters 2 through 4 present three keys to a productive training period. Following these guidelines can bring you to optimal readiness on the day of competition.

This chapter discusses training key #1: quality practice. It is vital that you effectively practice with respect to all aspects of your Master Plan (physical game, equipment, playing lanes, MENTAL GAME, and conditioning).

Concerning mental game skills, we recommend the following:

- Follow a sequence of four steps in the mastery and application of a new technique.

- Practice should enable you to "automatically" apply a psychological method in competition.

- Apply psychological skills in practice the same way you would when competing.

Use simulation to prepare for the wide range of game situations you'll encounter.

A crucial element of quality practice is setting specific goals. This should encompass all areas of development.

Plan practices so that the duration, frequency, intensity, and activities are appropriate for your personality, bowling schedule, upcoming competitions, and skill level.

3

MOVING AHEAD BY SETTING GOALS

A fellow competitor once said, "A man with a purpose is hard to beat."
"The purpose" is a well-defined goal.
Mike Lastowski

Setting goals is a vital part of the mental game and essential to preparation during the training period. Establish a series of goals for overall progress in each part of your bowling game. Then, as steps towards these aims, set specific goals for on-lane practice as well as other aspects of training (e.g., conditioning workouts and mental practice away from the center). Finally, set goals for competition as an event approaches.

Why Goal Setting Is Important

Setting goals focuses attention on the essential elements of performance. By clarifying expectations and creating achievable performance aims, goal setting can reduce anxiety, raise confidence, increase practice effectiveness and interest, and accelerate your learning of skills. This can increase your motivation and lead to greater persistence—a prime ingredient for success.

Let's see how you can lift the level of your game through goal setting.

Keys to Effective Goal Setting

Ask yourself the following six questions in order to set optimal performance goals:

1. Are My Goals Process-Oriented or Outcome-Oriented?

As much as possible, set goals that are within your control. If your goal depends on what others do, then it's not fully within your control. Winning a game, match, or title is dependent on how competitors perform. Therefore, winning is an outcome goal, not a process goal.

Naturally, you're playing to win and would find such an outcome very pleasing. However, since you can only be responsible for how you perform, in terms of personal achievement and the satisfaction that accompanies it, it makes sense to work towards goals you can reach through skill and effort. The number of pins you knock down on a given condition is based on how you perform—on your abilities and execution. A prime example of a process-oriented goal would be converting 90% of single pin spares.

The best any human being can do is to realize his or her potential. Defining success in these terms is a key to effective goal setting and ultimately a key to peak performance. John Wooden is hailed as one of the all-time greatest coaches in American sport. "The Wizard of Westwood" guided his UCLA basketball team to ten NCAA championships in 12 years and recorded a career winning percentage of .813. This is his definition of success:

> Success is peace of mind which is a direct result of self-satisfaction in knowing you did your best to become the best that you are capable of becoming ... as coach I tried to teach all youngsters under my supervision never to try to be better than someone else. That's something over which you have no control.[4]

Ironically, setting process goals can result in better competitive outcomes. Process-oriented goals can reduce anxiety, boost confidence, improve concentration, and lead to higher quality performance. Over time, this will translate into higher scores relative to other bowlers—i.e., into competitive triumphs.

2. Is My Goal Sufficiently Challenging?

Strive for a middle ground in terms of difficulty. If your goal is too tough, the likely result will be frustration and disappointment. If your goal is too easy, the potential to learn is limited and your interest, focus, and satisfaction will be adversely affected. Your confidence level won't be raised by simply repeating something you already know how to do. Make your goals tough enough so that you must "stretch" to achieve them.

Expecting perfection is a sure sign of goal setting that is excessively demanding. There's a world of difference between working towards perfection and expecting it.

3. Are My Goals Specific or General?

Make goals as specific as possible. This gives an exact target enabling you to know how you're doing. Then you can make adjustments in your program as needed. Whether you're working on spare conversions, arm swing consistency, ball velocity, release point, break point, entry angle, or equipment changes for a particular condition, clearly designate a goal. When possible, use numerical goals.

4. Is My Goal Short-Term or Long-Term?

There is a place for both short-term and long-term goals. However, on a daily basis, it's the short-term goals which can best guide you to improvement. Short-term goals provide more of a challenge, permit greater control, and create an opportunity for positive reinforcement. A goal ladder (illustrating a step-by-step progression) is a useful device for setting a series of short-term goals leading to a terminal goal. The following is an example of this approach:

Ultimate Goal:	Make 95% of my single pin spares
Step 5:	In practice, be able to hit the right, left, and center of each single pin on call
Step 4:	Spend 5 minutes on my 10-pin and 5 minutes on my 7-pin in each practice session
Step 3:	Get comfortable positioning my body so it's in line with my target throughout my approach

Step 2:   Seek out help on developing a better spare shooting system

Step 1:   Determine where I start, slide, and look for each of my spares and write it down

Present Performance: 68% single pin conversion

Mika Koivuniemi: 2004 PBA Player of the Year, 1991 FIQ World Champion, title winner in ten countries, native of Finland

5.   Are My Goals Realistic or Unrealistic?

It is most important that goals be realistic. Set your goals based on recent form. Sometimes goals are unrealistically high. This might be due to a number of factors such as the expectations of others, unfamiliarity with your true skill, your wish to succeed, or one tremendous performance. Unrealistically low goals could be attributable to factors such as an underestimation of your ability by yourself or others or anxiety about failing.

The "Additional Hints"* and "Goals for Competition" sections later in this chapter contain further suggestions for making goals realistic. Also helpful in this regard will be the "Effective Feedback" section and REALITY system in Chapter 7 and the "Be Realistic" section of Chapter 9.

6.   Is My Goal Set For an Individual or a Team?

There is a purpose for both individual and team goals. Both have a place in sports and can be useful. Team goals inspire motivation and encourage cooperation among athletes. Individual goals establish accountability.

---

* Note especially the second and third hints.

Examples of Goals

The goals below are consistent with the principles we've described:

- To increase consistency in shot making (hit my target 8 of 10 shots)

- To have good bowling posture on my approach

- To have equipment versatility: 4 balls that do 4 different things (e.g., different amounts of hook or differing arc pattern)

- To understand the difference between label, leverage, and axis balance

- To be able to loft the ball 12 feet onto the lane

- To be able to play outside the first arrow

- To increase ball velocity from 15 mph to 17 mph

- To develop a consistent pre-shot routine

- To master diaphragmatic breathing technique

- To reach the pocket on my first ball delivery 75% of the time

- To maintain proper nutrition by adhering to a dietary plan

- To increase endurance by engaging in an aerobic workout 3-5 times per week

" ONE STEP AT A TIME "

A GUIDE TO GOAL SETTING

1. Write a statement of your goal.

2. Is it sufficiently specific so you'll know when you've reached it? If not, rewrite it.

3. Is it positively stated? If not, rewrite it.

4. Is it under your control in that it focuses on your behavior—not someone else's? If not, rewrite it.

5. Is the goal important enough to you that you want to work on it and have the time and energy? If not, rewrite it.

6. How will reaching this goal make your life different?

7. What barriers might you encounter in working toward the goal?

   Knowledge roadblock. What more do I need to know?

   Skill roadblock. What more must I learn how to do?

   Risk taking roadblock. What risks must I take?

   Social support roadblock. From whom do I need support? What kind of support is it?

8. Goal Plan

   Identify the steps using the Goal Ladder. Are the steps small and manageable? If not, divide the most complex step. More than ten steps are possible.

Goal Ladder

Goal:_____

   _____

10 _____

 9 _____

 8 _____

 7 _____

 6 _____

 5 _____

 4 _____

 3 _____

 2 _____

 1 _____

Additional Hints

We offer a few final pointers to make your use of goal setting as effective as possible.

- Record your goals. This is the "ink it, don't think it" principle. Writing your aims ensures their accurate recall and keeps them in the front of your mind.

- Record your efforts. This enables you to see how you're faring generally and particularly with respect to your goals. In this way you can gauge your growth and modify your planning as needed.

- Reevaluate regularly. Goals must be continually updated and based on your ongoing performance. You'll want to consult your coach.

- Set positive goals, not negative ones. This is crucial. An optimistic, forward-looking attitude is conducive to peak performance. Setting a goal of what not to do (e.g., don't miss spares) contains a negative thought, and negative ideas generate anxiety, hinder concentration, and reduce confidence.

- Set practice goals. The training period is a time for establishing goals which will lead to optimal performance for a specific event and long-term development. As we noted, setting goals for each practice session is vital for quality practices and achieving maximum progress during the training period.

- Set target times. This is optional. Some athletes find it helpful to have a time frame for accomplishing goals. Others don't. Examples are mastering a pre-shot routine (one month); learning a new release (three months); and developing an equipment arsenal (six months).

- An acronym which covers all our goal-setting recommendations is S-C-R-I-P-T. "S" stands for specific and short-term; "C" for challenging; "R" for realistic, recorded, and reevaluated; "I" is for individual; "P" is for process, positive, and practice; "T" is time-targeted and team; SCRIPT your own success story.

Goals for Competition

An event, whether tournament or league session, is significant in three ways for your bowling career. First and most obviously, it represents a chapter in your competitive history. Excelling in competition is why you're training—it's the reason for your dedication, hard work, and collaboration with a coach. Second, competition enables you to assess your progress and adjust your training regimen as needed. Third, the combination of experience and assessment gives you the opportunity to improve. Success at any given event carries its own importance. At the time, it's the focus of your attention and something that matters intensely. Yet, what will determine the totality of competitive success in your career is the ability to grow your game, to evolve as a bowling athlete. That's why we suggest making improvement a primary goal. Incorporating overall improvement into your concept of success also reduces pressure. We discuss this goal in the following section.

When a competition approaches, it becomes meaningful to consider performance (i.e., process) goals for it. Seek to maintain and build on your level of competence previously displayed across the board in the five key areas of bowling excellence (physical game, mental game, etc.). To target progress in your game, simply apply the type of goals used in training to the event at hand. If your single pin conversion rate in practice has been 85%, you could make it a goal to shoot at or above that in the event. Here's a goal setting approach many athletes find useful: Set three goal levels. Level one would be an exceptional performance; level two, a very good one; level three, a solid effort. With respect to single pin conversion in this situation, the goals might be 95%, 90%, and 85%.

Setting specific outcome goals for an event can have the positive effect of boosting confidence and spiking motivation for individuals and teams. It hardly needs mentioning that you would like to achieve great results every time out. At its best this means winning a title and setting records. A great result could also be making the finals or cashing or besting your average. To be genuinely meaningful, outcome-oriented goals need to be realistically based on your skill level and, as much as possible, take into account the level of competition and conditions. Unlike the process of bowling, which depends entirely on what you do, results are affected by factors outside your control. You might execute well, make sound lane adjustments, and be mentally sharp, yet still be outbowled. Therefore, while outcomes matter, the true measure of your bowling is how you perform and that doesn't depend on what competitors do. As with process-oriented performance goals, you can also set three levels of outcome goals. For example, level one might be making the championship round; level two, winning a majority of matches; level three, making the finals.

The principle of updating goals applies to an event as well as to overall development. Event goals can be realistically adjusted before or during competition. Gordon Vadakin of Wichita State University is the winningest coach in the history of collegiate bowling. This is how he describes the value of reevaluating event goals while competing:

> I have found that this [reevaluating regularly] is something that is commonly overlooked and misunderstood. The average person sets a goal to bowl their first 700 series and they don't understand that with goals they need to be prepared to adjust them in the middle of competition. The thing that usually happens is someone will start out a night in their league with 248 and 239 and then in the last game they will still have the goal of bowling their first 700 series. Because of that, their focus is to get to that 700 number and this means they would need only a 213 game to reach 700. Mentally this is not perceived as a challenge since they just bowled two games that were better than that score. They mentally let down. Instead, the goal should be adjusted higher to bowl a 750 series, which would be a 263 game or better. This keeps the goal at a challenging level. If a player bowls 232 the last game they would fall short of the new adjusted goal of 750, however they would be over the original goal of 700.
>
> This problem with goals regularly occurs during tournament competition as well because the incoming goals are not viewed dynamically where they should be adjusted to fit the current situation. This includes someone who starts out slowly or someone who starts a tournament fast and should upgrade the goal to a higher expectation level.[5]

How much and when during competition you think of scoring is a matter of individual preference and personality. Some bowlers thrive on close attention to their score. Others perform best by limiting this sort of awareness (discussed in Chapter 14).

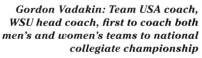

Gordon Vadakin: Team USA coach, WSU head coach, first to coach both men's and women's teams to national collegiate championship

Whatever goals you may set for an event, during competition we strongly advise a process orientation focusing on your own efforts. Staying in the "here and now" and following a pre-shot routine (Chapter 6) enhances concentration and reduces pressure. After the event, you'll want to thoroughly evaluate your effort (Chapter 15) and adjust training goals based on how you performed.

Overall Event Goal

For every event, we recommend a particular goal reflecting commitment to growth. The very act of setting this overall goal compels you to focus on the process of bowling and to make improvement a priority. The goal we have in mind is for you to emerge a better bowler at the end of the event than you were at the beginning. Your development can involve any area from the physical game to lane play to the mental game. In a team competition, the area may well be communication. Growth could occur in mastering a new skill or honing one you've already learned.

Advancing your skills, increasing confidence about what you already do well, and identifying that which needs attention in your game all represent steps forward. If you bowl great, it should be relatively easy to note what you did better than before and how you trust your game more. The far greater challenge will likely be noting where there is need for growth. Do that and you certainly will have emerged a better bowler. If you struggled overall, it's still quite possible that you improved some skills and gained confidence where you performed well. Perhaps you coped effectively with the adversity from an emotional perspective.

Then again, you may learn that this aspect of your mental game needs work. By learning from what didn't go right, zeroing in on that which can improve, and committing yourself to doing whatever it takes to grow, you move forward. We believe it's always possible, in one way or another, to be a stronger bowler at the end of the day.

Exercises

1. Review "Keys to Effective Goal Setting."

2. Using the keys and guide, set a goal for each area of your game.

3. Consider an upcoming event. Set three process goals and three outcome goals.

4. Describe how the last event contributed to your being a stronger bowler.

REVIEW

The second training key covered is goal setting. In Chapter 2 we provided specific examples of practice goals for each phase of your game. This chapter teaches you how to actually set goals.

Setting goals can serve several important functions. These include increasing practice interest, raising confidence, reducing anxiety, and accelerating learning.

Keys to effective goal setting are identified. You will generally derive the most benefit from goals that are

- Process-oriented,
- Sufficiently challenging,
- Specific,
- Short-term, and
- Realistic.

Both individual goals and team goals can be useful.

Use our Guide as an aid to developing productive goals.

Recording your progress and regular reevaluation are among additional hints offered.

Both performance and outcome goals can be set for events. We suggest that emerging a better bowler serve as an overall goal in every competition.

4

MENTAL PRACTICE FOR OPTIMAL TRAINING

On the TV show, right before I'd get up and at the ball return, I'd imagine where my feet were going to be, what I was looking at, then I'd see myself throw the ball over my target and strike. I'd see this happen from the inside as if I was actually bowling.

Lisa Noor

An essential psychological activity during the training period is mental practice.* This involves the use of imagination to rehearse your bowling. Using the imagination in this way is referred to as "visualization" or "imagery."

Visualization's Many Functions

Visualization is one of the most important psychological skills and is used by successful athletes in all sports. Imagery can be applied in many ways. Among its primary uses are

- Skill mastery,

- Priming for performance,

- Anticipating situations,

* Sometimes called "mental rehearsal"

- Confidence building,

- Relaxation and psyching up,

- Concentration, and

- Stress reduction.

These functions are described below. The first four are typically associated with mental practice because they involve images of an action you wish to execute.

Skill Mastery

Learning and sharpening skills are major functions of visualizing. Whether it's a physical game technique (e.g., a new release) or psychological method (such as thought stopping), your imagination can accelerate the learning process for all new skills and the honing of skills already developed. Every facet of your game can be advanced and maintained through imagery. Using visualization in this way is known as "process-oriented imagery." In this type of visualizing, the images concern what you do rather than the competitive results.

Priming for Performance

In order to successfully perform, skills must be mastered and then executed. One of the great potential benefits of visualization is to maximize the probability of your executing to full capability. In other words, the aim is to implement what you've learned. This involves process-oriented imagery during the training period and as part of your mental routines on the day of competition (Chapters 5 and 6 describe the use of visualization on the day of an event).

Anticipating Situations

Visualization can be used to prepare for the full range of situations you'll confront in competition and, for that matter, in life generally. In your mind's eye, you can conjure up any circumstance you may face and then rehearse the way you'll cope with it. Through such mental practice, all aspects of your Master Plan can be further developed and you can be optimally ready to effectively handle all conceivable competitive challenges. Following are some examples:

- See yourself bowl several games and adjust to changing lane conditions. Make the necessary moves, equipment changes, etc.

- Envision yourself faced with a variety of spare opportunities. Convert these using whatever techniques you would actually use.

- Imagine your team needs you to strike in order to win a match. Use relaxation techniques to maintain poise and then throw a perfect shot.

- Visualize game circumstances which might distract you. Maintain focus through concentration techniques.

- See yourself becoming distracted. Utilize refocusing methods to quickly regain your concentration.

- Visualize yourself using your pre-shot routine over several games. Regardless of distractions, the results of a game, or lane conditions, your routine is consistent.

- Imagine a teammate has an angry outburst and isn't relaying relevant information. Use communication skills to help him or her regain composure and contribute to the team process.

- See yourself rebound from various types of adversity: a slow start, missed shot, poor game, etc.

- Envision a rough day at work. Use stress management methods to prepare yourself mentally for league play that evening.

- Think of a family conflict. Call upon communication skills to resolve the conflict.

Confidence Building

Visualizing performance excellence contributes to confidence (Chapter 7). Your optimism can be boosted by seeing yourself properly execute skills and effectively cope with a wide range of competitive situations. In addition to this process-oriented imagery focused entirely on the quality of your execution, there is a second type of imagery which can raise confidence. "Outcome-oriented imagery" involves competitive results. Imagine winning a match, winning a tournament, or rolling an 800 series. These are examples of outcome-oriented visualizing. This type of imagery can inspire and energize as well as increase your confidence level. Visualizing actual successes you've achieved is another way to raise confidence.

Relaxation and Psyching Up

The ability to calm or energize yourself in order to create an optimally poised and energized readiness is crucial to peak performance. Visualization is a basic and invaluable tool that can be applied here (Chapters 13 and 16).

Concentration

Visualization is one of the psychological tools which can help you maintain concentration and refocus if you become distracted. We recommend that visual cues for concentration be a part of your pre-shot routine (Chapter 6). Even if you don't use visual cues on every shot, they can be included in your mental game repertoire. Then you'll be prepared to call upon this imagery when faced with distractions.

Kim Terrell: Won two major championships among nine PWBA titles, three-time recipient of Robby Award (most positive image of women in professional bowling)

Stress Reduction

Relaxing imagery can be used to calm yourself before, during, and after competition. Beyond this, using visualization to relax is a life skill (Chapter 13). Later in the book, you'll learn how some creative visualizations can enable you to leave behind the stresses of a day when entering the bowling center (Chapter 11).

To summarize: Visualization is a powerful psychological tool with multiple uses. Four functions, in particular, lend themselves to

---

MENTAL PRACTICE BOOSTS TRAINING PROGRESS

The setting was a Team USA training week at the United States Olympic Training Center. Peter Partridge, a veteran bowler who had enjoyed many successes in his career, was eager to learn from the coaching staff. Yet, he expressed concern during a sport psychology consultation about his ability to implement a significant correction in his physical game advised by the coaches. The advice was that he approach the foul line straight with shoulders open rather than using his characteristic angled approach in the direction of his target.

Through this athlete's experience in a group psychological skills training session for the full team and through an exercise during an individual session, it was discovered that Partridge had superior visualization skills. The athlete and team psychologist collaborated on developing a mental practice format for the new approach. Later in the week, Partridge reported that the visualization was "very, very helpful" and that he was feeling more confident and comfortable. In follow-up contacts, he again stated how useful the visualization process was. The coaching staff confirmed his progress.

The specific strategy involved the following sequence:

1. Diaphragmatic breathing
2. Imagine a wave of relaxation moving through the body
3. Visualize aiming between the 3rd and 4th arrows
4. Visualize a perpendicular approach to the foul line with shoulders shifted appropriately
5. Visualize the ball following the target line (what we call "the line in your mind")

An indication of this athlete's immersion in this process was his hearing the sound of pins during the mental practice.

In the following year, Partridge came through with a dominant performance at the United States Olympic Festival. Gold in the singles, doubles, and team competitions earned him the nickname "Three-Pete." He credited the type of adjustments noted above for enabling him to triumph despite a painful injury.

mental practice—skill mastery, priming for performance, anticipating situations, and confidence building.

The circumstance in the box on the preceeding page illustrates the use of mental practice. In this example, the function is skill mastery.

Increasing Visualization Skill

Aptitude for visualizing varies among athletes. However, we've found that most bowlers can master visualization sufficiently to derive benefit from mental practice applications and the other functions identified in this chapter. Even when bowlers don't readily experience non-bowling imagery (e.g., a scene of nature for relaxation purposes), more often than not, there has still been some capacity to envision themselves bowling. In other words, they could still use visualization to mentally practice. If you're like most individuals, the more you visualize, the better you'll get at it.

If you're unable to visualize at all, take heart. The array of psychological tools available means that no bowler is dependent on any one approach. The "secret" to an elite mental game is to find the methods which are effective for you as an individual athlete.

When to Mentally Practice

While there are no hard and fast rules, we recommend that you mentally practice at least once per day for a minimum of ten minutes. In addition to a continuous stretch of time, such as ten minutes, visualizing for any time period can be beneficial. Seeing yourself bowl one shot with perfect form doesn't take long at all and can be done numerous times during a day.

Increase the amount you mentally practice as an event approaches. Rainer Martens, one of the most influential sport psychologists and a longtime coach, specifically recommends mental practice at least three times per day for two days prior to the event.

On the day of competition, mentally rehearse before arriving at the center and then again inside the center prior to the start of competition. Based on research, the effectiveness of this technique at the center may be maximized by visualizing for one to three minutes immediately before you warm up.

How to Mentally Practice

As an introduction to visualizing, try this exercise:

1. *Close your eyes. Breathe slowly and deeply until you feel pleasantly relaxed. Use diaphragmatic breathing if you already know this technique.**

2. *See yourself in a theater, waiting for a movie to start.*

3. *Engage your senses. What do you see? Are there other people around? What do you hear? What do you feel? What do you smell?*

4. *Think about something you've always wanted to do but couldn't. This doesn't have to be about bowling. It could be any endeavor in life.*

5. *Now imagine the movie beginning. Picture yourself on the screen. You're doing something special that you've always wanted to do. Savor every detail. Enjoy the moment.*

6. *When finished, once more concentrate on your breathing. Slowly count "three-two-one," feeling more alert with each number. Open your eyes.*

Now that you're warmed up, follow this sequence:

1. *Close your eyes. Breathe slowly and deeply or use another relaxation method until you feel very calm.*

2. *Imagine you're aligning yourself in the stance. Start at the feet, working your way up the body.*

3. *Proceed through your approach using ideal form. You're perfectly aligned, balanced, and synchronized.*

4. *As you reach the finish position, see the ball following the line in your mind precisely on its way to the strike pocket.*

5. *Open your eyes. Stretch your arms and legs.[6]*

* Taught in Chapter 13

What to do

To mentally practice, simply close your eyes and imagine yourself bowling. If you're working on skill mastery, execute the targeted skill flawlessly. If priming for performance is your goal, envision yourself bowling with perfect form (as in the second exercise). To optimally cope with specific situations, picture those circumstances and see yourself coping effectively. If you're looking for a confidence boost, visualize excellent form and/or a competitive success.

Perspective

When you visualize, take note of the perspective. Do you see yourself bowling from the front, from the side, or from behind? See if you can change the vantage point. Does one seem clearer than the other? If so, stay with this perspective.

Now try to visualize from an internal frame of reference. In other words, the experience is identical to the way you perceive things when you're actually bowling. Instead of seeing yourself from the outside, you're on the inside looking out. If this perspective is as clear or clearer than the others, try using it. While no one perspective has been proven to be preferable to another, the internal perspective is most similar to the actual bowling experience. Therefore, all else being equal, we suggest you use the internal perspective. However, we must stress that all perspectives are effective. What matters most is the clarity of the imagery and your comfort with it.

Senses

As you visualize, try to experience your other senses in addition to what you see. Can you hear the sound of the ball on the lane or the sound of the pins crashing? Do you feel the ball in your hand or the approach beneath your feet? Are there smells you associate with a bowling center? Calling upon multiple sensory experiences during mental practice may add to the impact of the visualization. We want to emphasize, however, that this isn't necessary.

Relaxation

Note that the introductory exercises for imagery began with a relaxation technique. While some athletes find their visualization enhanced by relaxing, this isn't always the case. Experiment to learn whether or not a full relaxation process improves your imagery. It may be that a brief form of relaxation, such as a few calming breaths, is sufficient. Or you may simply be able to visualize very well by simply closing your eyes and beginning.

Even if a full relaxation process is best for you, we suggest you sometimes mentally rehearse with briefer preparation. This will help prepare you for competitive circumstances where you may not have the opportunity to complete a relaxation process.

On the other hand, even if relaxation doesn't seem necessary for effective visualization, you still may choose to go through a relaxation sequence before mental practice. There are two reasons for this. Using relaxing methods on a regular basis will enable you to master the techniques and keep them sharp. You'll also derive the health and other stress management benefits which relaxation can provide.

Exercises

1. Follow the instructions for the two introductory visualizations.

2. Proceed through our steps and suggestions regarding what you do to mentally practice and how perspective, senses, and relaxation are involved.

3. Practice your visualization skills by imagining the ten competitive challenges cited under "Anticipating Situations."

REVIEW

Mental practice is the third training key considered. This activity involves visualizing yourself bowling in order to master skills, prime for performance, anticipate situations, and build confidence.

Visualization has other valuable applications such as assisting relaxation or energizing, enhancing concentration, and reducing stress.

The ability to visualize usually increases with practice.

Recommendations are offered regarding the amount and timing of mental practice and what procedures to use.

GAME FACE TIME

P A R T   I I

Routines Before and During Competition

Time spent developing a mental routine allows improvement beyond most expectations.
Jeri Edwards

5

PRE-GAME PREPARATION

Getting a feel for the bowling center contributed to making the tournament go easier.
   Tony Manna Jr.

Our training guidelines can bring you to a state of maximum readiness as the day of competition arrives. In this chapter you'll learn what actions to take on the actual day of the event prior to its start. The next chapter will present actions we recommend repeating before each shot.

Routines

These pre-game and within-game routines are planned patterns of behavior designed to give you the greatest likelihood of performing to your full potential.

In order to execute optimally, adhering to a fixed routine before and during competition is essential. With respect to psychological skills, a routine guarantees that specific techniques will be used. Also, a fixed sequence of actions functions like a ritual of sorts, creating a sense of order, consistency, and familiarity. This may exert a calming effect, promote concentration, and help you refocus following distractions.

Pre-game routines consist of two segments: activities occurring before you enter the center and those you do once inside.

Activities Outside the Center

On the day of competition, we recommend a series of actions before you arrive at the center.

- A relaxation method is calming and may also enable you to derive the most benefit from visualizing. Choose whatever technique is effective for you, such as diaphragmatic breathing, Progressive Muscle Relaxation, meditation, or music (covered in Chapter 13).

- If you find yourself in need of energizing rather than calming, apply a "psyching up" method which you've previously practiced (Chapter 16).

- The two types of imagery, process-oriented and outcome-oriented, may both be useful. Close your eyes and visualize bowling with perfect form. Imagine ideal execution in regard to posture, timing, finish, and follow-through. Your arm swings freely and easily. See the ball travel perfectly on line and pass over the target. To boost confidence and intensity, bring to mind images of success. Setting a personal best, earning a check, or reaching the championship round are possible achievements you can envision.

- Set your mind for success prior to leaving for the center. "Mindset" is a psychological method to orient and prime you towards peak performance. It can be used any time. Its purpose here is to promote unwavering focus and unyielding determination. As an example, here's a mindset sequence you can say to yourself:

  I'm going to play my best today no matter what. Whether I start with three strikes or three opens, I'm not going to allow that to affect me in any manner. Each and every shot, I'm going to give it the very best I can possibly muster, both mind and body, attitude and delivery, mental thought process and flow to the line. I'm going to get those two, I'm going to put them together. I'm going to do my very best today on each and every shot no matter what. I promise to myself on every shot I ever throw in my bowling career, that's what I'm going to do.

- Keep your thoughts ("self-talk") positive before leaving for the center. This is vital. We suggest repeating affirmations used in your daily routine during training. Quickly apply thought stopping if negative self-talk occurs. Substitute positive ideas. (Chapter 8)

- Review event goals developed with your coach. Make revisions if circumstances call for it (e.g., equipment factors or injury).

- This would be an ideal time to play a performance audiotape (Chapter 16).

All of these methods can be used as you travel to the center, if your means of transportation permits.

Finally, be sure to "park" stressful thoughts concerning your daily life outside the center (Chapter 11). Whether these thoughts relate to work, relationships, or any other important matter, it's crucial that your mind be clear for bowling. Thought stopping and a relaxation technique such as a calming visualization are two methods for accomplishing this.

Systematically preparing in this way will gear you to excel as you enter the center.

Activities Inside the Center

When you enter the bowling venue, become thoroughly familiar with the surroundings ("acclimate"). Locate the paddock, tournament office, restroom, and other important areas. Determine where to go for water or a snack. Consider where to place your equipment during competition so it's easy to make ball changes if needed. Where are you going to stand or sit? Check out the entire center and get a feel for the big picture. The goal of this acclimation process is to become efficient in use of the competition environment and to be comfortable.

Most athletes like to reach the center 45 minutes to an hour prior to competition. Some only want 20 minutes lead time. What do you prefer? Develop a routine based on who you are. For instance, Lynda Barnes, a member of Team USA 2005 who has also bowled professionally, likes to arrive enough in advance to prepare mentally, tend to her equipment, and take her time. This helps her feel calm instead of rushed. In contrast, Mandy Wilson, a former Team USA player, found that waiting for an hour got her too fired up.

If you're part of a team and don't like to be there as early as the other players, what do you do? Wilson had to come up with a plan allowing her to deal with the extra time. So, she might walk around the center, play video games, or listen to her favorite music on headphones.

Two immediate activities inside the center are situating your equipment and completing any necessary administrative tasks. Next, tend to final preparations regarding the balls you're taking to the lanes and physical needs, such as hand-care. Then do some stretching and apply any number of psychological skills you've already been using. Determine if you're tense or need an energy boost and use a relaxing or psyching up technique. You may want to visualize using process-oriented imagery (the aim is to focus on what you can control rather than the final results). Repeating affirmations is another likely activity. Listening to a performance audiotape and/or music is also among your options.

With respect to communication, follow what works best for you. If talking to others (competitors, friends, etc.) is pleasant and typical of your pre-game pattern, then do this. If staying totally focused on what you're doing is preferable, then don't engage others beyond what courtesy or your team requires. In fact, tactfully deflect efforts to involve you in conversation. If you're unsure what amount of pre-game communication is best, try varying approaches and keep a log to see how your performance is affected. Discussion with your coach can help you arrive at the best approach.

Just prior to your warm-up, we suggest one to three minutes of process-oriented visualizing. Use the same type of imagery as in your regular mental practice. Imagine yourself bowling with perfect form. You might take a few relaxed breaths and close your eyes before starting the process.

Next start warming up. Develop your immediate game plan. Decide on the angle you'll play; choose the equipment which best matches this line and the condition; consider the ball velocity, rotation (wrist action), and loft.

Exercises

1. Of the activities recommended for outside the center, which ones are you already doing?

2. Which will you add to your routine?

3. Which activities suggested for inside the center are currently part of your routine?

4. Which one(s) will be added?

REVIEW

Pre-game preparation consists of routines before arriving at the center and routines within the center prior to competition.

Activities we recommend outside the center are

- Regulating your energy (for example, use a relaxation method);
- Visualizing—both process-oriented and outcome-oriented imagery can be used;
- Mindset—orienting yourself to all-out performance;
- Self-talk—repeating affirmations and applying thought stopping as needed;
- Reviewing/revising event goals;
- Listening to a performance audiotape; and
- Clearing your mind of daily concerns.

Inside the center, the following are suggested:

- Acclimating—familiarizing yourself in detail with the environment.
- Completing tasks relating to equipment placement and administrative requirements.
- Tending to final equipment preparation and any special physical preparation.
- Stretching.
- Applying psychological skill methods such as diaphragmatic breathing.
- Conversing to the degree that's competitively best for you.
- Prior to warming-up, visualizing using process-oriented imagery.
- Developing a game-starting strategy as you warm up.

6

PRE-SHOT PREPARATION

Pre-shot routine is very important in our sport. This means going through a methodical thought pattern and teaching your body to do the same thing every time.
Susie Reichley

It's time to bowl. Time to knock down pins and reap the benefits of your systematic preparation. Dedicated training has brought you to the point of maximum readiness. Pre-game routines have you set to perform. You now take the key final steps priming you to successfully execute.

These final steps to excellence comprise your routine leading to each shot during competition. Alternately referred to as "within-game routine," "between-shot routine," or "pre-shot routine," this sequence of actions is necessary for performing well. Bowling your best requires a consistent routine before shots. This point deserves highlighting. No matter how hard you train or how talented you are, what you do immediately before each shot will affect the quality of your game, and if your routine fluctuates, so will your pincount.

What to Do and Where to Do it

Pre-shot activities occur in three areas: the settee, by the ball return, and the approach. There are essential assignments to undertake in each of these locations. These actions prior to executing are equivalent to loading a computer before hitting "print."

In the Settee Area

Think of the settee area as your office. This is where you analyze and plan strategy prior to each frame. Your immediate game plan includes five essential decisions:

1. What angle?
2. What ball?
3. What speed?
4. What release?
5. What loft?

Make your decisions and adjustments before walking to the ball return. Determine what your target is and where to stand. Select the equipment best matching the condition and situation. Decide whether to be aggressive or throw the ball softer. Choose your wrist and hand action. Calculate how far to loft the ball.

At the Ball Return

Armed with your strategy, you now walk to the ball return. The area by the ball return is equivalent to the on-deck circle in baseball. We refer to this area as the "think circle." By thinking, we don't mean analyzing. That's been accomplished.* Instead, what you do here is engage in a series of brief mind/body methods designed to create an optimum psychological state for bowling performance.

We commonly recommend a sequence consisting of a concentration technique (A), relaxation method (B), visualization (C), and affirmation (D). Ten to twenty seconds should be sufficient to complete this sequence.

    A. With respect to concentration, a verbal or visual cue can lock you into high focus. You might say the word

---

* This applies to all but those spare shooting decisions and tenth frame adjustments made when you've already been on the lane. These take place at the ball return between shots. Then proceed as described here.

"focus" to yourself or think of your coach saying this to you. Or imagine a big banner hanging from the ceiling over your lane (anywhere from the pins to the foul line or even the scoring console). "FOCUS" is inscribed on the banner in bold letters. Choose any colors for the banner so long as the letters stand out. A white background with dark blue letters is one popular choice. Coach Borden, speaking as a competitor, observed, "I see that sign in every bowling center and I get the eye of the tiger." (Cues for concentration are covered in Chapter 11.)

B. To relax, take one or two slow, deep breaths, inhaling through the nose and exhaling through the mouth. We suggest diaphragmatic breathing. As an alternative, you can quickly calm yourself through another method you've practiced, such as recalling music or envisioning relaxing images. Some bowlers like to imagine tension dripping from their fingertips onto the floor. (Chapter 13 provides instructions for diaphragmatic breathing and other relaxation techniques.)

C. Visualize bowling with ideal form. Your stance, stride, swing, and release are perfectly balanced, synchronized, and smooth. Then picture the ball following "the line in your mind," traveling over the target, down the lane, into the pocket. If you choose to see the pins go down, that's fine. However, what's crucial here is the dynamic, coordinated movement of your body leading to a crisp, clean delivery and great bowling shot.

D. Recite an affirming statement which may include a performance cue to remind you of technique. "I'm a great shot-maker" represents a general affirmation, while "My swing is smooth and easy" is technique-related. (Chapter 8 teaches you how to create affirmations.)

An optional fifth step is playing a few seconds of music in your head. We recommend something that inspires (e.g., Survivor's "Eye of the Tiger" or the Wallflowers' "Heroes").

If your routine is interrupted at any point, simply "rewind"—i.e., start the sequence again. This is important for regaining focus as well as for deriving the full benefit of the psychological skills you're using.

(While most bowlers do this routine in the distinct steps provided, some prefer to merge steps. For example, the banner is pictured during one deep breath, perfect form is visualized on another deep breath, and then an affirmation is repeated as music is recalled. Even if you ultimately go this route, we recommend initially learning and applying the steps in sequence.)

Before stepping onto the approach, you go through a number of accustomed physical activities. Using a towel or rosin bag, turn and wipe your ball. Some bowlers will then blow on their fingers or the finger holes (others may do this promptly on the approach). This short series of actions constitutes a routine of its own and serves both a practical and comforting purpose.

Several examples of routines at the ball return are given in the box that starts on page 64. These illustrate the range of possibilities for each step (see "Individual Variations" on the next page).

On the Approach

You've planned and psychologically primed yourself to make a great shot. What you do next on the approach should be simple, efficient, workman-like. Step up, put your feet in position, flex your knees, and assume your stance. Make sure your focus stays external. This means concentrating on where you're throwing the ball. Then, just go. Keep your eyes forward and feel the overall flow of your entire body moving to the foul line and executing the shot toward the target.

School is Out

A frequent and costly mistake is overthinking by the ball return and on the approach. Excessive thinking can interrupt and otherwise interfere with the sequence of methods intended to optimally prepare you for the upcoming shot. Concentration may be broken and anxiety may climb. The expression "paralysis by analysis" graphically describes the way an overactive mind can impede your bowling process.

Instead, we say uncomplicate your bowling life and enjoy the fruits of your hard work. Your problem-solving "homework" is done by the time you leave the settee area. Now have some fun. Smoothly, automatically go through your pre-shot sequence at the ball return. When you're on the wood, it's time for action. The computer is loaded. Just hit print. As you walk to the line, don't think of your delivery, but rather where you're throwing the ball. Your mind is uncluttered and lasered into the target. You're not conscious of yourself at that moment and simply allow the bowling process to unfold.

Individual Variations

Bear in mind that the most effective pre-shot sequence is ultimately a highly individual matter. What produces the best results for you may vary considerably from what works best for your teammate. It's up to you and your coach to find the most effective routine. We have suggested a framework within which there are many possible variations.

For example, not only can the choice of concentration techniques vary, some bowlers don't feel the need for any concentration cues. The number of relaxing breaths may well differ from one individual to another. In fact, instead of using a calming technique, some may want to energize themselves with recall of upbeat music or some other psyching up approach. Visualizations may vary in numerous ways, including viewing perspective, senses involved, and starting and ending points (e.g., does the imagery stop upon release or do you see the ball on the lane?). If an athlete doesn't experience clear images, visualization may not even be part of the pre-shot routine. Affirmations may vary with respect to content, position in the sequence (some prefer to say them before the visualization), the number recited, or whether or not you include them at all. Finally, music is an option with endless possibilities.

There's no end to the variations in physical routine before and just after stepping onto the approach—whether it's the number of times the ball is turned, how it's held and wiped, the process of blowing in the thumb hole, and so on. Our only suggestion here is that you be efficient as well as consistent so that the transition from your psychological routine at the ball return to your delivery is brief.

On the approach, some bowlers recite a performance cue such as "ball out slowly." Others use counting or another technique to maintain a particular pace or prevent distraction. Regardless, strive to remain externally focused.

SAMPLE PRE-SHOT ROUTINES

- At age 19, Bill McCorkle qualified for a TV bowling show for amateurs seen across Ohio. The top amateur got to bowl against 1972 PBA Bowler of the Year Don Johnson for $10,000. McCorkle beat four competitors on TV and then bested Johnson in a stunning upset. At the age of 50, with many successes to his credit, he upgraded his mental game. This was the pre-shot sequence he started using in 2003:

  1. Visualize a banner with maroon background and gold letters ("FOCUS") suspended from the ceiling near the approach.
  2. Take one or two slow, deep breaths.
  3. Visualize bowling with perfect form. See the ball to the arrows. The perspective is from the right, midway between the back and side. Hear the ball hit the lane.
  4. Say to yourself: "I will do this," "I'm relaxed," "I trust my armswing," "I will carry."*
  5. Recall music—"Like a Rock," sung by Bob Seger.

  Using this routine, McCorkle averaged 233 for the league season, best in the Columbus, Ohio area. As credited in *Sports Illustrated*,[7] he also swept the Greater Columbus Bowling Championships, winning titles in the singles, doubles, and team event (becoming the first senior bowler to capture three Open Division titles in the same year).

- A dedicated bowler had immigrated to the United States as a teenager. His mental game evolved dramatically in 2004**. This was the pre-shot sequence he adopted:

  1. Visualize a red, white, and blue banner hanging from the ceiling in front of the pins (describing this image, he declared, "America is my country, America is my home.")
  2. Take two slow, deep breaths.
  3. Visualize bowling with perfect form. The perspective is from the back. Hear the sound of pins falling as the ball hits the pocket ("a great feeling").
  4. Say to yourself, "I'm a great bowler."
  5. Recall music—"New York, New York," sung by Frank Sinatra ("It's me. I'm New York!").

  Bowling with this routine, his average rose to the top of a high-caliber league.

- Teenage girls and boys in the People-to-People Sports Ambassadors Program*** received mental game coaching while bowling at international events in 2002 and 2003. Among the choices for each step of the pre-shot routine were as follows:

  (continued)

1. Visualizing a banner: Red background, white letters; black background, gold letters; red background, black letters; green background, yellow letters; gold background, red letters; triangular shape, yellow around the edge, white background, black letters.

2. Breathing: Take one, two, or three slow, deep breaths.

3. Visualizing perfect form: From stance to release; imagery ends there or ball is seen to arrows or to pins; perspective is from the side or back or internal (looking out); there are usually sounds heard (e.g., pins crashing) and sometimes sensations (e.g., fingers holding the ball).

4. Saying an affirmation: "I will make this"; "I'm an amazing scorer"; "Great timing, great release"; "My armswing is smooth and consistent"; "Perfect form, perfect shot"; "I'm a winner."

5. Recalling music: Start of Beethoven's Fifth Symphony; "We are the Champions" (Queen); "Hero" (Chad Kroeger, with Josey Scott); "Sweet Emotion" (Aerosmith); "Follow Me" (Uncle Kracker).

In both years, individual tournament winners used this type of routine.

---

* In 2004, "I will carry" was changed to "I will execute."
** A fuller discussion of this athlete's mental game is found in Chapters 12 and 13.
*** In this program, qualified young athletes travel to countries worldwide to compete and expand their cultural horizons.

Liz Johnson: First woman to reach a PBA Tour title match (on TV) and first to win a PBA regional (2005)

Round Out Your Routine

In addition to the basic routine we've presented, using psychological skill techniques throughout the time between shots is a vital part of pre-shot preparation. Every moment between shots can be covered by a useful activity.* In other words, you should consider all your actions in light of whether or not they are best preparing you for the next shot. For instance, socializing between shots is stress-reducing to some athletes, while others find this distracting. How does social contact in the settee area affect you?

Perhaps the two most commonly applied techniques are visualization and relaxation methods. As an example, diaphragmatic breathing and process-oriented imagery (visualizing a perfect delivery) may be used between every frame in the settee area. Any of the psychological tools you've developed can become part of your standard pattern of actions between shots. Your unique responses to the challenges and stress of competition will determine what's useful for you to do in the settee area along with strategizing.

Be Adaptable

Adaptability is an indispensable feature of a top grade mental game. Developing a versatile repertoire of psychological skills enables you to apply a well-practiced technique to cope with any situation encountered during competition.

Your pre-shot routine is designed to optimally prepare you to execute. Consistency is essential. Yet, you must be ready to make some changes as the need arises. The following are suggestions regarding some possible adaptations during a game:

- Use thought stopping whenever negative self-talk or images occur.

- Except for additional deep breaths as needed, your routine on the approach should typically remain set. However, if you become aware of a particular muscle group that's tight, you can instantly relax it due to your Progressive Muscle Relaxation training.

- At the ball return, consider changing the concentra-

---

* Such "wall-to-wall" (shot-to-shot) coverage by routines creates a seal of sorts against negative and other unwanted thoughts (Chapter 11).

tion cue if it's ineffective or introducing such a cue if you're distracted and haven't been using one.

- At the ball return, adjust your energy to its optimum level* through a relaxation method (such as the diaphragmatic breathing we've suggested) or through a psyching up technique.

- The ball path will, of course, change in your visualization at the ball return according to the game circumstance.

- Also at the ball return, you may choose to fit the affirmation to the specific situation you face (e.g., "I'm a very accurate spare shooter" or "I make all my spares" or "I always convert"). If you haven't been using affirmations, you may want to add one, for instance, as a confidence booster in the clutch (e.g., "I bowl great in the tenth frame" or "The tenth frame is mine" or "I own the tenth frame").

- The settee area is where you have the most time and opportunity to flexibly apply psychological skills. Use your selection of mastered techniques to create the concentration, optimism, and poise associated with elite performance.

During competition, decisions regarding mental game adjustments, like the ones just mentioned, are made, in the vast majority of cases, in the settee area. So, there are really two types of strategies developed in this "office" area: technique/equipment moves related to lane conditions and psychological skill moves related to your inner reactions.

Master Your Routine

Use mental practice and on-lane practice to become fluid and comfortable with a new routine. Mentally rehearse the routine on a daily basis. Visualize yourself bowling using the routine in complete detail. When practicing, go through your sequences as if you were actually competing. Through simulation of varying game situations and by mentally rehearsing a full range of competitive circumstances, you'll prepare yourself to effectively utilize the routine when you bowl.

* You will learn how to exactly determine this in Chapter 12.

Your aim is to learn consistency in the face of game stressors while also learning to adapt as called for by the situation.

Mental rehearsal and sufficient practice lead to the next step, which is using the routine in league play. Finally, you'll be ready to introduce the routine in a tournament setting. This progressive, step-by-step implementation of a routine is designed to "mentally toughen" you to increasingly demanding levels of competition. When competing, it's absolutely essential that you feel at home with your routine. The routine then functions as a secure base, warding off potential distractions and ensuring that you're primed to perform.

If changes in your pre-shot preparation are relatively minor, the process of integrating them into your routine will, naturally, be accelerated. However, don't take for granted your ability to apply an altered routine. Practice and mental rehearsal are recommended before any modified routine is used in competition.

Exercises

1. Describe in detail what you typically do between shots—in the settee area, at the ball return, and on the approach.

2. Does your pre-shot routine include any mental game methods?

3. Use visualization to select a focus cue and to see yourself bowling with ideal form. If you use a FOCUS banner, where is it located and what are its colors? From what perspective do you view yourself? Remember to use as many senses as you can.

4. Develop an affirming statement.

5. If you choose the option of music, what inspires you?

6. Visualize yourself proceeding through the four or five step pre-shot sequence at the ball return. Do this several times.

7. Visualize your physical routine.

8. Visualize yourself on the approach proceeding in a business-like manner. Remember, just hit print. Your

form is perfect, the ball is on line. Repeat this several times.

9. Visualize the four or five step routine, followed by your physical routine, followed by your approach. Do this several times until the sequence is smooth. When you settle on a full routine, this will be what is mentally practiced as a step to mastery.

10. Do you over-think at the ball return or on the approach?

11. Consider how factors unique to you may shape your pre-shot sequence.

12. In addition to choosing how much to socialize, select psychological methods (taught throughout the book) to round out your routine between shots.

REVIEW

The pre-shot routine is a final step preparing you to perform. Building on your training and pre-game preparation, the pre-shot routine primes you to bowl at your highest level.

The sequences comprising your routine take place in the settee area, by the ball return, and on the approach.

- In the settee area, you strategize. The frame-by-frame game plan involves decisions concerning five condition-related adjustments: angle, ball, speed, release, and loft.

- At the ball return, we recommend a four step process. This sequence consists of a concentration cue, relaxation method, visualization, and affirmation. An optional fifth step is music. A brief physical routine follows and then you transition to the approach.

- On the approach, two keys are efficiency and external focus. You position yourself, promptly start forward, and concentrate on the target.

Overthinking at the ball return and on the approach is a common mistake. Having completed your analysis in the settee area, it's important to fluidly proceed through your planned sequence of psychological skills and physical actions.

Ultimately all athletes develop a pre-shot routine which is unique in some ways. Using our recommendations as a guiding framework, work with your coach to find the combination of methods which is most effective for you as an individual.

Every moment within a game provides an opportunity to prepare for a great shot the next time you throw the ball. Consider what psychological techniques you can regularly apply in the settee area in order to optimally ready yourself.

Elite bowling execution calls for the ability to adapt your application of psychological skills to varying game situations. Most variations in what you do will occur in the settee area.

Mastery of a pre-shot routine is best achieved by combining mental rehearsal, practice, and a step-by-step application in competition. An effective routine is completely familiar, smooth, and efficient during an event.

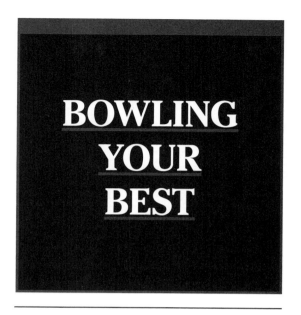

P A R T   I I I

Keys to
Peak Performance

*Successful application of the mental approach
to sport creates greatness.*
Fred Borden

7

MAINTAINING POSITIVE PERSPECTIVE I: CONFIDENCE

The best advice I ever received: You have to believe in yourself to be successful.
Jason Couch

A positive perspective is crucial for bowling to your potential. Chapters 7, 8, and 9 cover the three main aspects of this perspective: confidence, positive ideas, and self-acceptance. To kick off this discussion, we show you how to develop and maintain confidence.

Confidence

One of the most meaningful and enduring quotes in all of sports was the rallying cry of the 1973 New York Mets—"You Gotta Believe!" It was uttered by ever-colorful, ace reliever Tug McGraw and came to symbolize his team's mental toughness as it rallied from far behind to win the division title.

Jason Couch: Only bowler in PBA history to win three straight Tournament of Champions, PBA career earnings top $1,000,000

Whether it is a team or individual, confidence is a highly significant factor in performing optimally. Your expectations about performance can drastically influence your state of mind. If you trust your own capabilities, if you believe in yourself, then eagerness will result. However, if you anticipate failure, if you doubt your capacity to perform, then you'll likely experience significant anxiety.

A confident, optimistic outlook is conducive to performing at your best. A highly confident athlete is more likely to be energized and focused. In sharp contrast, a viewpoint characterized by lack of confidence and pessimistic beliefs can seriously hamper your efforts. An athlete with low confidence is more likely to become discouraged and distracted.

Be Aware of Crisis Signs

The methods of building confidence described in this chapter are valuable for all bowlers. Their prompt application becomes especially important for athletes suffering a crisis in confidence. A primary step to overcoming a confidence deficit is recognition that a problem exists. Awareness keys for low confidence include

- Lack of eagerness,
- Critical attitude towards oneself,
- Body language reflecting discouragement,
- Expressions of doubt, and
- Signs of anxiety.

Once alerted to the difficulty, you can take corrective action to raise your level of confidence.

How to Build Confidence

Building and maintaining confidence is a process. Like all parts of the mental game, this requires ongoing attention and effort. The potential benefits you'll experience in terms of success make this commitment of time and energy a highly rewarding investment on your part.

Competence → Confidence → Competence

The realistic basis for believing in your bowling game derives from your actual skills. In other words, competence forms the rational core of confidence. Any and all methods of increasing your bowling mastery, therefore, potentially contribute to heightened confidence.

Interestingly and importantly, confidence then promotes greater competence (i.e., performance capability) due to the psychological factors identified earlier. Think of confidence in terms of a racing metaphor and finishing kick: Through confident eyes, the finish line looms in front of you. Tasting success, a jolt of energy catapults you forward with determination. The feeling that you will not be denied represents the will to win. It is the hallmark of a champion.

Quality Practice

In discussing the essentials of quality practice, we stressed its importance. Quality practices are absolutely vital to the development of all aspects of your game. By raising the level of your competitive performance, confidence will be hiked. In addition, belief in your capability will be boosted by experiencing a general sense of accomplishment and by gains in specific skills during practice sessions. Finally, trust in the quality of your practice regimen raises overall confidence since you know you're doing what it takes to reach your goals.

Effective Feedback

The fastest and most efficient way to acquire skills and confidence in those skills is to receive effective feedback about your efforts. In fact, the quality of such feedback can make a critical difference in your growth as a bowler. The key is to receive input that is prompt, specific, and makes clear where you need to improve. In this way, the reality of your performance is reflected back to you and the door opened to future success.

Input from a coach is likely the major and most important source of information about how you perform. Such coaching should identify what you've done correctly and constructively point out what you can do to improve. Positive coaching reinforces an overall successful effort and the successful parts of efforts where the success was limited. Our long-standing advice to coaches: "Say, 'This is what you are doing, and this is what I would like you to do.' Never say, 'This is what you are doing wrong.' Instead say, 'This is how you do it right.'"[8]

A simple, readily available, "low tech" method of getting feedback about accuracy is white bowler's tape. Place one piece at the arrows and then two other pieces separated by one to one-and-a-half feet to target your breakpoint. The usefulness of this aid is its immediacy in providing essential information.

Videotape is an extremely valuable tool for providing performance-related feedback. If you know what to look for, the external viewpoint videotape provides can enable you to make the necessary analysis to correct a flaw or upgrade in a specific way. It can enable your coach to pinpoint what you're doing and to convey this picture to you.

As an example, Coach Borden recalls working with Chris Barnes at the Olympic Training Center on his start:

> We were out on the lanes and not making the progress we wanted, so I told Chris, "Let's take a look at your start when we review your videotape." We did just that and Chris saw immediately what we were talking about. Chris was inconsistent with the initial movement of his arm and ball in relation to coordinating it with his footwork. This played havoc with his timing. Once Chris saw this on the television screen, he could understand exactly what we were trying to get him to do. In this case, a picture was truly worth a thousand words.

Barnes enjoyed a storied amateur career and, beginning with PBA Rookie of the Year honors, has continued his winning ways in the professional ranks (including the 2005 US Open Championship).

A limitation of video is that bowlers must know exactly where to look and how to evaluate what they find. Coaches and top level players are the most likely to have this awareness. Two high tech tools we'll discuss shortly can accomplish this video analysis for you.

Coaches may also call your attention to performance keys by providing audiotapes. These can reinforce and remind you of the feedback given during practice or during an analysis of a videotape. In addition to straightforward descriptive feedback, audiotapes can be formatted in various ways to enhance motivation. You'll learn about the design of audiotapes in Chapter 16.

Finally, two devices at the cutting edge of bowling technology can contribute to the accurate assessment of your performance. The Dartfish video training system and the BowlersMAP Motion Analysis Program* enable you to copy video onto a software program whether the video source is a camcorder (digital or analog), TV, or VCR. The images can then be analyzed through a variety of advanced features.

These video analysis systems represent a quantum leap in receiving feedback about your physical performance. Armswing, steps, release, and other facets of posture and action can be precisely depicted and quantified. For instance, how you use your trail leg for leverage. This digital technology can superimpose one bowler's movements over another's. This allows the closest possible comparison of your form to a great bowler's, such as Walter Ray Williams. The systems can also "stroboscope" your actions. This means that the dynamic bowling motion, from first step to follow through, is viewed as a series of still images. Initial and average ball speed, release RPMs, and distances and angles can all be calculated.

Such technological innovations eliminate all guesswork as to how well you're throwing the ball. They can answer questions you or your coach have about a specific aspect of your game and, overall, remove doubts in your mind about where you must improve. After the initial assessment, progress can then be tracked. The end result? Developing a delivery which makes you proud.

These tools can be effectively used to restore your game to its best level should your performance drop off. The efficiency of doing this is enhanced by measuring your performance when you're at the top of your game. If you slide or slump, you can then pinpoint what needs correcting by comparing your present form to your best form.

To learn about these devices and how to obtain them, visit these websites: *www.dartfish.com* and *www.bowlersmap.com*. Pro shops which provide quality teaching will also be able to assist you.

It is vital to recognize that such advanced systems aren't substitutes for coaching the physical game, but rather aids to it. Interpretation of the data requires expert input. More importantly, a coach is needed to develop and monitor a plan for improvement here as well as with other parts of your Master Plan. And of course, there's no substitute for the overall guidance and support so necessary for development. Bear in mind that a qualified coach possesses the observational, analytic, and

* Distributed by Dartfish Ltd. and Ebonite International, respectively

communication skills needed for your growth. Technological devices can be viewed as potentially enhancing an already effective process. As an example, a 74-year-old bowler whose scoring had slipped didn't accept feedback from friends that his velocity was down. However, when his ball speed was measured at 15.2 mph, he recognized the need to increase velocity. With just 30 minutes of coaching, the speed of his armswing and footwork increased and ball velocity jumped to 17.1 mph. That year his league average increased by 18 pins.

All feedback about performance, regardless of the technology involved, can increase confidence by pointing to what's solid in your game as well as identifying what can be improved. Carolyn Dorin-Ballard, 2001 PWBA Player of the Year, had a high tech evaluation during the WIBC tournament* one year. She was extremely pleased to learn that her physical game didn't require any change. In addition to raising her confidence level, the feedback allowed her to concentrate on honing her mental game. Over the next three months, she was the tour's top scorer.

Encouragement

The impact on confidence that encouragement can provide is enormous. The significance of encouragement as a factor is summarized in the following passage from a prominent bowling publication:

> Nothing is more important than encouragement. Your coach and others on your "support team" (e.g., family and friends) can exert a tremendous impact on how you view your game and yourself. The feedback here goes beyond reinforcement regarding a specific effort or skill. The encouragement can be in the form of explicit statements about your skills in general, your potential, your capacity to learn, or your past achievements. Encouragement can counter negative expectations and give you renewed hope. Encouragement tells you that your coach/supporters will not abandon you and can directly boost belief in yourself.[9]

While the confidence-enhancing benefits of encouragement are triggered by a source outside yourself, you play an essential role. It is your responsibility to select a coach who can offer this type of support. This means you must appreciate the value of encouragement and be able to identify this capacity in a coach. In addition to what

* As of 2006, renamed the USBC Women's Championship

you sense about the person in face-to-face contact, we suggest you ask how he or she might communicate with you in various situations. Describe hypothetical circumstances and see if the encouragement you would want is forthcoming. You might also inquire about the coach's perspective or philosophy on the subject of encouragement and other aspects of feedback.

Surrounding yourself with supportive friends and making clear to family and friends what you expect in the way of support are other steps you can take to establish an optimum interpersonal environment. Sometimes, people who would readily provide encouragement aren't aware of your needs. Therefore, another area of responsibility is expressing your state of mind to your coach and other support team members.

In order for encouragement to meaningfully register and raise confidence and spirits, you must be receptive. Openness to the positive information directed towards you calls for trust in the honesty and wisdom of the source. It is also necessary to feel deserving of support. If you're consumed with self-anger and direct harshness towards yourself, you may well be closed to the impact of encouragement. A self-accepting attitude allows you to resonate with, and gain strength from, the encouragement. The topic of self-acceptance is covered in Chapter 9.

Master Plan & Goal Setting

The design of a Master Plan and the principles of goal setting have already been discussed. These contribute to confidence in three ways.

First, as we stressed, your use of a Master Plan and goal setting are vital to increasing skill level. In other words, they help develop competence, which forms the core of confidence.

Second, your belief in the realism or feasibility of your Master Plan and specific goals or steps along the path to fulfilling the plan is highly conducive to increasing confidence. Simply stated, belief in your game plan for development readily translates into heightened conviction about your ability to succeed. As you achieve goals and set new ones, skill increases and belief in yourself should likewise increase.

Third, an unwavering commitment to growth, such as setting improvement as an event goal, makes success attainable. This brings with it a sense of optimism.

Visualization & Review of Past Successes

We've pointed out that two types of visualization, process-oriented imagery and outcome-oriented imagery, can increase your confidence. With respect to time frame, these involve "here and now" images of your bowling performance.

Confidence can also be raised by visualizing your previous successful efforts. This type of a review can direct your expectations towards optimism. The logic is straightforward: "I did it before, so I can do it again." The great Pelé, perhaps the world's best-ever soccer player, would spend time before every match visualizing in the quiet of his locker room. With feet raised on a bench, Pelé first relaxed by visualizing himself playing on the beaches of his youth. He then played back in his mind triumphant performances on the soccer field.

While this type of review can include spontaneous recollections, we advise you to develop the technique as you would other psychological skill methods. That is, mentally practice the technique away from the lanes, apply it during practice sessions, use it in league play, and ultimately make it part of your mental game repertoire in tournament action.

Self-Scouting

A scout is someone who assesses an athlete's potential. The firm foundation of confidence resides in an accurate appraisal of your capacity to develop as a bowler as well as your current ability. In a sense then, you must be your own scout.

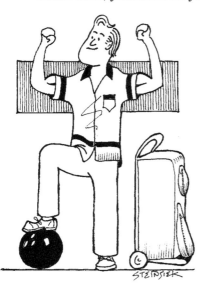

Various sources of information for this kind of assessment were cited in our discussion of effective feedback. Input from coaches, information from other trusted advisors, videotapes, and data from specialized high-tech systems can each play a role. Your prior achievements represent an expression of talent and naturally are an essential part of self-scouting. Most important, however, is your mastering of skills, your process of development. For this, look to the specific ways your talents are growing. Review the goals you set and met. Then look ahead to future goals and the gains in your game which will result. You're traveling on a path of increasing bowling skill mapped out by your Master Plan.

Self-Talk

The inner dialogue we all carry on within ourselves is referred to as self-talk. Keeping this positive is critically important to confidence building. This topic is covered in the following chapter.

Mindset & Reframing

Two valuable methods for bolstering confidence are mindset and reframing. These involve ways to control the content of your thoughts so that they are success-oriented. Mindset was previously discussed; reframing is discussed in Chapter 10.

Self-Hypnosis

Providing positive self-suggestion through the process of self-hypnosis can help increase confidence. In this process you actually hypnotize yourself.*

Hypnosis is an altered state of consciousness characterized by high focus and receptiveness to suggestion. In addition to its many clinical uses (e.g., smoking cessation, pain management, and weight control), hypnosis has varied sport psychology applications. Among these are confidence building, discussed here, and relaxation, considered in Chapter 13.

Hypnosis can be thought of as a guided three-step process: induction, deepening, and intervention. Induction most often involves instructions leading to eye closing. An example is staring at a spot on a wall and following the suggestion that your eyes are gradually closing and that you're becoming more and more relaxed as they do, until finally, when they do close, you feel fully and deeply relaxed, yet completely aware. At the same time, you can listen to instructions as well as communicate. The deepening process relaxes you further. Imagining yourself slowly descending a staircase and becoming increasingly relaxed with each step is a classic deepening technique. Once you're in a deeply relaxed, receptive state ("trance"), you're ready for an intervention.

An hypnotic intervention is a suggestion to influence your thoughts, emotions, or actions. In self-hypnosis, you provide your own intervention by reading a script, listening to a tape recorded by yourself or someone else, or simply speaking silently to yourself.

---

* We advise reading "Essential Tips" in Chapter 13 before engaging in self-hypnosis.

The intervention may be in the form of an affirmation or a scenario. Affirmations can be brief, such as those presented in the next chapter, or somewhat longer, as in the following:

> *I'm talented and mentally tough. I've practiced hard, I'm set to execute. I will make decisions quickly and trust them. I will be poised and focused on every shot. My swing will be loose and smooth. I will hit my target and hit the pocket. I'm sure and eager and ready to go.*

This type of suggestion can be in the present tense (as in a typical affirmation) or combine present and future tenses (as in the above example). Use the form which feels most inspiring. The suggestion can be repeated throughout the day in a normal state of consciousness.

Scenarios in self-hypnosis are detailed accounts of successful performance. For confidence building, describe a game exactly as you would like it to go. Note your pre-shot routine and physical execution. Adjust to varying game situations. Emphasize your confidence and overall positive perspective as well as your consistent concentration, optimum intensity level, feeling of comfort, and the fun you're having. Stay in the present, use the first person, and stick to process.

In addition, you can develop a confidence "trigger" by internally repeating a word or words at intervals throughout the scenario. Examples are "zone," "confident," "tough," "dialed in," "loose," and "pocket hit." What you repeat becomes associated with feelings of success and your ideal state of mind. At the end of the scenario, while still hypnotized, reinforce this association. Tell yourself that these same confident feelings can be later experienced by recalling or reciting the trigger.

When you're ready to regain full alertness, say the following to yourself: "I'm now going to wake up fully. I will count to five and become more and more alert with every number. When I reach five, I will be totally alert, completely awake, and feel absolutely great." Next, slowly count to five and enjoy the feeling of being refreshed and alert.

In self-hypnosis, you completely control the entire process. If you're interested in standard hypnosis, be sure to enlist the services of a qualified professional (e.g., a sport psychologist trained in this modality). This individual will inform you that, as with self-hypnosis, you'll remember everything, be able to talk, and can return to full alertness at any time you choose.

· T H E   C O A C H I N G   C O R N E R ·

Coaches' Guide for Confidence Building

The impact of coaching on your confidence level, as well as all other aspects of your bowling, can be immense. In his nationwide training programs, Dr. Lasser presents coaches with a guide for instilling confidence in their students. This framework, known as the REALITY system, is outlined below. The guide can serve coach and athlete as a handy summary of key confidence building methods.

R – rehearsal, reflection, reinforcement

E – encouragement

A – aiming

L – looking

I – imagery

T – talk

Y – yourself

- The R in REALITY stands for 3 Rs. *Rehearsal* refers to quality practice. *Reflection* is a reference to feedback, an accurate mirroring of your performance. *Reinforcement* calls for immediate and constructively expressed reactions to your specific actions.

- The E in REALITY stands for *encouragement.* Encouragement is second in line here, yet its importance is primary. Encouragement can make the difference between discouragement and determination, between feelings of futility and eagerness about the future.

- The A in REALITY stands for *aiming*—that is, goal setting. Effectively setting goals provides a ladder for skill development and a foundation for optimism.

- The L in REALITY stands for *looking.* The reference is to review of past successes (looking to the past) and accurate self-assessment (looking at present skills and potential).

- The I in REALITY stands for *imagery.* Mentally practice with process-oriented and outcome-oriented imagery.

- The T in REALITY stands for *talk,* meaning self-talk. This is a reminder of how important it is to maximize positive self-talk.

- The Y in REALITY stands for *yourself.* What this refers to is a coach utilizing himself or herself as a model for learning. This is described on the following page.

(continued)

• T H E   C O A C H I N G   C O R N E R •

(continued)

Coaches' Modeling

A coach can exert influence through modeling in several ways.

One means is by straightforward physical example. This involves demonstrating a facet of the physical game, such as a particular release. The athlete sees firsthand what the coach expects and thereby develops a clear mental picture of the learning goal.

A second way a coach can model is by self-disclosure—communicating experiences he or she has undergone in order to make a point. For example, a coach may describe actual situations encountered to powerfully illustrate distraction control in the face of noisy fans, the importance of pre-game routine, or the value of a piece of equipment.

Also, personal disclosures in the form of errors committed can effectively illustrate what to avoid (e.g., revealing how an opponent's comments once rattled the coach and led to a poor shot). In addition to being a useful tool for illustration purposes, this type of negative self-disclosure can free athletes to admit mistakes less self-consciously, without concern of being harshly judged. By following examples of mistakes with examples of later successes in the same situation, the coach then models and encourages successful learning.

A third means for a coach to teach by modeling is by actually behaving in the way described. For instance, a coach teaches focus by maintaining concentration during lessons and competition, and teaches confidence by displaying optimism if the bowler starts slowly or has a rough stretch.

On the following page is a clear example of how a coach can assist a bowler through modeling:

Michelle Mullen is a professional bowler and coach. She is a former national collegiate champion, the woman who represented the United States in the World Cup in Seoul, Korea, and the winner of multiple pro tour titles. She has served on the Team USA coaching staff.

(continued)

Undoubtedly, you can learn from the modeling of a good coach. Keep in mind that you also stand to benefit from the model provided by athletes and others having desirable skills/attributes. Look to emulate those possessing such positive qualities with respect to the mental game and life in general.

Mullen was instructing a relatively new bowler*. This woman was unmistakably talented, with high aspirations. Struggling at one point in the lesson, the student expressed discouragement, stating that she shouldn't still need all this coaching. Mullen recognized that the bowler was pressing and realized that this attitude was adversely affecting performance and limiting her learning potential. So, this coach said to her student, "Adjustments are something we all need to do, even at the pro level." Mullen then proceeded to receive some coaching herself from another instructor directly in front of the student. The bowler later commented, "It helped me to see Michelle work with the coach—she's a pro and still needs to work on her game."

Mullen's words and actions made a difference. The bowler relaxed, gained confidence, and felt more accepting of herself. She enjoyed and benefited from the rest of the lesson. This experience made a lasting impact, favorably influencing her attitude towards training and her own development. This athlete went on to win a NABI** tournament for the first time and has continued to enjoy success.

---

* At the time, Mullen was an owner/coach for Professional Bowling Instruction (Pbi)—a group of the world's top coaches offering affordable schools to bowlers wanting to upgrade their game.
** National Amateur Bowlers, Inc.

Exercises

1. Do you regularly experience any of the signs associated with low confidence?

2. Circle the rating which describes how much you use these confidence builders:

   1=No Use   2=Slight Use   3=Moderate Use   4=Great Use

Quality Practice	1	2	3	4
Effective Feedback	1	2	3	4
Encouragement	1	2	3	4
Master Plan	1	2	3	4
Goal Setting	1	2	3	4
Visualization	1	2	3	4
Review Past Success	1	2	3	4
Self-Scouting	1	2	3	4
Self-Talk	1	2	3	4
Mindset	1	2	3	4
Reframing	1	2	3	4
Self-Hypnosis	1	2	3	4

3. What steps will you take to implement or increase the use of these approaches? (Add to these as you become familiar with methods new to you.)

4. As a reminder, note what each letter stands for.

R   =

E   =

A   =

L   =

I   =

T   =

Y   =

5. Describe the way a coach and/or another person have been good models for the mental game. How about for other areas? Who in the present fits this role?

6. If you're a coach, cite one or more instances where you taught students through modeling or where you might have done so. Identify one or more situations where you can use this teaching method in the future.

REVIEW

Attaining a consistently positive perspective is fundamental to your bowling success. In this chapter, we consider a major component of this perspective: confidence.

Confidence is a highly significant performance factor. Awareness of problem signs is a primary step towards correcting a deficit in this area. Confidence can be increased and maintained by various actions. Competence is the realistic core of belief in your ability. A total effort to develop your bowling skills is, therefore, vital to becoming consistently confident. We suggest a confidence-building strategy consisting of 12 specific approaches. These include

- Quality practice,
- Effective feedback,
- Encouragement,
- Master Plan,
- Goal setting, and
- Visualization.

A coaches' guide based on elements of this strategy (the REALITY system) is offered. The model provided by a coach and others can serve as a powerful tool to increase an athlete's confidence.

Walter Ray Williams Jr.: 1990s' Bowler of the Decade, six-time PBA Player of the Year, PBA Hall of Fame

8

MAINTAINING POSITIVE PERSPECTIVE II: POSITIVE IDEAS

If you're not positive then you're negative and you're thinking of something that's going to take you backward instead of forward. There's only one way to go and that's ahead.
Pat Costello

Bowlers have vastly more control over their thinking than they realize. In this second chapter on positive perspective, you will learn extremely effective ways to manage your thoughts so they work for you instead of against you.

Positive Ideas

Belief about our abilities on and off the lanes clearly influences the way we think, feel, and behave. Confidence is all about such expectations. The mind's eye is also impacted by internal images and words which, at least initially, aren't full-fledged beliefs. Images of success* (seeing yourself roll a strike) or a phrase describing success ("I deliver in the clutch") can potentially influence us even though a firm expectation isn't involved. Such positive ideas are directly constructive and can also contribute to confidence. Whether in the form of a positive idea or a fully formed belief, your immediate thoughts (sometimes referred to as "current dominant thoughts") are tremendously important to performance. The psychological process of self-talk concerns such immediate thoughts and, therefore, is central to your mental game.

Self-Talk

Self-talk is our ongoing internal communication. We all engage in such inner conversations, which consist of words, phrases, sentences, and paragraphs. These verbal forms can combine in differing degrees with images. Self-talk is undoubtedly among the most vital psychological skills for bowling and other sports. What accounts for this importance?

Positive vs. Negative Self-Talk

When self-talk content is positive—meaning optimistic and supportive—your confidence, energy, and concentration tend to increase. In contrast, negative self-talk—expressions which are pessimistic and/or critically judgmental—can impair concentration, lower energy, and spike anxiety.

The following illustrates the differences between positive and negative self-talk: One of the top collegiate bowlers in the nation reported struggling to an emotional extreme with tough lane conditions he couldn't readily solve. Finding himself in such a situation, the bowler cursed. Then he said to himself, "Some of the other guys are bowling well. I should be better than these guys who are beating me. I don't belong here." The competitive impact of this negative self-talk was typically damaging, sometimes disastrous. His performance deteriorated. Frustration further mounted, and ultimately the caliber of his play could plummet.

Using a pre-set affirmation, as well as thought stopping technique (if necessary), the bowler was able to steer his self-talk in a positive direction. Instead of harsh, doubt-filled ideas, his mental content shifted to success-oriented, inspiring thoughts: "You're a winner. You can do this. Stay calm, confident, and solve it." No longer was the athlete undermining himself with self-defeating thought content. Now he was placing himself in the best possible position to maximize pincount.

---

* As discussed in Chapter 4

Self-Fulfilling Prophecy

Self-talk can become a self-fulfilling prophecy. In other words, positive self-talk can lead to favorable results and negative self-talk to unfavorable results. This creates the potential for a continuing outcome spiral in one direction or the other. A satisfactory outcome lends itself to further positive self-talk, while a disappointing outcome lends itself to negative thought content. This spiraling may continue over a game, series, block, tournament, or beyond. Whether a streak or slump develops may well depend on the type of self-talk you use. Therefore, it's essential to do what you can to maintain positive self-talk and to curtail self-talk that's negative as soon as possible.

Awareness of Self-Talk: Keeping a Log

If your self-talk tends to be positive due to confidence, personal style, or psychological techniques you may use, this area of the mental game will require less attention than if your self-talk tends to be negative. Nevertheless, since we all have some negative self-talk, and since positive self-talk is a psychological asset, it's useful for all athletes to develop techniques to maximize positive self-talk.

As with other areas of the mental game, awareness is essential to exerting control. Since most self-talk isn't conscious, we suggest you keep a log, at least initially.

The directions for a self-talk log are straightforward:

- Make notes of the self-talk which occurs before, during, and after you compete.

- Jot down both positive and negative thoughts, word for word.

- Record the situation which triggered the self-talk (e.g., "two opens to start last game of the first block").

- Indicate how you performed after this situation.

Excerpts from the self-talk log of a dedicated, several-leagues-per-week bowler are presented on the page that follows. As you read, carefully observe the type of descriptions provided. In particular, note the contrast between positive and negative self-talk as this bowler begins to work on his attitude while he competes. Reflect on how such self-talk compares to your own.

ENTRY A

Synthetic lanes and approaches.
Game #1: Open 1st two frames. Stay with it—don't let it destroy your day. 33 in the 4th frame. Very hard to get back into focus, but I'll try. I don't want to give up. 137—five opens. But I still have three games left. I can't become negative, but it's hard not to.

Game #2: Timing off—too fast on my feet. Next shot was perfect, but I speed up and don't even realize it. Maybe I should put weights on my ankles (JOKE)! 7th frame—I realize by this time that I'm not going to do anything here today. However, I'm bowling a little better this game than the first. Right now all I want is to improve the next two games and go home on a positive note. Shot 131— gave up counting the open frames. [Curses] It's the same every time I come to one of these matches. Maybe I'm just a house mouse and just can't bowl any place else. Maybe I just think I'm better than I really am! Got a lot to learn it seems.

Game #3: More relaxed but still not throwing ball the way I do back home. Shot 168. Wow—moving up in the world. Just a little more relaxed than before.

Game #4: Starting to drop my right shoulder. Nothing more to say—just a bad night. AS USUAL! Total: 600, four game series.

ENTRY B [Three days later; one day following a sport psychology consultation]

Warm-up before league—everything went well. I'm good and loose at this time.
Game #1: So far into 5th frame my thumb is slow—got to get it out faster. Not throwing the ball well. I'm trying to make it happen instead of just letting it happen. Score 180, two opens. It seems I was aiming the ball instead of swinging at it—will try for a better armswing into the 2nd and 3rd frames.

<u>Game #2:</u> So far at the end of the 6th frame, throwing the ball much better, more relaxed now. Scored 196, one open. Throwing better, in the pocket. Can't throw a strike every time, but I'm pleased. Babe Ruth didn't hit a home run every time at bat, or should I say Mark McGuire.

<u>Game #3:</u> Throwing well but missed 10-pin in the 4th. I tried to help the ball. Got to stay loose. Shot 193, split in 10th frame. 193 + 196 + 180 = 569. Not too bad considering my 1st game.

I'm at home now and going over my game tonight. I have to say, even though I didn't shoot as high tonight as I did last week, I feel I threw the ball better after the first game than I did last week. During the 2nd and 3rd games, I visualized myself making a good smooth delivery every time I got up on the approach and it worked. Also, I'd like to add this to my approach each time before I make the shot. NO NEGATIVES TONIGHT.

<u>ENTRY C</u> [Next day]

Practiced about 30 minutes. I feel good, throwing the ball well—nice and loose. I pictured myself making a perfect shot again while I was on the approach. I'm going to incorporate this into my game if it continues to be successful. We'll see how it works out today in league play.

10 minute league practice went well.

<u>Game #1:</u> Scored 202 with three opens. Started to rush towards the end of the game. In spite of this, I'm throwing well. Just have to keep focused on my rushing. I feel very good about myself and my game.

<u>Game #2:</u> Throwing well. But can't make a 7-pin. Missed about four so far, but I'm still okay. Next frame, I finally made a 7-pin. Although my score so far isn't that great, I feel I can come back and have a decent three game series. I'm good and loose and relaxed. I'm still seeing myself make a perfect shot. I like this idea for my approach. Strike out from 6th frame to end. 214 score. 7 timer. I'm doing OKAY SO FAR. KEEP IT UP.

> Game #3: Before I missed in the 4th frame, I threw ten strikes in a row—seven from the 2nd game and opened up the 3rd game with a triple. Score 190. Two opens. I'm pleased with myself.
>
> Today, I had about eight opens in three games. I shouldn't have that many opens. However, it was a good test. I never got down on myself and, for the entire match, I never missed the pocket except for the very first ball I threw. It looks like things are starting to pick up for me.

The general principle concerning the time to record your thoughts is to write notes as soon as possible after the self-talk occurs, without disrupting your concentration and routine. The best time for you may be between frames, games, or blocks.

Your self-talk during actual competition can immediately influence your performance. However, your thoughts at all other times also exert an impact on your psychological readiness. Therefore, be sure to record self-talk occurring before and after competition as well as thoughts away from the center. The latter includes thoughts on the day of competition as well as thoughts on the days leading up to the event.

A log serves three purposes. The first is to make you aware of the type and amount of self-talk. What you discover may surprise you since many, if not most, athletes aren't conscious of this internal process. A second related function is to gauge your progress towards increasingly positive self-talk. The third purpose of a self-talk log is making you alert to negative self-talk as it occurs. The log will teach you what self-talk is triggered by what circumstances. By acquiring the ability to quickly spot negative self-talk, you can prevent negative momentum from building and turn yourself in a direction that's positive. We will now teach you a method for accomplishing this critically important shift.

Thought Stopping

You've bowled quite well in the first five frames against a tough opponent. The match is dead even. Leading off the sixth frame, the other bowler throws a Brooklyn strike. You're in the pocket, but leave a ringing 10. You say to yourself, "Why don't I get the breaks?" The spare shot misses. As your stomach knots up, your inner voice says, "Oh no, here we go again. Don't choke."

Because you keep a self-talk log and know your own tendencies, you quickly recognize the negative self-talk. What do you do next?

A technique we recommend for quickly and effectively controlling negative self-talk as well as negative images is thought stopping. Let's see how it works.

We suggest four thought stopping options:

1. Say the word "STOP" silently or envision another person saying this to you.

2. Visualize a stop sign.

3. Visualize a red light.

4. Combine the first option with either the second or third.

In order to learn which method works best for you, try the following exercise:

Sit back. Make yourself comfortable and close your eyes. After a few easy, relaxing deep breaths, think of an unpleasant situation—perhaps bowling-related or possibly being late to work or in a fender bender. Then say the word, "STOP" to yourself. Note the way this affects the negative thought. Now conjure up the same thought. This time visualize a stop sign. Observe how effective this is in erasing the thought. Then experience the negative thought yet again. Imagine a red light. Note the impact. Re-experience the negative thought one more time. Now say the word "STOP" to yourself as you see either a stop sign or red light. How does this affect the thought?

These four thought stoppers are by no means the only options. If envisioning a red flag, hearing a whistle, or any other sight or sound works for you as a brake on negative self-talk, use it.

Once the negative self-talk is halted, take a few slow, deep breaths* (diaphragmatic breathing technique is recommended), then immediately substitute positive self-talk and/or other positive thought content such as nature imagery or a visualization of your bowling with perfect form. In addition to their own performance-enhancing qualities, these positive thoughts can block the return of negative self-talk and imagery. For this reason, such substitution is essential. An optional final step is briefly recalling music for a calming effect or an inspiring lift. Then resume your normal routine. If negative thoughts recur at any point, simply repeat the thought stopping process.

A thought stopping sequence, even if it consists of five steps (e.g.,

* One, two, or three is typical.

"STOP," two relaxing breaths, imagery of pins flying, an affirming "I've got a great delivery," and a blast of "Born to Run") can be completed relatively fast. A common range is 15 to 30 seconds.

As with other mental game techniques, thought stopping must be automatic to be effective. To master it we recommend practicing the sequence you develop as follows: ten times each day for a week, then five times each day for a week, then once a day thereafter. The practice repetitions needn't be consecutive. You can do them anywhere, even while walking around. Also, you don't need a negative thought to practice. The immediate aim is a seamless, effortless process. Effectiveness will follow. Also, visualize yourself using the technique when competing, followed by perfect form and a great shot. We generally suggest a week's preparation of this type before applying the method on lane. Then, once you feel comfortable with it in practice sessions, you're ready to use in competition.

Bowlers regularly tell us that thought stopping is one of their most useful mental game skills. It is also a valuable life skill since negative thoughts can impede functioning and generate stress throughout the day.

A key to the effectiveness of thought stopping is its prompt use. That's why it's vital that you be aware of your tendencies (i.e., what situation tends to elicit negative self-talk). The self-talk log should prove very helpful by increasing your awareness and priming you to rapidly respond.

An extension of the self-talk log which can accelerate the process of awareness/response is a "situation analysis" like the one which follows. In this actual example, a bowler first identifies his thoughts and some accompanying reactions at key points in a game ("Awareness"). Knowing his tendencies, he then notes what is or would be counterproductive at those times ("The Do Nots"). Finally, effective actions are listed ("The Solution").* As you acquire more psychological tools in the pages ahead, your options for the third column will expand.

---

* These actions are typically useful for the various issues raised (not only for their row). The self talk in quotes is sometimes repeated. References to past and future time correspond to previous and upcoming shots.

SITUATION ANALYSIS

Three Starts

Bad Start

8-	9-	X	9-						

Awareness	The Do Nots	The Solution
Getting upset	Get mad, give up	"Next frame, new frame"
Forcing shots	"Must make this"	Breathing
Getting down on self	Think bad of self	Thought stopping
		Process thinking, not outcome
		Be a friend to myself, front of hand only*

Ok Start

8/	8/	X	9/						

Awareness	The Do Nots	The Solution
Begin to worry	Pessimistic thoughts, panic	Relaxation method in settee area
Wonder about form	Look for perfection	Thought stopping
Want to make something happen	Focus on end results	Realistic expectations, self-tolerance
		Focus on routine

Great Start

X	X	X	X	X					

Awareness	The Do Nots	The Solution
Become excited	Too pumped	PMR**
Want to keep it going	Try to control shot	Trust routine, trust delivery
Think of remaining frames	Dwell on future, score	Stay in here and now

* As you would for any teammate, give yourself a hand—the front, not the back.
**Progressive Muscle Relaxation

Complete Game

A			B			C	D		
9-	81	X	X	9/	8/	7/	9-	X	X8/

A

Awareness	The Do Nots	The Solution
Body becomes tense	Past thinking, frustration	Use thought stopping
Want to make shot happen	Results thinking, pressure	Use breathing
Self-doubt arises	Thoughts of failing, no confidence	Then focus on looseness of body
Self-judgment starts	Bad thoughts of self	Remember: only one of many frames ahead
		Respect myself, think only positives

B

Awareness	The Do Nots	The Solution
Want to make quality shot	Give shot great importance	"Just one of a million frames"
Mind wants to control shot	"Have to be perfect"	Use breathing in settee area
Upset about early frames	Look back, question, and regret	Stay in the here and now
Thinking of later frames	Attention away from present bowling	Follow routine
		Have fun—"Let it go"

C

Awareness	The Do Nots	The Solution
Feeling tense	Past/future thinking	Use breathing & PMR
Feel pressured to make a shot	Must make shot to value self and skills	Use thought stopping
Discouraged	Negative thoughts	"I will make the next one"
		Appreciate my effort, my fight, my abilities

D

Awareness	The Do Nots	The Solution
Thinking of end	Think ahead	Use thought stopping
Want to finish game strong	Make it feel necessary	Have perspective
Get excited	Get too anxious/eager	Use PMR
Concern about competitive results	Lose concentration	Focus on routine

Tom Baker: PBA Hall of Fame member, two-time recipient of PBA's Steve Nagy Sportsmanship Award

How to Generate Positive Self-Talk

There are two types of positive self-talk: spontaneous and planned (pre-selected). To learn how adept you are at the spontaneous approach, do the following—apply thought stopping and practice substitution of positive self-talk as it comes to mind in the moment. The fluidity of such impromptu self-talk can improve through practice. Yet, we've found that for most bowlers, it's best to have pre-selected positive self-talk ready to be applied.

In order to create your own affirming statement (affirmations), we recommend the following guidelines.[10]

- Use self-assuring statements which are realistic.

- Be goal-directed.

- Create positive emotions and expectations.

- Stay in the present.

- Express statements only as a positive—what you will do.*

- Focus on performance, not results.

- Focus on controllable factors.

- State affirmations in the first person ("I"/"We").

An alternative to developing original affirmations is to use affirmations successfully applied by other bowlers. The advantage of creating your own self-talk is that it rings true and is easily recalled. On the

---

* Telling yourself not to do something (e.g., "Don't miss this spare.") is, in essence, negative self-talk, since it brings to mind what you want to avoid.

other hand, if an affirmation is genuinely meaningful to you, it truly becomes your own whether or not you were the first to use it.

Team USA provides its athletes with a list of individual and team-oriented affirmations used by the 1991 squad. Some of these are listed below. Read each out loud and then to yourself. See if any resonate based on your experience and outlook.

— PERSONAL AFFIRMATIONS —

- *I've practiced enough and I'm ready for this competition.*
- *I'm ready to give it my best.*
- *I have a really smooth motion today.*
- *I always have a relaxed, natural armswing.*
- *I have a loose, smooth, free-flowing, powerful motion.*
- *I'm a winner.*
- *I respect myself and my opponent.*
- *I prepare for the unexpected.*
- *No lane beats me. I can always figure them out.*
- *I observe my ball action and make the right adjustment.*
- *I always think positive thoughts.*
- *I maintain the same level of intensity on every shot.*
- *I'm alert, aggressive, confident, and in control.*
- *I'm working on my release and it's getting better and better.*
- *I'm a champion class player and person.*
- *I Carry Everything (ICE).*
- *I always stay calm and make appropriate adjustments.*
- *I have the best mental equipment for all lane conditions.*
- *I always play to the highest level of my abilities.*
- *I'm a hard worker at practice.*
- *I get the most out of every practice session.*

— TEAM AFFIRMATIONS —

- *I'm your teammate, and I'm here for you, no matter what.*

- *Whatever we do we'll do together.*

- *I always encourage and support my teammates.*

- *My teammates are helpful and beneficial to my game.*

- *I'm an asset to my team, and they're an asset to me.*

- *I'm positive and helpful in all my expressions to my teammates.*

- *I'm ready to give my best effort for my team.*

- *We have total confidence in each other.*

- *Positive is the only energy source we know.*

- *Our greatest successes are those we share.*

Be versatile in your self-talk planning. We suggest developing multiple affirmations which you can apply in different situations. For instance, "I'm grooved to the pocket," "I'm a great spare shooter," and "I'm coming back strong" are situation-specific. An affirmation such as "My swing is loose and smooth" is broadly applicable.

Consider switching affirmations once in a while. Keeping them fresh in this way sometimes adds to their effectiveness. If you discontinue using an affirmation for this reason, this doesn't mean it needs to be permanently retired. At some point in the future, it can be reintroduced and will likely be fresh again.

When to Use Positive Self-Talk

We've focused on the use of positive self-talk as a substitute for negative self-talk in the context of thought stopping. However, the potential benefits of positive self-talk go beyond this use. In fact, positive self-talk should be used as much as possible. Repeating affirmations on a regular, ongoing basis can enhance confidence, motivation, and other psychological dimensions important to performance. Additionally, the consistent use of self-talk may minimize the incidence and intensity of negative self-talk. In a sense, it functions as a shield against the intrusion of negative thoughts.

Mike Aulby: 1980s' Bowler of the Decade, PBA/USBC Halls of Fame, twice PBA Player of the Year, 27 titles

Affirmations can be used in a variety of ways in your routines. They may be included in your pre-game routine or the routine you use between shots. As part of your pre-shot sequence, affirmations can be recited in the settee area or by the ball return. Keep in mind that affirmations are a tool in your mental game repertoire. Even if not a fixed part of your routine, they can be used as needed. For instance, affirmations might be called upon if you want a confidence boost or if your team needs an emotional lift.

Many athletes benefit by repeating affirmations throughout the course of a day. Ingenuity is the order of the day here. Bowlers report to us that they tape affirmations to their refrigerator, night table, and bathroom mirror. We even know of a PBA Hall of Famer who tapes affirmations to the visor of his car.

Exercises

1. To what extent is your self-talk negative? (circle one)

   Not At All   Occasionally   Fairly Often   Frequently

2. Cite situations leading to any negative self-talk you experience.

3. What do you say?

4. Note how this affects your performance.

5. How might those around you be affected?

6. Following our instructions, develop a thought stopping sequence.

7. Using the guidelines, create two affirmations.

8. Which of the Team USA individual affirmations resonates most with you? Which of the team affirmations is your favorite?

9. During a day, the best time for you to repeat affirmations is _____ .

10. Where can you use one or more affirmations in your pre-game preparation? Consider activities both outside and inside the center. Visualize their use. Repeat each visualization several times.

11. How can your affirmation(s) be used as part of pre-shot preparation? Consider time spent in the settee area and at the ball return. Remember, we recommend including an affirmation in your routine at the ball return. Visualize these pre-shot uses several times.

12. Plan on using a self-talk log and situation analysis to help monitor and manage your thinking.

REVIEW

It is vital to success that your thoughts stay positive. The methods in this chapter are designed to bring this about.

The internal communication, or conversation, in which we all engage, is referred to as "self-talk." Because your inner words and images greatly influence performance, keeping self-talk positive is essential to the mental game.

We recommend using a log to increase your awareness of the content, context, and impact of your self-talk; to record progress towards using positive self-talk; and to help you quickly identify the occurrence of self-talk that's negative.

Thought stopping is a technique that can effectively shut down negative self-talk. Prompt use is key to its being effective.

A situation analysis can increase your efficiency in applying thought stopping and other coping methods.

Affirmations are succinct statements of positive self-talk. Guidelines for their formation are presented along with personal and team examples. Such planned positive self-talk can be used as part of thought stopping, in routines, and throughout the day.

9

MAINTAINING POSITIVE PERSPECTIVE III: SELF-ACCEPTANCE

You are a person who bowls, not a bowler who happens to be a person.
Eric Lasser

If you take its message to heart, this third chapter on positive perspective may prove to be the most valuable in the book. That's because self-acceptance is a key to both excellence and a life well-lived.*

Self-Acceptance

Consistently valuing your effort, your achievements, and, ultimately, who you are overall is of utmost importance. We cannot stress this enough. The psychological dimension of self-valuing—acceptance of oneself—affects an athlete's attitude about performance and can affect the quality of the effort and the adjustment to the results. Beyond this, self-acceptance is vital to your inner peace and sense of fulfillment in life.

* Central ideas in this chapter are rooted in the classic approaches of psychologists Albert Ellis and Carl Rogers.

Why Self-Acceptance Matters

Tremendous pressure can result when an athlete's feelings of worth depend on his or her performance. If self-acceptance rides on the caliber of performance or competitive outcome, this can ratchet up anxiety and trigger an extreme emotional response (such as depression or rage) to defeat or an otherwise disappointing effort. Concentration can be diminished, performance impaired, and motivation reduced.

Self-acceptance has implications for team play as well. First, the type of reactivity noted above can hurt a team by lessening an athlete's contribution and by interfering with communication, undermining confidence, and creating a distraction. The bowler who angrily curses or kicks a ball return or is withdrawn and non-expressive due to anxiety or despair can hardly inspire, uplift, and provide useful information. Second, if a bowler's self-regard depends on the performance of teammates, there is the distinct possibility that that athlete will overreact to how his or her teammates do individually and how the team does as a unit. In addition to the previously mentioned problems which can result, this type of team-related overreaction may lead a bowler to put pressure on team members or berate them.

The effectiveness of coaching can be significantly influenced by the stability of self-acceptance on the part of both coach and bowler. If a coach's self-worth rises or falls with the performance of the athlete, it's virtually assured that the quality of coach-athlete interaction will be adversely affected. The coach's reactivity may come through in the form of agitation, anger, worry, demandingness, or other negative qualities. These can readily undermine the trust, confidence, and support so essential to effective coaching. If bowlers believe that their worth depends on pleasing the coach by a successful result, performance pressure is significantly heightened. This can also produce tension in the relationship and tempt a bowler to hide or deny perceived weaknesses in his or her game. Such an attitude could seriously impede the bowler's growth.

Passion vs. Desperation

We make a sharp distinction between motivational intensity and emotional over-investment. Intensity involves a passionate commitment towards reaching your goals. An all-out striving fueled by this intensity is at the core of the sporting experience. Such motivation makes determination and perseverance possible and accounts for both the satisfaction and disappointment which competitive participation produces. In contrast, when feeling good about who you are strongly depends on how well you perform or whether you win or lose, you've crossed over from passion to desperation.

Awareness

How can you tell if you're operating with the irrational belief that your worth as a person is determined by how you bowl?

Several words which you may generally attach to your performance can give a good indication. These key words include "should," must," "have to," and "ought to." The following exercise suggests the power of these words alone to influence attitude towards performance.

With your eyes closed, take several slow, deep breaths. Enjoy a feeling of calm. Totally clear your mind. Now imagine you're about to bowl in a league or tournament event. Thinking of the first game, select a score which would represent an outstanding start. For approximately 30 seconds, repeat to yourself, "I must bowl [the score]," "I must bowl [the score]," "I must bowl [the score]," and so on. When 30 seconds have elapsed, take a few deep, relaxed breaths and once again clear your mind. For 30 seconds, silently repeat, "I'd like to bowl [the score]," "I'd like to bowl [the score]," "I'd like to bowl [the score]," etc.

How did these two brief experiences compare? In our experience, most bowlers report that the first 30-second segment is characterized by a sense of pressure with various signs of anxiety and tension commonplace. These include both physical signs (such as accelerated heart rate) and thought-related signs (e.g., pessimism). During the second 30-second segment, bowlers report feeling much calmer and poised. When the words, "should," "ought to," or "have to" are substituted for "must" and the words, "want," "prefer," or "love" are substituted for "like," the reported experiences are comparable.

This simple exercise demonstrates the potential impact of words which orient you very differently towards performance. It also shows your ability to control your attitude towards what happens in competition (this topic is taken up in the next chapter).

A straightforward indication of emotional over-investment is your actual reaction to competitive situations. The emotions of rage, depression, and panic suggest that your self-worth may be linked to performance and results. These extreme reactions are disproportionate to what has occurred. Because you desire to succeed, when you encounter competitive frustration, some emotional reaction is expected.

However, anxiety, disappointment, and irritation or passing anger aren't extremes, and these don't suggest an irrational dependence on performance to maintain or boost self-esteem.

Be alert to three common misconceptions relating to self-image which can exaggerate performance pressure.

- If I don't perform at a particular level today, then I'm not good enough as a bowler. Frequently, thoughts of future failure accompany this attitude.

- If I'm not the bowler I'd like to be, then I'm not worthy as a person.

- If my performance doesn't satisfy my coach or parents or spouse or friends or fans, then I'm not worthy as a person.

Carrying around such misconceptions represents a significant obstacle to your success and is a heavy burden. It's hard to imagine anyone enjoying herself or himself with these beliefs. With self-acceptance at stake, bowling becomes more an emotional survival test than a sporting activity.

Be Realistic

One of the keys to reducing excessive performance pressure is being realistic about your ability—your current skill and potential to develop. If you're as realistic as possible, there won't be an overpowering need to prove your ultimate talent in any given competitive moment.

An overall steady belief in your bowling talent creates a reassuring context for processing your performance. A specific shot, game, block, or tournament can never predict how you'll perform in the next event and cannot prove what your career capabilities are. Relying on a specific outcome to prove your ability can generate pressure before and during competition, as well as later triggering various negative emotions if the outcome is disappointing. It's also important to not overestimate your talent as a result of a successful performance. Overconfidence can produce a range of detrimental effects, such as insufficient preparation, inconsistent concentration, and non-adherence to routine (Chapter 10).

In the previous discussion of confidence building, we covered several approaches to acquiring a realistic belief in your ability. These include quality practices, sound feedback, consistent encouragement, use of a Master Plan, effective goal setting, regular mental practice, review of prior successes, and positive self-talk.

Value the Person You Are

To perform at your best and to enjoy bowling to the utmost, it is vital that you value yourself independently of how you do. In other words, it is essential that your self-worth not be equated with execution and competitive results. The words of Anne Marie Duggan, member of the USBC and Women's Professional Bowling Hall of Fame, ring true: "No matter how good a day or how bad a day you have, you go to bed at night and wake up still the same person." Your qualities as a person and your worth as a human being do not depend on the number of pins you knock down. Simply put, when you go to the line, your self-esteem should not be on the line.

Maintaining a consistent, positive sense of oneself is a truly crucial attribute for living, aside from allowing you to cope with the ups and downs of your bowling efforts. While it's beyond the scope of this book to cover this topic in depth, we offer several hints for enhancing self-esteem.

— SUGGESTIONS TO ENHANCE SELF-ESTEEM —

1. Identify your skills—your competencies—in different areas of your life.

2. Review your successes. Experience these moments in as clear and intense a way as possible, in as many sensory modalities as you can.

3. Recall positive feedback received from others.

4. See yourself as a whole person. Recite the qualities in yourself you admire, including values which remain constant.

5. Value your striving, your effort, your intensity, your heart—treasure the part of you that goes all-out.

6. Realize that this all-out striving, as well as your learning and developing, are behaviors which you can control.

7. Visualize yourself succeeding.

8. Visualize yourself coping well with disappointments, remaining centered and self-accepting; learn from the

experience and feel more prepared for the future; orient yourself towards the next challenge.

9. Challenge irrational beliefs about self-worth, such as a link between a specific event and your value as a person.

10. Seek to live a balanced, well-rounded life with varied sources of fulfillment spanning the realms of work/school, social life, and recreation.

11. Develop relationships where you feel supported, accepted, and free to express your feelings.

12. Value your giving to others and society and realize this is something you can always do.

13. Set realistic and challenging goals and work steadily towards them; see progress as an achievement.

14. Engage in activities and practices which you find rewarding and leave you feeling good about yourself.

15. Maximize positive self-talk-using a log, thought stopping, situation analysis, and affirmations as tools.

Excel as a Self-Coach

Self-acceptance can contribute to inner harmony and feeling centered. Self-rejection, in contrast, means that you're not at ease with yourself and likely not with others.

"Self-coaching" concerns guiding yourself and living with yourself in a self-accepting way. Its aim is that you be your own best friend rather than your own worst enemy. Contact with others, even in the closest relationships, isn't continuous. There are gaps. Yet there is never a gap in the contact with yourself. No hockey player in a Stanley Cup final could be shadowed closer than you shadow yourself.

Try the following exercise to experience the boost which can be derived from good self-coaching:

Imagine you've suffered a competitive disappointment. Visualize this outcome in detail. Allow yourself to react emotionally as if the event had actually occurred. Then take a few calming breaths. Next, bring to mind words previously expressed to you at a trying time by a coach, parent, friend, mentor, or the like. These are words which meant a great deal as well as conveying support and commitment. These uplifting words instilled hope and determination and enabled you to better cope with adversity. In the present, say these same words to yourself. Let yourself feel both comforted and energized.

You can use the same or similar words whenever the need exists, for situations involving bowling, other sports, or, for that matter, any life circumstance.

Many athletes find it easier to support others than to support themselves. If you're like that, ask yourself what you would say if a teammate, friend, or family member experienced a setback. If you can readily "be there" for others, you can learn to give yourself the same respect and support. Or consider how you would react if a child with whom you were walking tripped and fell. Undoubtedly, you would extend a hand, not hit the child. Then why would you even symbolically hit yourself if you trip along the way? Instead, give yourself a hand—be a great self-coach and enjoy the emotional and performance benefits.

Exercises

1. Would you describe yourself as more passionate or desperate with respect to performance?

2. Based on the methods covered in Chapter 7, are you doing all in your power to be realistic about your game?

3. Cite what you value about yourself.

4. Note which of these qualities don't depend on bowling performance.

5. How much do you rely on others' approval to feel good about who you are?

6. Review the 15 suggestions for enhancing self-esteem. How many are you already doing? Of the others, list those you can do immediately. Then note the steps needed to implement all of them.

7. Rate how good a self-coach you've been. (circle one)
   Poor   Fair   Good   Excellent

8. Write the supportive, uplifting words which emerged from the self-coaching exercise.

9. Is it easier to give support to others than to yourself?

10. Identify the person who comes to mind when you think of supporting someone else.

11. Will you make a commitment to excel as a self-coach?

REVIEW

Self-acceptance is important for bowling and life generally. Consistent valuing of yourself independent of performance can reduce competitive pressure and enable you to effectively cope with results. Level of self-acceptance can impact team play and the coach-athlete relationship.

There is a distinct difference between motivational intensity and emotional desperation. To determine if your self-worth hinges on bowling performance, identify any overreactions in competition and possible misconceptions about self-image.

Realism concerning your ability is a key to limiting performance pressure. Various methods enabling this type of accurate appraisal are reviewed.

Consistent self-valuing in the face of bowling's ups and downs is vital to optimal performance. We provide 15 suggestions for building your self-esteem.

To excel as a "self-coach" is to guide yourself in a self-accepting way. Challenges in and out of the center are better handled if you're at peace with yourself. Treating yourself in a quality way goes hand in hand with quality performance.

10

HANDLING PERFORMANCE UPS AND DOWNS

I don't let anything bother me. Nothing gets under my skin so that I throw away the next shot.
Parker Bohn III

Coping with adversity is one of sports' great challenges. Performance disappointments are an inherent and inescapable part of athletic competition and present a gigantic emotional hurdle. Possessing the psychological wherewithal to handle bowling's frustrations and setbacks is an absolute requirement for performing to your potential. Unquestionably, if you're equipped to roll with the punches, then you'll enjoy a tremendous competitive edge over those lacking the same ability. Bouncing back from adversity is an essential element of mental toughness and a key to the mental game. Success also presents challenges. This chapter teaches ways to handle adversity and success within an ongoing game. In Chapter 15, the same principles are applied to overall outcomes, such as the end of a match or a tournament.

Emotional Turmoil is Self-Defeating

Your distress or agitation is a pin's best friend. The more emotionally upset you are, the more likely it is that a pin will remain standing and unscathed. Put another way, you become a great teammate to your competitors—you help them win—if you lose control psychologically. Despair or rage represents an extreme emotional response to within-game adversity. Since you alone are responsible for your emotional reactions to events, you are, in fact, defeating yourself.

Concentration, poise, fine motor control, and problem solving (i.e., adjusting) can all suffer due to emotional unrest. Since bowling success requires excellence in execution, as a competitive bowler, you simply can't afford to indulge in emotional extremes. Despair and rage, whether apparent to others or not, are counter-productive and contrary to peak performance. Temperamental outbursts (such as kicking the ball return, cursing, or calling yourself names) or despairing withdrawal (downcast eyes, sulking, or holding head in hands are examples) can easily hurt your team. Competition is stressful enough without the added burden of a teammate's emotional overreactions. Communication will obviously be hampered. Seething anger often spills out, and this may produce tension, if not outright conflict. Beyond this, bowling can be a psychologically health-promoting and pleasurable experience. Anguish or explosiveness represents neither. You owe yourself as well as those around you more than that.

There are some athletes whose performance seems to benefit from extreme emotional reactions and displays. The reality is that most— and, in all probability, you—do not. Also, an unsettling outburst could adversely affect teammates even if your performance doesn't suffer. Even those athletes who seem to perform better after outbursts might perform equally well, if not at a higher level, were they to develop different psychological tools. As an example, John McEnroe, the all-time tennis great, known for his angry outbursts, has remarked that he probably would have been even better had his emotions been more in check.

Be Alert to These Reactions

In addition to overt emotional extremes, adversity can produce other counterproductive responses. Pessimism or discouragement is a common reaction. Self-doubt has the potential to lower energy, hinder focus, and heighten anxiety. Additionally, specific types of self-doubt can affect your strategy. For example, if you unrealistically believe your

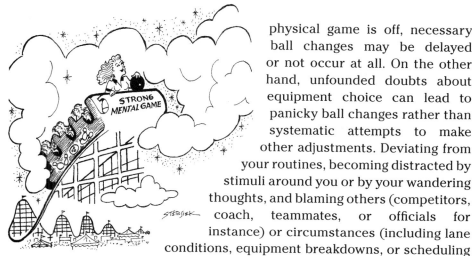

physical game is off, necessary ball changes may be delayed or not occur at all. On the other hand, unfounded doubts about equipment choice can lead to panicky ball changes rather than systematic attempts to make other adjustments. Deviating from your routines, becoming distracted by stimuli around you or by your wandering thoughts, and blaming others (competitors, coach, teammates, or officials for instance) or circumstances (including lane conditions, equipment breakdowns, or scheduling changes) for your performance are frequent responses to competitive disappointment. All of these can detract from pinfall.

Rally in the Face of Adversity

We use the acronym R-A-L-L-Y as a guide for coping with competitive adversity. As every bowler knows all too well, what you experience as adversity during a game comes in many forms: slow start, lack of carry, unfathomable split, missed single pin spare, poor shot in the clutch, stoppage in play, an opponent's behavior (e.g., pace, comments, or actions), strong performance by other bowlers, falling behind in a match, etc. In our experience, the most intense reactions tend to be triggered by situations where bowlers see themselves as failing to execute.

Once a threshold of emotional upset has been reached, distress can be touched off by an actual or perceived occurrence (such as lane conditions favoring lefties). Our guide presents a sequence of responses to moments of adversity which can enable you to effectively "move on" and bowl your best. Specific psychological tools for helping you follow this sequence are cited in the next section.

"R" stands for "react." Feelings of disappointment are a natural emotional response to situations where a goal isn't reached. On any given shot in competition, your immediate goal is to knock down pins (the fill ball may be considered an exception) or to execute in a way designed to ultimately achieve this result (getting the desired ball reaction and getting to the pocket). Therefore, it's understandable that a sense of letdown/frustration will occur if the desired result isn't attained. If you're motivated to achieve, then of course you'll feel some degree of

emotional pain when you don't. The significance the event holds for you and the intensity of your overall desire to succeed influence the potential impact of moment-to-moment ups and downs.

Our emotional "hard-wiring" is such that we can't experience joy unless we can also experience sadness. Denying or judging yourself for some emotional response to disappointment is counterproductive. Unacknowledged emotions tend to build and may interfere with physical and mental execution. Stifling your emotions in the early frames could lead to an overly strong reaction later in the game or in a subsequent game. Sitting on or burying emotions could easily be draining and tie you up in knots. Even a subtle tightening of muscles can affect your performance. Unacknowledged emotions can also throw off your decision making. Your mind needs to be clear to get a clear read on ball reaction. So reacting is fine. Underreacting or overreacting is not.

Reactions to competitive adversity may take various forms. The most straightforward response can be described as a sense of disappointment, a feeling of letdown. Very often athletes experience anger in addition to the disappointment. Sometimes anger replaces the disappointment so quickly that you're only aware of the anger. We believe you may well be able to shape the type of emotion you experience. Yet, whatever your emotional response may be, ultimately what matters is the strength of your reaction and your ability to "let go" and move forward.

A constructive emotional response to moments of adversity would be brief and non-extreme. Your reaction may or may not be apparent to others. That's your choice. An appropriate physical gesture (such as a clenched fist), facial expression (grimacing, for instance), or utterance (e.g., a grunt) may help you release the emotion. Extreme displays, in contrast, can disrupt your rhythm and concentration, distract and disturb teammates, and signal competitors that you're unraveling.

The second letter in RALLY is "A" for "accept." A disappointment in bowling and other sports is akin to loss in any of life's arenas. We all have the capacity to process loss and move on. This requires an emotional response and an acceptance of the reality. The grieving process when you miss a 6-10 spare is certainly a lot briefer and shallower than when you lose a job or someone dies; however, there's a fundamental similarity. To the extent that the loss or adversity is seen as unbearable, there will be a tendency to resist the reality—to hold on to what you want rather than accept what is. Acceptance is made considerably easier by a perspective characterized by self-trust and self-acceptance. Catastrophizing when confronted with a setback (e.g., a moment's adversity becomes a sign of complete futility) or devaluing yourself (as when pinfall becomes a measure of worth) can transform a momentary sting into a punishing emotional body blow. A positive perspective accelerates acceptance. Acceptance clears your path to the next shot.

The third action in the RALLY sequence is "learn," represented by "L." At this time, your task is to analyze information from the last shot together with information from the last series of shots. You're seeking to understand the relationship between conditions, equipment, and your physical techniques. What is the ball reaction telling you? What adjustments, if any, are needed? If you're switching lanes, what do you know about the new lane or pair based on your own history there, or what you've seen of others' reactions? Is there something you can do to execute better? Is there a particular psychological skill method you can apply? If needed, speak to your coach or a teammate or consider information volunteered to you. You quickly evaluate the available information, make decisions, and are prepared to move forward with a "shot plan" (game plan) for the spare attempt or next frame.

Now you orient yourself toward the upcoming shot. We say "lean" into the future, a phase represented by the second "L" in RALLY. What's happened before has been processed. You've reacted to the disappointing moment. You've accepted the reality. You've learned and decided on a possible adjustment. This is the time to be forward looking, literally looking forward to throwing the ball. Determined and focused, you continue with your pre-shot routine.

Moving successfully through these steps will place you in a position to throw a great shot—that is, your best shot given how you match up. Adapting to adversity means you are coping with reality. You are taking care of business. You are answering "yes" to the question of whether or not you are mentally tough. You are saying "yes" to your potential as a bowler. You are saying "yes" to yourself. Therefore, the fitting and final letter in RALLY is a symbolic "Y."

"RALLYing" is a sequence which routes you towards optimum readiness for the next shot. Be aware, however, that for any given instance of adversity, your progress through the sequence may vary. The time spent in each phase can differ. More than this, there can be some back and forth among phases. For instance, you may be in the learning phase (L) only to find that you're again experiencing a strong emotional reaction (R). You would then take the needed steps to regain full acceptance (A) and move on to the end of the sequence. What's essential is to regard all such "rerouting" as part of the coping process, not a sign of its failure.

Parker Bohn III:
Twice PBA Player of the
Year, PBA Hall of Fame,
four PBA Steve Nagy
Sportsmanship Awards

Keys to Resilience

You may apply any number of psychological skill methods in order to help you cope with competitive adversity. In effect, these techniques allow you to handle tough moments in a way consistent with the RALLY guidelines.

We must emphasize that managing adversity isn't simply a matter of applying a psychological technique at a specific moment in competition. That's true even if the method is a good one. Rather, the ability to cope at any given moment comes from your previous hard work in developing mental game skills expressly for such moments. You must have mastered a technique, mentally rehearsed its application, and practiced it. The more you apply it in competition, the better prepared you'll be to utilize it again.

Use mental rehearsal and practice simulations to anticipate the specific situations you may encounter. While our recommended approach can apply to all kinds of adversity, it's definitely to your advantage to have already experienced in these different ways the handling of the exact circumstances you now face. In addition to honing your skills for managing adversity, this preparation will develop your core optimism about dealing with competitive rough spots. This optimism can contribute to overall confidence and lower anxiety generally. Also, recall that your pre-game routine can help you solidify skills and your confidence level. Most importantly, to best handle adversity in competition, it's necessary to enter the event feeling solid about your game and about yourself. Building yourself up in these areas is central to the preparation you undergo in training.

We recommend the following as aids for effectively managing adversity. These are options in addition to your regular within-game routine which may already incorporate these methods in some form.

1. <u>Stay realistic.</u> First, use your reasoning power to remain in touch with your actual bowling talents. Avoid the logical error of drawing unwarranted conclusions from what just happened. Your last shot or shot sequence doesn't prove your essential competence as a bowler and doesn't predict how you'll perform on your next shot or series of shots. Review of previous successes and recall of feedback from your coach and objective sources can contribute to your reasoning. Second, any other aspect of the confidence building process which you can quickly apply (e.g., imagery and affirmations) may reassure you about your overall skills and potential as well as immediate capabilities.

2. <u>Choose self-tolerance.</u> Tolerate your fallibility. Everybody makes mistakes. Missteps of one sort or another are part of being human. Even computers don't spare us from errors and fumbles of all types. As Robert Strahan put it, "The embarrassment of riches that the computer has given us is just that. It is so easy to do fantastically complicated things totally wrong." Dallas Green, when he was GM of the Cubs, nearly ruined a trade for a star pitcher (Rich Sutcliffe). His comment at the time was, "What am I going to do, deny it? Lie about it? I don't lie. I made a mistake. I'm human." In other words, don't knock yourself for being imperfect. That can only waste energy, distract you, tense muscles, and impede your thinking. Instead, be self-accepting and move forward. Should you have a spiritual sensibility, this can help promote tolerance towards yourself (discussed in Chapter 17).

3. Regulate your excitement level. Most commonly, you'll want to calm yourself using one or more brief relaxation techniques or activities. A few deep breaths is probably the most widely used method—either by itself or followed by other approaches. Serene imagery, Progressive Muscle Relaxation, and music are among the options. If you're feeling depleted, an energizing technique, such as visualization, can be applied.

4. Manage your thinking. Emphasize positive images, ideas, and beliefs. Introduce or increase process-oriented visualizing and affirmations or other forms of positive self-talk. Control negative thinking. Negative thoughts can be quickly erased by your individual thought stopping sequence. Remember, this includes the substitution of positive images and/or words.

5. Be tuned-in. Maintain concentration and refocus attention if necessary. Apply distraction control methods you've developed. Cue words and images can allow you to retain or regain concentration. Maintain a "here and now" attitude (*immediacy*). Adhere to your between-shot routine.

6. "Hear voices." Imagine your coach or another person whose bowling expertise you trust offers encouragement and assurance that you can definitely rebound. Hear these words as distinctly as possible.

7. Communicate. Seek out the actual input/support of these valued persons. Or, if they volunteer information/encouragement, welcome it.

8. Set your mind to cope. Tell yourself that you will effectively deal with the adversity you've encountered. You might also suggest to yourself a particular emotional response to the situation, such as staying on an even keel or reacting briefly and non-extremely with disappointment.

9. Believe you will cope. Reason your way to optimism about managing adversity. Recall your specific training and prior successes, as well as feedback and other evidence of mastery in this area.

10. Use "Edited Instant Replay." After an unsuccessful shot, some bowlers like to immediately visualize the shot again. Only this time your execution is perfect and, if your imagery extends to the pin deck, the ball reaction and pinfall are exactly what you were aiming for. This mental rehearsing may ease the frustration and bolster confidence.

11. Be process-oriented. A worthwhile goal contributes to motivation and realistic expectations. Recall that we generally recommend striving for achievements that are process-oriented, challenging, and attainable. Aims related to skill development, including mental skills, are ideal. Ironically, your adversity creates the opportunity to further develop the ability to cope with setbacks. Concerning the number of pins you knock down, the only relevant matter now is what you can do in the frames ahead. Striking out, marking each frame, or even an adjusted possible score can be specific targets if you're inclined to look beyond your effort in the immediate frame.

12. Reframe. Constructively analyzing what's happened involves identifying that which is useful or otherwise positive in your performance. First of all, consider that your ball reaction is providing valuable information about how to play (i.e., what adjustments to make). Instead of raging at the condition, seize the learning moment. Coach Edwards' description of this potential benefit is a classic example of reframing:

You are watching and looking for feedback all the time as to what the lane is telling you. The lane is acting as your friend every time you throw a bowling ball down that lane. The lane is telling you by the reaction the ball gives whether you want to be playing there or not. It's telling you, "yes, this is the area to be playing in," or "you'd better move because this is the wrong area because you have no area."[11]

Beyond obtaining specific information that can lead to adjustments, consider what was positive about your effort and what opportunities have been created. What did you do right in terms of physical technique, equipment, adjustments, and the mental game? Are you clearer on where your game needs work? What opportunity is presented for developing psychological tools (like coping with adversity)? What opportunity is there to work on adjustments (such as equipment selection)? How you view events depends on your vantage point. Is the spare shot you face a sign of failure or an opportunity to add to pincount, hone your spare shooting, and display professionalism by being methodically cool, in control, and consistent?

Recall our suggestion that you make emerging a better bowler an overall event goal. Setting this goal is highly conducive to reframing, since all you do can in some way serve as a stepping stone to improvement.

13. <u>Try a change of pace.</u> Sticking to your routine between shots is a primary principle. However, sometimes a change of pace is needed to break the spell of an "emotional funk." This involves a brief but significant shift in what you do. For instance, talking to others even if you usually keep to yourself. Another example would be engaging in some physical activity, such as stretching or, if time permits, taking a fast walk. Parker Bohn III, a perennial PBA star and Hall of Famer, might crush a paper cup to relieve built-up frustration. With enough time (such as between games), he sometimes walks to a restroom and splashes water on his face. This enables him to snap out of the mood. Listening to music or a different type of music, listening to a comedy tape, or visualizing non-bowling situations are other examples of activities which can effectively free you emotionally. Then resume your normal routine.

14. <u>View the moment in life perspective.</u> Realize that while bowling is important, what's happening competitively is not a matter of life and death. Consider what's valuable in yourself and in your life that goes beyond and is unchanged by your immediate performance. Reflect

on what you're grateful for and/or what you can look forward to in the future. Think of those you love. A senior tour bowler had a tendency to become angry and agitated after a rough stretch. He now pulls out a photo of his grandchildren at these times and reports becoming quickly centered and focused. Viewing your adversity through the lens of life perspective can help keep you emotionally grounded, up and running.

15. <u>Cue & Preview.</u> Say "RALLY" to yourself as a reminder of how to cope and as inspiration to do just that. Visualize your successful progress through the comeback process.

As you can see, the list of coping tools for managing emotions during a game is long. But the time to implement them is relatively short. During a game, you must quickly adapt and get on with the business at hand. The good news is the time between shots is more than enough if you've

Michelle Feldman: 2002 PWBA Player of the Year, first woman to bowl a perfect game on national television

adequately prepared. For example, say you've missed a series of spares you felt were makeable and sense frustration and anger mounting. Doubts about your skill are entering your mind. Immediately alert to what's going on, you first use thought stopping to erase the negative thoughts and replace them with positive images and words (30 seconds). In the settee area, you take several deep breaths (30 seconds) and listen to part of a favorite music track either on a Discman, iPod, or in your head (1 minute). To wind down further, if you feel a need, you might recall or read a joke you find extremely funny. Perhaps you think of someone who matters greatly to you and once again are in touch with what is most important in life. (The times cited for each activity are purely estimates of how you could budget time. The actual durations are a matter of individual preference and can vary significantly from these examples.)

Shape Your Emotions

Your emotional response to events, competitive and otherwise, relates directly to how you view what has happened. Another way of saying this is that the meaning you give to something shapes its emotional effect. We've made the point that emotional overreactions can result from drawing irrational conclusions about your abilities and your self-worth based on immediate bowling results. We believe that if you're realistic about yourself and consistently value who you are as a person, then responses to competitive adversity won't reach an extreme that's self-defeating. Consequently, we've suggested a variety of approaches enabling you to be realistic and self-accepting.

In addition to the intensity of your emotions, certain beliefs and attitudes you hold may help determine the type of reaction. In particular, rage during competition may be related in some ways to beliefs such as these:

- "Mistakes deserve to be punished."

- "Losing means you're a loser."

- "I can't stand myself if I'm not perfect."

- "I need to be yelled at to succeed."

- "If I'm angry, I'm tough."

- "Feeling disappointed is weak."

- "If I feel disappointed, I'll get discouraged and won't snap out of it."

If such underlying beliefs are changed, a bowler's response to adversity—at least certain types of adversity—can change. Anger may be toned down or may not even occur in circumstances which used to bring on rage.

Do you tend to become readily angered by competitive adversity? If you want to diminish such a tendency, identify the underlying assumptions which may be influencing your reactions. Ask yourself whether or not you hold beliefs similar to the ones just cited. Actively challenge the validity of these notions.

To help identity underlying beliefs and see them in perspective, it's sometimes useful to consider their source. Ask yourself these questions:

- How have my mistakes in bowling and other activities been treated by the significant people in my life (such as family, coaches, and teachers)?

- How do these persons react to their own errors?

- Are they more reward-oriented or punishment-oriented?

- How do they respond to adversity in general?

- Have my family and/or coaches encouraged me to express emotions openly and spontaneously?

- How direct or indirect is their expression of feeling?

- Do they verbalize disappointment and other vulnerable feelings or find it easier to be angry?

- Growing up, was there an important adult with a bad temper?

What you learned from others about coping and emotions presents you with choices. As an independent person, you're not bound to follow what you're told or imitate what others do. Decide for yourself what's most constructive on the lanes and in your overall life.

The alternative to a harshly critical type of response is a supportive, encouraging approach. We advocate this approach as a coaching style and as a self-coaching style. Even if a punitive approach apparently leads to success, there is often a significant internal cost. Threat of punishment creates a fear of failure. This can generate anxiety as well as severely detract from enjoyment. It can result in young bowlers being turned off to the sport and contribute to burnout in long-time participants.

Minimizing or even eliminating anger doesn't leave you emotionless. Recall the "R" in RALLY stands for "react." You will have emotions. You will feel frustrated/disappointed when goals aren't met. However, the explosiveness or seething anger will no longer be characteristic.

Professional Consultation

Work closely with your coach to implement the approach we've presented. If your emotions remain self-defeating despite all efforts, consulting a sport psychologist or another qualified professional is a step to consider.

Perhaps you and/or your coach simply need guidance in designing an individually tailored psychological skills strategy. Possibly other bowling-related stressors such as injuries, conflict with your coach or teammates, or symptoms of burnout are increasing your emotional reactivity in competition and need to be addressed. Or, it may be that your emotional sensitivity on the lanes is related to life issues which might well be resolved by a clinical intervention. These issues could range from a family or marital problem to alcohol abuse, depression, an eating disorder, work impairment, or any other psychological condition. The point is, any issue affecting your functioning and well-being merits attention.

The ideal choice for a consultation would be a sport psychologist. This professional's familiarity with athletes as a distinct population could be enormously useful in terms of assessment and intervention. While there are advantages to using the services of a sport psychologist for the evaluation and treatment of psychological conditions, it's perfectly appropriate to initially consult and/or receive treatment from another type of licensed mental health professional. (The topic of referrals is addressed further in Chapter 17.)

Awareness

The awareness necessary for growth can be increased in various ways. You're seeking to know the situations which trigger reactions and the nature and impact on performance of the emotions. As you make an effort to cope more effectively, you'll want to monitor changes in your reactions and modify your approach as needed.

Feedback from your coach and other observers can be an invaluable aid, especially if you're inclined to outwardly show your emotions. Your coach should be the world's expert in reading your body language, and this is an excellent time to benefit from the expertise. Video of you competing could be helpful as a learning tool, although you would need to run a great deal of tape to cover the full range of situations which can trigger your emotions. In addition to its obvious potential to help you during a match, "live" feedback during competition or practice is most meaningful due to the immediacy of the emotions and the possible continuation or recurrence of the triggering situations.

We strongly recommend keeping a journal of your emotional reactions. The closer in time to the actual response, the better. Record as much detail as possible regarding the situation and the type, intensity, duration, and performance impact of your emotions. Note the methods you apply in order to cope and the effect these have. Systematically logging your reactions will increase the knowledge of how you're handling adversity and increase alertness to reactions when they occur in competition. You also become more quickly alert to situations which can potentially produce disruptive emotional responses. Your alertness concerning situations and reactions increases the probability of effectively coping with the adversity.

Use the worksheet at the end of the chapter to increase awareness of your highly individual emotional responses to adversity during competition. The worksheet is a guide to understanding and skill development. It helps you assess your present response tendencies and develop a plan for effectively managing your emotions. Periodically reevaluating yourself using the worksheet can contribute to the monitoring/modifying process and keep your awareness as high as possible.

Coaching feedback, the journal, and the worksheet are tools to assist your development and also provide reinforcement and reassurance that you're on the right path.

Coping with Success

If you're bowling very well, all would seem to be well. However, to maintain your performance level, it's necessary to avoid four potential pitfalls of success. These are overexcitement, complacency, the pressure of expectations, and "attitude."

Overexcitement

It's natural to get "pumped up" when succeeding. It's also possible to get too pumped up. That occurs when your excitement level exceeds what is optimal for you. A drop in the quality of decision making, concentration, and execution are among the possible consequences. To prevent this from happening, learn what your optimal activation level is (this is a very individual matter) and how to stay there (Chapters12, 13, and 14). Monitor your intensity and adjust if necessary (e.g., use a relaxing visualization). Sticking with your pre-shot routine is a key to maintaining, or regaining, the groove you've hit.

Complacency

With success comes the risk of complacency. This overconfident attitude can produce several consequences which knock down your game. These include discontinuing or varying routines, wavering concentration, decreased awareness/learning/reaction necessary for adjustments, and flattening of your emotional edge. Avoid complacency about performance by valuing your skills and the hard work that developed them. Successful bowling is a feat of athletic excellence. Even if you

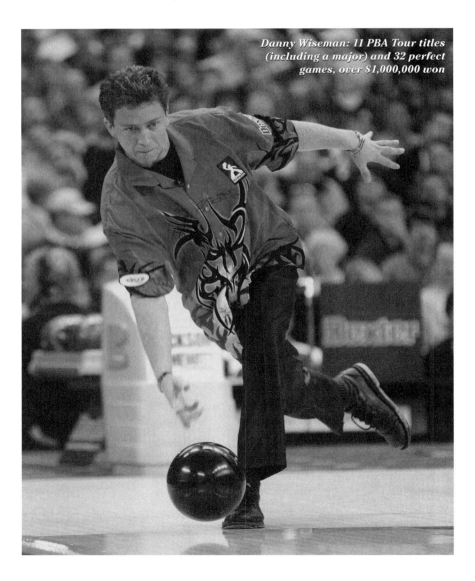

Danny Wiseman: 11 PBA Tour titles (including a major) and 32 perfect games, over $1,000,000 won

make it look easy, it's not. It's like driving a high performance auto—if you keep your eye on the road, hand on the wheel, foot on the pedal, and motor running, you'll have a great ride. In other words, keep doing what you've been doing, shot by shot, frame by frame. Respect your game by continuing to play it.

Bowling well sometimes leads to overconfidence about the final score and outcome of a game. What can result are the same consequences we've just described, hampering your performance. Even if you're realistic in anticipating a successful result, it's important to not become lackadaisical. Your sharpness will be lost and regaining it in the next game may not prove easy. If it's your last game, maintaining form— physically, mentally, and lane play-wise—will set you up for the next block or event and not risk the development of bad habits. The surest way to avoid these and other potential problems caused by anticipating outcomes (distraction and anxiety) is to focus on the process of bowling with a "here and now" attitude.

Pressure of Expectations

When performing well, bowlers may feel intense pressure due to their own expectations or their sense of others' expectations (e.g., coach, teammates, family, and fans) that the success will continue and lead to a specific outcome. This can throw off your game by distracting you or stressing you. Later chapters deal in depth with ways to offset competitive pressure. Here we offer several keys for defusing the burden of expectations:

- Adhere to mental and physical routines.

- Adopt a "here and now" attitude.

- Apply thought stopping to avoid thinking of expectations.

- Use relaxation methods if such thoughts have made you anxious and refocusing methods if they've distracted you.

- Avoid looking at those whose expectations may concern you.

- Be process-oriented.

- Stay optimistic and otherwise positive in your perspective.

- Know that your worth as a person does not depend on how you bowl.

- Know that your worth as a person does not depend on others' reactions to you.

- Tell those who matter to you what would be most helpful in terms of their communication and attitude during competition.

(The suggestions offered here and in Chapter 15 regarding expectations generated by success can also be generally applied to other times when expectations may affect you.)

"Attitude"

Arrogance in response to success may give competitors added incentive and alienate teammates and others around you. We suggest reacting with class and centeredness. You can be exuberant and grounded. Ultimately, bowling is its own antidote to arrogance. It is a humbling sport. If you're humble to start with, the inevitable spills will sting less. And that could enable you to rebound faster.

COPING WITH ADVERSITY: WORKSHEET

Part One: Becoming Aware

1. List the various types of adversity you encounter during a game. For example, slow start, missed single pin spare, lack of carry, and physical game mistakes.

   _____

   _____

   _____

   _____

   _____

2. Next to each situation listed in Question 1, rate the intensity of your emotional response using the following scale:

   1 = no response

   2 = slight response

   3 = moderate response

   4 = strong response

   5 = extreme response

Situation   Intensity (circle one)

_____   1   2   3   4   5

_____   1   2   3   4   5

_____   1   2   3   4   5

_____   1   2   3   4   5

_____   1   2   3   4   5

3. For each situation, briefly describe the type of emotion you experience, such as anger or feeling down.

Situation   Emotion

_____   _____

_____   _____

_____   _____

_____   _____

_____   _____

4. For each situation, note how much your emotional reaction negatively affects your bowling performance. Use the scale below:

1 = no impact

2 = small impact

3 = moderate impact

4 = large impact

5 = great impact

Situation   Effect (circle one)

_____   1   2   3   4   5

_____   1   2   3   4   5

_____   1   2   3   4   5

_____   1   2   3   4   5

_____   1   2   3   4   5

5. Describe in as much detail as possible, the exact circumstances which trigger your emotional reactions. For example, do you become significantly upset after one missed 10-pin or only when you miss three? If you're not getting the desired ball reaction, how many frames will it take until your emotions become intense?

Situation   Circumstances

_____   _____

_____   _____

_____   _____

_____   _____

6. Describe the nature of your experience for each situation. What are your actual thoughts? What is the quality of your thinking (e.g., focused, organized, and normally paced or distracted, chaotic, and racing or blank)? What are your physical reactions (e.g., rapid heart beat, feeling very warm, and tightness in shoulder)?

Situation _____

Thoughts: _____

Quality of thinking: _____

Physical reactions: _____

Situation _____

Thoughts: _____

Quality of thinking: _____

Physical reactions: _____

Situation _____

Thoughts: _____

Quality of thinking: _____

Physical reactions: _____

Situation _____

Thoughts: _____

Quality of thinking: _____

Physical reactions: _____

Situation _____

Thoughts: _____

Quality of thinking: _____

Physical reactions: _____

7. Describe the start, ending, and duration of your emotional reactions in general (refer to Question 3). Do you tend to react suddenly or do your emotions build gradually? Do you settle down quickly or do the feelings pass slowly? How long do they last?

Use the following code:

S = sudden

G = gradual

Q = quick

SL = slow

Emotion	Start (circle one)		End (circle one)		Duration (# frames or games)
_____	S	G	Q	SL	_____
_____	S	G	Q	SL	_____
_____	S	G	Q	SL	_____
_____	S	G	Q	SL	_____
_____	S	G	Q	SL	_____

8. If your performance is hindered by any emotional response (Question 4), indicate how this occurs in the space below: For instance, "Frustration over not carrying makes me irritated and then angry and this leads to becoming distracted and muscle tension; my swing then becomes erratic."

Part Two: Learning to Cope

1. Evaluate your overall emotional processing in terms of the RALLY guidelines (*React-Accept-Learn-Lean-Yes*). For each phase on the following page, note the degree to which your reactions to adversity match the recommended response. Use the scale that follows.

1 = no match at all

2 = slight match

3 = moderate match

4 = close match

5 = full match

Match (circle one)

R:	1	2	3	4	5
A:	1	2	3	4	5
L:	1	2	3	4	5
L:	1	2	3	4	5
Y:	1	2	3	4	5

2. For each phase, describe specifically how your present reactions are *in keeping with* the recommendations.

R: _____

_____

A: _____

_____

L:_____

_____

L:_____

_____

Y:_____

_____

3. Describe the ways your present responses *do not* match the guidelines for each phase.

R: _____

_____

A: _____

_____

L:_____

_____

L:_____

_____

Y:_____

_____

4. Which of the Keys to Resilience (pp. 118-122) do you now apply when encountering adversity? Note these in the space below.

5. List each situation identified in Part One (Questions 4 and 8) where your emotional reaction detracts from performance. Next to each, using the Keys to Resilience as a guide, cite the methods which can enable you to more effectively cope with adversity.

Situation   Coping Methods

■ _____   _____
                                 _____
                                 _____
                                 _____
■ _____   _____
                                 _____
                                 _____
                                 _____
■ _____   _____
                                 _____
                                 _____
                                 _____
■ _____   _____
                                 _____
                                 _____
                                 _____
■ _____   _____
                                 _____
                                 _____
                                 _____

Exercises

1. Use awareness tools to learn about your emotional response to competitive adversity.

2. Use the worksheet to develop a coping plan.

3. If you easily become angered by adversity, identify and write down beliefs which may be contributing to this reaction.

4. Correct these beliefs.

5. When successful, do you experience any of the following? (circle one or more)

   Overexcitement   Complacency

   Pressure of Expectations   "Attitude"

6. If you're affected by a pitfall of success, note the actions you'll take to change this.

REVIEW

Recovering from adversity is a key to successful performance in bowling and other sports. Coping with this challenge represents a crucial application of the mental game.

Emotional overreactions during a game are self-defeating. Concentration, fine motor control, and decision making can readily be impaired by excessive anger or despair. Furthermore, outbursts and other signs of emotional agitation or distress may interfere with team communication and upset your teammates. Adversity can also lead to other counterproductive responses, such as self-doubting.

A guide for coping with competitive adversity is represented by the acronym, R-A-L-L-Y. There are a variety of methods—Keys to Resilience—which bowlers may apply to successfully follow these guidelines. Use mental rehearsal and practice simulation to anticipate specific situations where the methods can be applied.

Underlying beliefs contribute to emotional reactions in the face of adversity. By identifying and challenging certain assumptions, both the intensity and type of your response may be changed so that you more effectively cope.

If your emotional reactions continue to be self-defeating, a professional consultation may prove beneficial.

Feedback, a journal, and our worksheet are tools for developing the awareness needed to master emotional control when confronted with adversity.

Success poses its own challenges. Avoiding pitfalls such as complacency is essential for consistent excellence.

11

HOW TO COPE WITH DISTRACTIONS

(Don) Johnson was focus personified. His concentration was so intense that he was virtually deaf to voices or noises that would rattle or disturb the average player—particularly in clutch situations.
John Jowdy

Successful shot making calls for the capacity to concentrate. This involves maintaining attention and quickly refocusing if you're distracted.

Make consistent concentration a cornerstone of your mental game. Focus on the tasks at hand. These include strategizing and all other aspects of your within-game routine. Above all, top flight bowling requires your steady focus when on the lane. Regardless of how skilled you are, if your mind wanders while you bowl, the ball won't be delivered as planned.

What Can Help You Concentrate

In addition to specific distractions, your attention may be hindered by anxiety, pessimism, inner turmoil, and lack of enthusiasm. It's difficult to be fully focused if you're worried or agitated, don't have confidence, and feel insufficiently motivated. Consequently, all psychological techniques which enable you to be optimistic, eager, emotionally poised, and optimally energized can contribute to concentration. These are cited throughout the book. In this chapter, we recommend a cluster of actions considered most essential for consistent concentration in the heat of battle where potential distractions abound.

Lock into Focus

We believe in a proactive approach to maintaining concentration. Your front-line defense against the disruptive effects of distraction is a series of steps locking you into focus.

Routines

The primary tool for sustaining concentration is adhering to your pre-game and pre-shot routines. Sticking to these planned sequences guarantees your use of specific psychological tools, like visualization or self-talk, minimizes anxiety by creating a sense of familiarity, and leaves little room for intrusive, jarring thoughts. Think of routines as a home base of sorts—shielding you from distractions as you stay comfortably on track towards a successful shot.

Visual and Verbal Cues

Taking the return of the ball as a signal to be sharply focused is an example of a purely visual cue. A straightforward verbal cue is saying the word "focus" in order to maintain complete attention. A variation of this is a complete statement, as in the affirmation "I'm locked into focus." Cues sometimes combine visual and verbal elements. One PBA Tour bowler was reminded to "zone in" mentally by the word "Zone" inscribed on his ball. Recall the focus cue we recommended for your pre-shot routine at the ball return: Visualize a huge, colorful banner with "FOCUS" written on it suspended over the lane. If not used as a fixed part of your routine, this cue or any other can be part of your "psychological skills bench," available when needed.

The effectiveness of these cues in competition may be increased by reciting and/or visualizing them while you recall peak performance involving acute concentration (see "Recall" below). This anchoring in genuine experience can enhance the capacity of the performance cues to trigger similar states.

Recall

Visualize. Call to mind your best prior performances (lead into this imagery with a brief relaxation process if that heightens the realism and intensity). Re-experience the exceptional focus involved in these efforts. Re-create this same perception of acute focus in all your pre-game and pre-shot visualizing.

Mindset

Direct yourself to remain fully focused. Commit yourself to steadfastly following your routines. Be determined to stay in the present moment and to exclude thoughts of competitors, stressors from daily life, and results. Resolve to maintain attention to the process of bowling in every competitive situation. Trust your refocusing skill.

Process Orientation

Devote your attention to the act of bowling. Focus fully on the actions involved in the current shot. Attend to form and execution, rather than score and results. The aim of this approach is to involve yourself in doing instead of worrying or fantasizing about competitive outcome.

Immediacy

Adopt a "here and now" approach. Stay in the moment with a "one shot at a time" philosophy. What happened on the last shot or in the last frame or game is bowling history. Leave history to the historians. All that matters is the immediate future, the shot in front of you. It is equally important to limit your thoughts about the frames or games ahead. Think of it this way: If your attention drifts to the future, your ball will drift in the present.

Immediacy applies to space as well as time. You can get valuable information in some circumstances by watching the ball reactions of other bowlers. However, continually looking at competitors out of desperation will throw off your own game. The philosophy here is "one lane at a time." Don't rubberneck.

Don Johnson: PBA/USBC Halls of Fame, twice PBA Bowler of the Year, won a PBA title in 12 consecutive years

Reframing

Keep your outlook positive. Doubts, regrets, judgment, and other negative thoughts are distracting. A key to an upbeat, optimistic attitude is looking at events in a constructive light. For instance, rather than dwelling on the shot you didn't make in the last frame, you might reflect on what you did right or learned and think of the opportunity to display and hone mental toughness by coolly striking on your next shot.

Be Aware of Lapses

Breaks in concentration occur to even the best and most "tuned in" of bowlers. The ability to rapidly adjust to such lapses is crucial to competitive success. Awareness is key to regaining your focus. Quickly becoming aware that you're distracted is vital for a couple of reasons. Logically enough, the longer your attention is diverted, the longer you'll be performing with a psychological handicap. In addition, redirecting your attention may simply prove more difficult the longer your thoughts have strayed.

Two types of knowledge can help you become more quickly alerted to concentration lapses:

Know Your Vulnerable Situations

Countless situations may be distracting. These include the three "bads"— "bad" shots, "bad" breaks, and "bad" blood (meaning tension between you and competitors or teammates)—delays in play, fan reaction, family advice, clutch circumstances, and events in your daily life.

Knowing those circumstances that tend to distract you can enable you to more quickly catch yourself and refocus if attention wanders. Knowledge of potential distractions also allows you to take preventive actions during competition. For instance, say a stoppage in play tends to impair your concentration. Faced with this situation, you can use verbal or visual cues, mindset, or any other focusing method described in this chapter to protect you against a disruption of concentration. Knowing what tends to distract you has another important benefit. You're now able to practice coping with these specific situations.

Know Your Lapse Indicators

Knowing how you react when distracted is a vital step to becoming aware of concentration lapses during actual play.

- Common indicators of concentration lapses are
- Thoughts unrelated to the process of bowling,
- Varying your between-shot routine,
- Looking around,
- Uneven performance,
- Continuously watching competition on other lanes, and
- Feeling distracted during play.

Other possible signs of breaks in concentration are the common signs of excessive anxiety (noted in Chapter 12), low confidence (Chapter 7), or limited motivation (Chapter 16).

Which of these signs of distraction apply to you? The ways that breaks in concentration reveal themselves vary from one bowler to another. Your psychological and physiological responses and your visible actions when distracted may involve any combination of these common signs and/or other reactions.

Ways to Become Aware

We recommend the following steps to become aware of situations which tend to distract you and your reactions when distracted.

<u>Reflect:</u> Think back to past events. Which situations (such as competitors' psych-out attempts, media presence, or a teammate's display of anger) have disrupted your concentration? When distracted, how did you react? What steps, if any, did you take to refocus attention and how effective were they?

<u>Keep a log:</u> Record variations in concentration during competition. Note the circumstances that triggered any lapses—what happened, in what frame of what game, in what competitive context. Describe your state of mind—where your attention was directed, as well as accompanying thoughts, emotions, and actions. Jot down how long you remained distracted. Indicate the impact on your performance. Cite the methods you used to refocus and how successful they were. Instead of writing, you may prefer to use a tape recorder.

The following is what a log entry might look like:

> 1st frame of final game. We had all struggled last game, but were still in contention. John [teammate] was in the pocket, but left a ridiculous split and cursed loudly and then said, "Here we go again!" I began dwelling on what he said, worried he might be right, then felt angry that he made a comment like that. My stomach began to tighten. I stared back at him, then at the other team to see if they were reacting to his comment. I saw one of them smile. I wondered if he thought we were coming apart. I made a terrible shot, somehow I didn't make an obvious ball change. I told myself to forget about it, but I couldn't settle down until the 9th frame and by then it was too late. I closed strong but we still lost by a few pins.

<u>Receive feedback:</u> Call upon others who know your game. Whether coach, friend, family member, or teammate, you're seeking input about changes in your customary actions. These observations can confirm or add valuable information to what you've noted in your log.

<u>View videotape:</u> Videotaping can sometimes be useful for discovering what body language and actions correspond to your internal states, such as your concentration in specific game situations.

Defuse Distractions

If you encounter a situation that's potentially distracting or if you actually become distracted, the first course of action is to renew the application of methods we've already recommended. That is to say, maintain or regain concentration by adhering to your routines, using visual and/or verbal cues, recalling past successes, committing to steady attention, immersing yourself in the process of bowling, remaining in the "here and now," and looking at events constructively.

We want to underscore the importance of quickly returning to your mental and physical routines—your "home base"—if you get distracted. Reentering the flow of activities which comprise your routines creates a focused corridor to shot execution. The instant you're distracted is the time to invoke "The 15 Second Rule." This means getting your mind back to your routine within 15 seconds. Do this and you'll have met the challenge posed by the distraction.

Four other techniques in particular can be very effective for coping with distractions:

Thought Stopping

This technique can be used to quickly "delete" a distracting image or idea. Promptly recognize the disruptive thought and immediately apply your preferred verbal or visual thought stopping method (e.g., say "stop" or envision a stop sign). Then take at least one calming deep breath and substitute a positive image and/or affirming statement. You may briefly recall music. Finally, transition to your routine. Repeat this process if the distracting thought returns.

Visualizing

We've found three types of imagery especially valuable for deflecting distractions. "Tunnel vision" is a method in which you imagine the lane is a tunnel, totally sealed off from any sights or sounds outside your lane. A related technique entails blurring your peripheral vision on either side of the lane, while straight ahead your sight is totally sharp. Another method involves imagining yourself inside a transparent protective bubble. This bubble shields you from all potentially distracting stimuli that could potentially distract you (such as an adversary's comments). One example of this bubble imagery is provided in the box on the next page. The directions call attention to this method as a tool for handling interpersonal distractions.

VISUALIZE A SPHERE OF POWER[12]

Focus your attention on the center of your stomach, in the area of your navel. Feel that this is an area of tremendous strength. Visualize a clear sphere, a dome of energy surrounding your entire body, which is supported by your own will-power. Positive thoughts, feelings, ideas, and vibrations can pass through this sphere and reach you. But, as long as you visualize this sphere of clear energy surrounding you, negative thoughts, hostilities, anger, and aggressive feelings of other persons and situations cannot reach you.

While you imagine this sphere of clear energy surrounding you, feel that you are consciously directing energy from the center of your body, in the area of your navel, throughout the sphere. Feel that the energy of your willpower can easily deflect tension-causing feelings and frustrations that are directed toward you from the outside world. The more you practice it, the easier it becomes to visualize this sphere of energy and to stop the negative energy of others.

Slowing Down

Distractions, together with the anxiety they can trigger, may lead you to rush and feel mentally scattered. A way to counter this tendency is to slow down all your movements, even if briefly. In addition to the direct correcting of your pace, such a slowing redirects your attention from the distracting stimuli to the actions involved in the process of bowling. Resume your regular routine once you're refocused.

Centering

Centering is an action, part physical, part mental, which can help you manage distractions. *The state of being physically centered (described by Robert Nideffer) involves distributing your weight evenly while your feet are positioned approximately 18 inches apart. Place one foot a bit ahead of the other. Relax your muscles. Bend your knees slightly. Inhale deeper than usual, breathing steadily and somewhat slowly. Momentarily focus attention one to two inches below and behind your navel.* This anatomical spot is your center of mass. Centering creates a sense of balance and readiness. Being clear-thinking, grounded, and calm are the accompanying feelings.

When to Apply These Four Techniques

Thought stopping is specifically used here as a countermeasure in order to refocus once you're distracted. Visualizing, slowing down, and centering can be used to prevent the disruption of concentration or for refocusing.

Managing Outside Stress

Events from daily life have the potential to intrude on your bowling performance. If not properly managed, concerns from the day can impair your concentration as well as make you tense. To achieve success inside the center, your external stress must, in effect, be left outside.

The following are methods for coping with stress related to external events:

- "Decompress" before arriving at the center. This is a good idea in general and becomes especially important on days of high stress. Among the activities available to you are listening to music, lightly exercising (e.g., a brisk walk), reading, using a calming technique such as Progressive Muscle Relaxation, and viewing a favorite segment from a comedy or other video. Social interaction can be enormously helpful, whether this involves talking about your day or simply relaxed contact.

- Direct yourself to park worries and other thoughts and feelings concerning your life outside the center. If you want to be literal, visualize storing them in the trunk of your car. These concerns can be picked up (if you still choose) when you're done bowling.

- Think of the bowling center as your sanctuary. Because the sport of bowling is so significant in your life, the center has special meaning. It's a place where you've known many triumphs and faced adversity, related intensely to others, and ultimately grown as a person. Inside the center, commit yourself totally to the activity which means so much: the act of bowling. Once you enter, the outside world fades away.

- Imagine the center is surrounded by a force field. You're able to pass through this invisible wall. However, stress from your day is fully blocked. Bowlers sometimes refer to this as "the Star Trek technique." A variation is the "Stargate" visualization where a "portal" is used instead of a force field.

- Once inside the center, especially during play, "banish" thoughts related to outside matters through the prompt use of thought stopping. Any of the other techniques discussed in this chapter can be applied as needed.

- Keep in mind, the more effectively you cope with daily stressors in general, the less they'll tend to intrude when you bowl. The effective management of life stress can also help your bowling by promoting your health, boosting your energy, and increasing your resilience to the emotional demands of competition. The psychological tools in this book can enable you to better handle the challenges of living.

Mastering Concentration Skills

By now you're familiar with the step-by-step process for mastering psychological tools. This same approach applies to readying yourself to use the methods for maintaining or regaining concentration.

1. Learn the technique. Whether it's centering, thought stopping, reframing, use of cues, or any of the other methods we've cited, the initial step to mastery involves learning what to do.

2. Mentally rehearse for competition. On a regular basis, mentally practice the application of these various techniques. See yourself compete and encounter potentially distracting situations. Visualize two scenarios using methods at your command: a) maintaining full attention, and b) refocusing attention after becoming momentarily distracted. End both scenarios with images of yourself bowling successfully.

3. Apply in practice. To acquire and retain competence in methods for sustaining and regaining concentration, use these methods in practice. As part of this preparation, simulate competitive situations having potential distractions. For instance, enlist the help of teammates to create distractions involving the actions of others (such as an adversary's provocative comments or a teammate's repeated complaints about lane conditions). You're seeking to reach the point where you can automatically apply these techniques in the midst of competing.

A series of practice exercises and tips are provided in the box which follows. The first three suggestions can be done anywhere.

PRACTICE EXERCISES AND TIPS[13]

- Sit quietly, let yourself relax, and focus on looking at something (whether a ball, your hand, the pins, or a banner). Really focus on it; look closely at its unique design; get absorbed in it.

- Line up several targets or objects. Become aware of all the targets. Then begin to narrow your focus until you're aware of only one target, then the center of that target, then the center of the center of the target. Let all other visions blur into the background; let all external sounds become inaudible. Connect with that target.

- Focus on a specific thought (or target), then let your thoughts wander, then refocus on the specific thought or target.

- As you learn a skill, focus on being totally connected to your moves.

- In mind and body, feel yourself execute a skill or shot through imagery, letting the movements unfold naturally. Then perform the actions.

- As you ready for competition, allow yourself to execute your own moves without evaluation. Just let go and see what happens. Go by feel. Go by instinct. Free yourself to flow.

- On the approach, tune out awareness of everything that's going on around you and totally connect to your target.

- Try to re-create the mental and physical conditions that allow you to experience the feelings and focus associated with your best performances.

- Use reminders to enter the state of mind that allows your best performance focus.

- Work on holding that focus for short periods, and try to gradually increase the time you're fully focused. The ultimate goal is to be able to hold that best focus, that total concentration, throughout your entire performance.

---

4. <u>Apply in competition.</u> After learning, mentally rehearsing, and practicing methods for maintaining attention and refocusing, the next step is using them in actual competition. Recall the sequence we generally advise for introducing new psychological techniques in competition: league play first, then tournament play.

Remember, You Are an Individual

As a unique person, characteristics of your ability to concentrate can differ from those of others in various ways. These include your capacity to initially keep your attention focused on a particular activity such as bowling; what occurrences or situations tend to grab your attention; and how readily you can redirect your attention if distracted. Also, as we've discussed, your internal and visible external reactions, when distracted, may well be different than another athlete's.

Due to such differences, it's essential to discover the exact attention-sustaining and refocusing methods which work for you. What functions very effectively as a concentration skill in your case may have the opposite effect for someone else. A common variation concerns socializing between shots. Some bowlers are distracted by such interacting, while others find that talking relaxes them and contributes to their concentrating during the next shot.

Even general principles don't apply to everyone. As an example, we've recommended a process-oriented focus as a means of assisting you to maintain attention. Yet, the attention of some bowlers becomes more riveted when they think about results. Another prime example of individual variation related to concentration concerns angry outbursts. Typically, intense anger is distracting, especially when aimed at oneself. However, you no doubt have encountered the occasional bowler or other athlete whose concentration is sharpened by this emotion.

It is essential that you try different concentration-enhancing approaches and gauge their effectiveness by your assessment and by the feedback of your coach or others qualified to evaluate your game. Bear in mind that the type of techniques as well as the exact way you apply them can and should change based on what you discover. The principle is Master-Monitor-Modify. Furthermore, as your game evolves, you may place less emphasis on, or even phase out, some methods while adding others to your repertoire of skills. The key is matching the technique to your current style and reactions.

Exercises

1. Name the methods you now use to lock into focus.

2. Cite additional ones you'll employ in the future and visualize applying them.

3. What are your vulnerable situations with respect to distraction?

4. Write down your lapse indicators.

5. Do you adhere to the 15 second rule?

6. What is your thought stopping sequence?

7. Visualize the three types of imagery we suggest for regaining attention. Which do you prefer?

8. Follow the directions for centering yourself. In the future, give centering and slowing down a try as ways of refocusing.

9. Which activities for managing outside stress seem best suited for you?

REVIEW

Bowling excellence requires the ability to maintain steady attention and to quickly refocus should you become distracted. Concentration can be broken by negative states of mind as well as specific distracting events. Therefore, all psychological skill methods priming you to perform can positively impact your focus. Being confident, poised, and alert contributes to optimal concentration.

To "lock" into focus, we recommend seven methods. These include adhering to routines (the primary tool), verbal and visual cues, and immediacy ("here and now" approach).

Rapid awareness is essential for refocusing attention if you become distracted. We suggest ways to acquire the two types of relevant knowledge: knowing which circumstances tend to distract you and knowing your reactions when distracted.

If you actually become distracted or encounter potential distractions, intently reapply the methods used for locking in. Returning to your between-shot shot routine is fundamentally important. Thought stopping and centering are among other valuable methods for regaining focus.

To clear your mind for bowling, it's necessary to separate from the stress of daily life.

Mastering concentration-enhancing skills consists of the standard four-stage process.

A list of practice exercises and tips is provided.

Which methods you use to bolster concentration as well as when and how you apply them is a highly individual matter. As your game evolves, adapt your approach accordingly.

12

WHAT YOU NEED TO KNOW ABOUT PRESSURE

*My legs were wobbling on that first shot.**
Norm Duke

The ability to prevent, limit, or reduce pressure is a primary mental game skill. Controlling its potentially adverse impact is a key step towards placing yourself in a focused, optimally energized, and optimistic state of mind.

In this chapter, we first discuss the significance of pressure and its relationship to anxiety. We then teach you how to acquire the types of awareness needed to handle competition-related anxiety. Equipped with this knowledge, you'll be ready to apply the coping methods presented in Chapters 13 and 14.

Impact of Pressure

Bowlers, and all athletes, are continually tested by the challenge of crucial game situations. Such key moments are a big part of the excitement and fun of sports. At these times, when outcome rides on

---

* Duke, twice PBA Player of the Year and USBC Hall of Famer, was referring to the initial shot of a sudden-death, one ball roll-off to determine the winner of a Tour event. After knocking down nine pins on the first shot, he won the title with two straight strikes.

immediate performance, there is the potential to feel pressured and become tense in mind and body. For example, your concentration can be broken, thoughts race, or mind go blank; your legs, arms, or hands may become weak, shaky, or tight. Because of the coordination and precision necessary to deliver the ball properly, all it takes is a small change in stride to affect timing or balance, or a slight tightening of the arm or a subtle squeezing of the ball to affect your release. Or decision making may be thrown off if your thinking is slow or scattered.

It's not hard to imagine the impact of these changes. Your shot can't be on line or carry well if the ball's direction, velocity, rotation, etc. is off. If you're not poised, clear thinking, and focused, your ability to quickly make a necessary move or equipment change is compromised. Since even a single pin can make a world of difference in the outcome, response to pressure situations can readily affect results. In team play, if someone's performance drops off, teammates may in turn feel heightened pressure to take up the slack. Also, under pressure some team members may stop communicating or display anger. This can further impair the team effort.

These types of psychological and physical effects and their negative impact on performance are commonly referred to as "choking." No athlete is immune. Grappling with the potential effects of feeling pressure is part of the sports experience from Little League to the Major Leagues, from youth league bowling to the ranks of the PBA. In one situation or another, in some degree, at some time, all who participate in competitive sports are affected.

Close your eyes and envision Walter Ray Williams in a championship round on TV, coming through again and again. If you ask Walter Ray, he'll tell you of the times in his career he didn't come through. Or ask Marshall Holman. Or Carolyn Dorin-Ballard. Or Betty Morris. Or any professional or elite amateur. All have had their share of events where the pressure they felt lowered their score. Yet to enjoy so many triumphs, these great athletes have consistently coped with the stress of clutch situations.

The same principle holds true for every bowler. You'll undoubtedly face countless situations where a result hangs in the balance. Those who bowl at or close to their best at such critical times enjoy a distinct competitive edge. Acquiring the skills to handle your reactions in these clutch circumstances is a mental game must if you are to reach your bowling pinnacle.

Pre-Game Pressure

Feelings of pressure are by no means limited to the actual competition. As competitors in all sports will attest, the period of time preceding play can be the toughest in terms of "nerves." While some pre-competition "butterflies" are, to borrow a sports metaphor, par for the course, excessive emotional and physical tension can have detrimental impact. Some possible negative effects include not adhering to pre-game routine, diminished energy, poor quality warm-up, distraction, and carryover of a pressured feeling into actual play.

Pre-Day Pressure

The experience of pressure can also affect your training. Some bowlers feel intense pressure to perform during all practice sessions. Others may feel it only at specific times, such as when team members, coach, or family are present. Sometimes bowlers will start to "press" during practice as the event approaches. Just as in actual competition, the quality of your bowling can drop if you start to tighten up. As we'll describe shortly, feeling pressure can produce different psychological and physical reactions. Difficulty sleeping is an example of a pre-competition reaction which could hinder your performance readiness.

Pride in Coping

Bowlers cite several essential characteristics of the sport which can contribute to a "pressure cooker" atmosphere: the isolated position on the lane with all eyes on you; the pause between shots leaving time to ponder what's ahead; the proximity of spectators and adversaries; the small margin for error; the glare of the lights and the stare of the cameras on the show, along with a single elimination format; the need to think quickly on your feet as you adjust to ever-changing conditions; the minimal opportunity to release tension through physical activity. Add to this the common combination of close competition and limited stakes. All the more reason to develop finely honed psychological tools and all the more cause to feel proud of managing the stress.

Pressure and Anxiety

When speaking of pressure, we're referring to an instance of the mind/body state known as "anxiety." Anxiety arises in situations where a person considers the possibility of something undesirable occurring. The greater the anticipated negative impact of the occurrence and the greater the expectation of it happening, the higher the anxiety.

Think of the anxiety response as a reaction to a perceived risk. The risk may be an auto accident, a social rejection, or a lost qualifying match. Pressure is the experience of anxiety when performance is involved and the risk concerns failing to succeed.

The reactions in the anxiety response are of two types: psychological and physiological. Later in the chapter you'll learn the common signs of both types. A widely used definition (coined by Charles Spielberger) refers to anxiety as an "emotional" reaction which combines *(1) feelings of tension, apprehension, and nervousness; (2) unpleasant thoughts (worries); and (3) physiological changes.*

The very positive implication of all this is that there are many ways to modify anxiety. Pressure is not at all a fixed, unchangeable reaction—it's not "built into" a situation. Pressure is triggered by anticipated negative outcome. By exercising control over thoughts related to outcome and your psychological and physiological responses in the moment, pressure can be successfully managed.

A prime example of how anxiety can affect bowlers is illustrated on the opposite page.

An essential step to coping with all circumstances that can elicit anxiety is awareness, our next topic.

Awareness

To equip yourself to handle competition-related anxiety in all forms, three types of awareness are needed:

- Know the situations which trigger anxiety in you: "pressure points"

- Know your signs of anxiety: "pressure indicators"

- Know your optimum anxiety/excitation levels: "optimal activation"

As you can tell by our references to "you" and "your," the anxiety response in competition is very much an individual matter. While aspects of your response are most definitely shared by others, the exact combination of anxiety-generating situations, anxiety signs, and optimum anxiety/excitation levels is unique to you. Also unique to you is the effectiveness of specific coping methods.

THE THRILL IS GONE

Bowling had always played a significant role in Yuri Kalinov's life*. It was a continuous source of joy, accomplishment, and pride. This talented athlete aspired to make Team USA and worked diligently on his physical game, equipment, lane play, and conditioning. Yet, though his overall game was stronger than ever, in 2004 Kalinov was on the verge of quitting the sport due to anxiety.

On a typical night before league play, the crippling effects of anxiety would begin with worries about performance. Even if he had bowled well in a practice session that day, he asked himself doubtfully, "But how am I going to do tonight?"

During the pre-game warm-ups, he couldn't shake a sense of dread. As competition got underway, a feeling of nervousness produced a knot in his stomach. Tightness then spread to his neck and shoulders. He found it difficult to breathe. He felt "uptight" and squeezed the ball. Kalinov expressed it simply: "I'd freeze." Not surprisingly, he bowled poorly and experienced intense frustration and disappointment.

In addition to pessimism about performance, Kalinov felt pressured by other factors. He was self-consciously aware of those watching in the stands. He could also be affected in this way by bowlers around him. After missing a shot, he might say, "Here I go again," and before the next shot, "Oh, I'm going to miss it again." This is how Kalinov described his attitude towards himself: "I'm very hard on myself, there's nobody harder. I call myself names. I expect perfection. Sometimes I hate myself after bowling."

With such enormous pressure on his shoulders, is it any wonder that Kalinov was performing far below potential and having a rough time emotionally? As he put it, "My mental game is destroying me." Fortunately, his coach recognized the reason for the gap between well-honed skills and actual execution and referred him to a sport psychologist. Feeling this was his last chance, Kalinov eagerly followed through. In the next chapter, you'll see how he tackled this challenge.

---

* This bowler's pre-shot routine was cited in Chapter 6 (the second sample routine). For confidentiality, his actual name is not used here.

Know Your Pressure Points

Certain game situations obviously tend to generate a feeling of pressure: competing on TV, approaching a perfect game, needing a strike or mark to win a match for you or your team or to qualify or cash. It's also quite common in sports for athletes to experience "jitters" at the outset of an event. These are all classic anxiety-generating situations.

However, bowlers can experience the anxiety response across a wide range of game circumstances. Some tend to feel intense pressure at the start of a block; others in match play; some more in team play than in individual competition or vice versa. Playing against strong competition, falling behind, encountering a difficult oil pattern, adjusting to changing conditions, and competing on a new level (e.g., a more competitive league, international competition, or a professional event) are frequently associated with pressure.

Sometimes anxiety is set off by an interpersonal situation. Playing with new teammates or the presence (and possible actions) of spectators, media, family, or friends creates pressure for some bowlers. A coach's presence is comforting for many, yet adds pressure for others.

There are also bowlers who feel "under the gun" virtually all the time. Here most obviously the pressure is self-imposed. However, in a real sense this is always the case. We've found extensive variation in those things that trigger anxiety in bowlers. Such variation reflects this reality: Pressure is in the eye of the beholder. As you'll see when we discuss pressure-reducing strategies, the positive implication is that your response to situations can be modified. You can then view a competitive circumstance differently. Instead of feeling worried and playing tight, you can think positive and play loose.

Knowing your pressure points can be of great value both for preparation and actual performance. Awareness of those situations which tend to trigger strong competitive anxiety enables you to mentally rehearse your coping with these circumstances and to practice coping through simulation. In competition, awareness of triggering situations allows you to take necessary preventive measures as the circumstances arise and to more quickly counter anxiety which may occur.

Pre-Competition Situations

Awareness of those circumstances when your pre-game anxiety tends to be particularly high is important due to the reasons mentioned earlier. Excessively high anxiety prior to the event can negatively affect your pre-game routine, concentration, energy level, and warm-up, as well as carry over into play. Pre-competition pressure may be felt to different degrees from the moment you wake until competition starts. One athlete may become worried and tense when driving to the center, another when entering the bowl, and another during warm-up.

Finally, identifying times of significant anxiety during training can enable you to counter potentially adverse effects (such as inconsistent concentration and insomnia). In this way, you can maintain the quality of practices and your overall psychological and physical preparedness.

Know Your Pressure Indicators

What are your psychological and physiological responses when feeling pressure?

This knowledge is essential for monitoring anxiety before and during competition. Awareness of your anxiety creates the opportunity to immediately apply whatever techniques are needed to establish an optimal outlook and excitation level. Making an adjustment promptly is a key to blunting, if not blocking, any negative impact. That's because the duration of the anxiety has been brief, limiting its effect and its chances of becoming entrenched.

The box below lists common signs associated with anxiety.

ANXIETY RESPONSE[14]

PSYCHOLOGICAL INDICATORS	PHYSIOLOGICAL INDICATORS
• Lacking sense of confidence	• Active stomach "butterflies"
• Decreased sense of control	• Unusual feelings of nausea
• Disrupted attention	• Increased respiration rate
• Pervading sense of worry, fear, doubt, and dread	• Increased blood pressure
• Worrisome expectation of failure	• Increased muscle tension
• Negative concern about performance	• Disrupted sleep pattern
• Impaired ability to concentrate	• Dilated pupils
• Diminished sense of well-being	• Yawning
• Increased indecision and apprehension	• Increased perspiration
	• Increased heart rate
	• Increased shakiness

These lists don't cover all possible responses. When identifying your own pressure indicators, look for any characteristic signs, psychological or physiological, which occur when you feel competitive pressure. Full awareness of your psychological signs includes knowing your specific thoughts.

Also make careful note of your behaviors at such times. Do you fidget? Do you pace? Do you look at the score? Do you look for your coach? Do you talk to others? Is your speech hurried? Some behaviors may contribute to anxiety as well as reflect it.

Know Your Optimal Activation

While excessive anxiety interferes with performance, athletes vary considerably in the level of anxiety associated with their best performances. For example, research and our own survey of bowling competitors point to noteworthy differences in preferred pre-competitive anxiety. While most prefer low levels, some report performing best with moderate levels, and a significant number associate high pre-competition anxiety with their personal best.

Knowing the level of anxiety (before and during competition) associated with your own top performances enables you to make the necessary adjustments. If, for example, you've performed at your best with moderate pre-competitive anxiety, then experiencing this degree of anxiety need not concern you. In fact, you may feel reassured that you're primed to perform. If your anxiety is very high, then you'll need to reduce it accordingly.

We've known bowlers who learn a relaxation technique in order to handle emotional reactions, such as anxiety, and then run into a totally unexpected problem: They become too calm and passive. "I've lost my edge," "I didn't feel gung ho the way I like to," and "I felt tired" are some ways over-relaxation can be reported.

This illustrates the principle that all athletes have an ideal or optimum level of excitation* for performing in their sport. Actually, there is an excitation range within which you're at your best**. Above or below— either over or under-stimulated—and you won't feel most comfortable nor be fully ready to perform at your peak.

We like to think of this ideal range of excitation in terms of a mind/body engine. You have an optimum rpm performing range. Use your brake or accelerator to keep within it. Rev too high and you can redline. Drop the rpm too low and you can stall.

In the next section, ways to identify your optimal activation are presented. Once you know the anxiety and overall excitation levels associated with your best performance, monitor your levels in competition and adjust accordingly. The aim is to be consistently as close as possible to your ideal. Remember, you have leeway on the "up" and "down" sides of these (averaged) levels. Methods presented in the next two chapters are primary tools for lowering anxiety/excitation. Techniques for increasing excitement are considered in Chapter 16.

You may be over-excited or "too pumped" for various reasons. Anxiety and anger are two "negative" emotional states associated with over-excitement. However, you could be too excited simply from the

---

* We use "activation," "excitation," and "arousal" interchangeably.
** The technical term is "zone of optimal functioning" (ZOF).

stimulation produced by the event or the setting. As unlikely as it may seem, the thrill of success can sometimes have a detrimental impact. This can happen during a game (as previously discussed) or after one (Chapter 15). For example, following a big match play win, you might need to settle yourself down for the next game.

Under-arousal may be due to any number of factors. Fatigue and discouragement are frequent reasons for "low energy." At times, inadequate concentration can deflate intensity. You may have a tendency to start slowly. Then there are athletes who simply tend to perform in low gear. While that tendency may be advantageous in certain pressure situations, at other times it might be far from ideal.

Kim Adler: Winner of 15 PWBA titles, including three majors, first woman to roll 800 series on Sport Bowling condition

How to Become Aware

In order to acquire these three types of awareness (pressure points, pressure indicators, and optimal activation), we recommend the following approaches:

Reflection

Ask yourself a series of questions. Start by recalling clutch situations you've faced.

1. How did you perform generally compared to less crucial moments?

2. Were there particular circumstances where you tended to tighten up?

3. In what ways was your performance affected at these times?

4. When you were successful in the clutch, did you or someone else do something which helped you handle the stress?

5. When else (other than in obvious clutch situations) have you felt significant pressure before and/or during competition?

6. To what extent, if any, did this pressure adversely affect you?

7. Do you tend to perform better in practice than in competition? This pattern often reflects the impact of pressure.

8. What specific psychological reactions have you experienced in clutch circumstances or other circumstances where you felt pressure?

9. What specific physiological reactions did you have at these times?

10. What were your specific behaviors at these times?

11. Now think back to your best competitive performances (try to recall at least four). Would you say your anxiety before the competition was low, medium, or high? During the competition what was it?

12. On a scale of 1 to 10, with 1 representing no anxiety (total calm) and 10 representing extreme anxiety (panic), how would you rate your pre-competition anxiety before your best efforts? If the ratings differ for various events, average them. How would you rate your anxiety during these efforts? Again, average the ratings if they vary for different events.

13. Again, recalling your top performance, what was your level of overall excitation before competition—low, medium, or high? What was it during the competition?

14. On a scale of 1 to 10, where 1 represents no excitement (listlessness) and 10 represents extreme excitement (very charged up), rate your overall excitation level before these most successful efforts. Average the ratings if they're not the same for each event. Now rate your excitation level during these efforts. If your ratings differ from event to event, average them.

Keeping a Log

Whether you write or use a tape recorder, your goal is to keep a detailed record which enables you to confirm answers or more fully answer the questions just posed. Describe the exact content of your thoughts as well as your specific emotions, behaviors, and physical responses. We suggest rating your pre-competition anxiety/excitation levels at regular intervals as the start of competition approaches (e.g., four hours before, two hours before, one hour before, half an hour before, and at completion of the warm-up). With respect to anxiety/excitation during competition, rate levels for as many individual frames as you can as well as for the game as a whole. If possible, do this immediately after the game is over. Rate with the same ten point scales used for reflecting.

Receiving Feedback & Viewing Videotape

Our thoughts about these aids to awareness parallel what we noted in the chapter on concentration. Input from your coach or another person familiar with your game can help identify changes in physical game technique and routine, as well as other overt behaviors and physiological responses occurring in clutch situations. Video can also capture these changes. Reviewing the tape with your coach provides the surest way to identify subtle reactions.

Exercises

1. After answering awareness questions one through seven, cite your pressure points.

2. List your pressure indicators (reflected in questions eight, nine, and ten).

3. Note your optimum activation levels, before and during competition (reflected in questions 11 through 14).

4. Set a target date for starting your pressure awareness log.

REVIEW

At key moments, feelings of pressure can trigger various physiological and psychological responses which interfere with execution. Pressure may also be experienced pre-game and even in training. Particular aspects of bowling can heighten pressure.

Pressure is anxiety related to performance. Anxiety has been defined as an emotional reaction that includes tense feelings, worried thoughts, and physical changes. You can learn to control this reaction.

Three types of awareness are needed for handling competitive anxiety. The first is knowing those situations where you tend to feel pressure (pressure points). The second is knowing how your mind and body respond when pressure is experienced (pressure indicators). The third is knowing the range of anxiety and overall excitation in which you perform best (optimal activation). Reflection, keeping a log, receiving feedback, and viewing videotape are ways to increase your awareness.

13

COMING THROUGH IN CLUTCH SITUATIONS: RELAXATION

When you're a kid, you dream about throwing two strikes in the tenth to win.
Brian Voss

In all of sports, there is no moment more thrilling, more supremely satisfying, than delivering in the clutch. The satisfaction is twofold: attaining an important result and mastering the pressure.

Ask any bowler about career highlights and inevitably you'll hear of events where individual or team came through when the chips were down. Of course, as all bowlers know only too well, there's the other side of the coin: those times when success proved elusive. And in many of these disappointing situations, the experience of pressure will have been the deciding factor.

Coping Methods

There are a range of psychological tools available for managing situations which can trigger feelings of pressure. To develop a consistently effective pressure-coping strategy, we recommend you master multiple approaches. Coping methods may be part of your pre-competition and pre-shot routines and/or used as needed.

In this chapter, we focus on behavioral relaxation methods. In Chapter 14, we discuss other means of coping and then offer overall suggestions concerning the mastery and application of skills for "crunch time." The mental game program described in the box below provides an introduction to the array of techniques covered.

THE COMEBACK

In the last chapter, we described how anxiety eroded both quality of performance and pleasure of participation for Yuri Kalinov. Over several months in 2004, he focused on his mental game (guided by a sport psychologist) while continuing to work on the other areas crucial to performance. He bowled in two leagues and practiced three times a week.

Assisted by reflection and a log, he increased awareness of pressure points, pressure indicators, and optimum activation as well as negative self-talk.

He mastered diaphragmatic breathing, using it in daily practice periods, as part of his pre-shot routine, and as needed when anxious during competition.

He developed a thought stopping sequence which was applied in practice as well as in competition. This dramatically limited pessimistic and self-disparaging ideas and beliefs. Eventually, the disruptive impact of any such thoughts became negligible.

Every day, he played a tape guiding him through a Progressive Muscle Relaxation (PMR) process and "The Blue Sky" visualization. During the PMR segment, he experienced a feeling of deep relaxation with sensations of warmth and heaviness. The visualization created a serene sense of floating which he described as highly realistic.

During competition, he employed the pre-shot routine described in Chapter 6. At certain pressure point moments and/or noticing pressure indicators, he used diaphragmatic breathing or brief PMR. Knowing his optimal activation, he reserved use of "The Blue Sky" for the most stressful situations. If applied at other times, he would become too relaxed.

In the settee area between shots, he often communicated or listened to music. Sometimes he mentally rehearsed and, if needed, applied thought stopping. Additionally, he could call upon another relaxation technique in his repertoire.

(continued)

Relaxation Techniques

A variety of mind/body methods exist to counter the effects of anxiety. For example, these techniques can slow heart rate and lower blood pressure, loosen muscles, and clear your mind of worrisome, racing thoughts. In fact, depending on your mastery of these calming methods and the exact circumstances or environment, different degrees of tranquility and complete physical ease can be achieved. As we noted in the last chapter, it's even possible to become too relaxed

---

Periodically during the day, he mentally practiced. This involved visualizing different releases and various competitive situations. The imagery always depicted success.

Two components of his pre-game routine were a mindset statement and a method for managing outside stress. The method used was the sci-fi "Stargate" visualization. He imagined a "portal" through which he passed as he entered the center. No concerns about his daily life could go through with him.

He made improvement ("emerging a better bowler") an overall competition goal. This oriented him towards growth and combined with reframing to maintain a sense of forward movement no matter what happened. He also set and met weekly goals for mastering psychological skills. This boosted optimism.

Most crucially, his capacity for self-acceptance expanded. A key to becoming a good self-coach was being as supportive to himself as he was towards others. This enhanced positive perspective meant there was less riding on each shot.

Another relaxation tool he developed was visualizing a favorite place. In a hypnotic state, he envisioned himself in such an ideal setting: on a comfortable couch, watching ESPN! The relaxation switch (verbal trigger) for this experience was "Paradise."

He successfully confronted a teammate whose harsh and otherwise negative comments were disruptive and increased tension. His genuine, direct, constructive approach proved effective.*

Finally, adopting a life perspective helped lessen the pressures of bowling. Given Kalinov's tough childhood circumstances and the challenge of adapting to a new country, he felt grateful for his current life.

The application of these methods profoundly affected Kalinov's attitude and execution:

He felt in control of his emotions. Instead of nervousness and "freezing," he literally

(continued)

---

* "Constructive confrontation" is taught in Chapter 19.

during competition! The point is, the proper application of relaxation techniques enables you to control anxiety and regulate your overall excitation.

As with all parts of the mental game, what you comfortably and reliably turn to in the clutch is a matter of personal preference. Experiencing the full range of methods presented in the pages that follow will enable you to discover those that are right for you.

Essential Tips

It is highly important to experience such techniques, especially when you're learning them, under ideal conditions. A quiet, comfortable setting is conducive to relaxing. Particularly at first, dim lighting is helpful. Remove jewelry and be sure your collar is loose. Loosen your tie or belt if you're wearing either. We recommend sitting so that you stay awake and are practicing in a position you can use during competition (e.g., in the settee area). Place your feet flat on the floor. Sit upright, flush against the back of the chair or couch. Your hands may rest on

---

THE COMEBACK (continued)

experienced calmness and warmth. The start of competition, adversity, and others around him no longer led to a flood of anxiety. Distress and distraction were replaced with eagerness and focus. He stayed positive, remarking, "I don't have the negatives any more." Trusting his game and his reading of the lanes, he more and more adjusted quickly to changing conditions.

The pincounts reflected this growth. His overall steady performance was punctuated with games above 260. That summer, he attained the top league's high average of 224—five pins better than the nearest bowler. During the next full season, he again led a high-scoring league in average. He capped off the league year by winning a stepladder playoff (beating three opponents). In the final game, with the title at stake, Kalinov bowled a 300.

Kalinov's transition was best expressed in his own words: "From where I started, it's day and night. I thought I was getting burned out. I was very tense. Now I have peace of mind. Bowling's nice and simple. I enjoy it again. I'm overwhelmed."

Due to his strengthened mental game, continuing skill development, and consistently solid performance, Kalinov's confidence soared. He started to have dreams of winning tournaments. In a burst of enthusiasm, he even exclaimed, "I could have Parker Bohn in front of me and I'd say, 'Bring it on.'"

At the same time, this athlete was well aware of the hard work ahead on the road to tournament success. Unmistakably, he now felt prepared to embark on the journey.

your legs, by your side, or on the arms of a chair. If you choose to lie down, do so on your back. Some athletes feel more comfortable with knees slightly raised, perhaps supported with a pillow. Arms can be extended at your side or on your legs.

We suggest keeping your eyes closed when using these methods away from the center. This is generally conducive to relaxation, but not absolutely essential. (If you have hard contact lenses, either take them out or keep eyes open.) Inside the bowl, pre-game and within-game, let whatever makes you most comfortable determine whether your eyes are open or closed. If you intend to keep your eyes open, practice the technique with open eyes at least some of the time at home and regularly on-lane.

Tranquil music tends to promote relaxation. In fact, listening to music is among our recommended approaches. Consequently, you can practice calming techniques with music playing softly. However, it's crucial that you be able to use the various methods without music since they'll be applied in a competitive setting. Therefore, we suggest experiencing them initially with no music. Once mastered, you can then listen to music at least some of the time when practicing the techniques.

Before starting each technique, take several deep, slow breaths, inhaling through your nose and exhaling through your mouth. Once diaphragmatic breathing has been learned, you can use this method. Imagine you're breathing calmness in and tension out. Learn the amount of such "warm-up" that works best for you (e.g., prior to visualizing).

Athletes and others who experience these relaxation methods commonly report feeling refreshed and re-energized. However, it may take a few minutes to become fully alert after completing a relaxation process. Walking, stretching, talking, and listening to up-tempo music are some ways to accelerate the return to full alertness.

If you use a relaxation technique prior to driving, be absolutely certain to regain your normal level of alertness. Due to the potential for drowsiness during use, it is inadvisable to utilize any of these methods, even briefly, when behind the wheel.

You now have an opportunity to experience a range of classic relaxation methods. The signs of relaxation are both psychological and physical. Psychological effects may include a sense of peace, well-being, timelessness, and a dream-like quality. Among the possible physical reactions are feelings of muscle looseness and heaviness (as if you're sinking into the chair, couch, or floor) and a sensation of warmth. You may experience a tingling in some muscles and even brief twitching. Everyone is different and some individuals experience other sensations. For example, some report a sensation of lightness instead of heaviness and visualize colors or hear music.

The vast majority of people find relaxation techniques completely pleasurable. However, some experience anxiety as they feel themselves "letting go." Relaxation is ultimately a passive state in which you allow yourself to "be" rather than "do." In a sense, you relinquish the conscious control of mind and body which characterizes our active existence at other times. If you experience anxiety, see if it passes. If not, try another technique, at least on that day. Do not continue any method which creates ongoing discomfort—either psychological or physical.

Give these relaxation methods a "tryout" and find the ones most effective for you. Preferences vary from athlete to athlete, and we all tend to more readily take to particular techniques. However, we've found that with practice most all bowlers can become sufficiently proficient in calming themselves through one approach or another.

Diaphragmatic Breathing

This method of breathing—sometimes referred to as "deep, slow breathing" or "controlled breathing"—is a primary relaxation method. Its great effectiveness is reflected in its use in clinical treatment settings for diagnosed anxiety conditions.

Diaphragmatic breathing involves filling the lungs completely and then emptying them completely with an easy, consistent rhythm. The method can be used at any time before or during competition to achieve a calming effect.

Breathing in this way also increases the amount of oxygen circulating in the blood. This can facilitate athletic performance.

The box on the following page describes the technique and how to learn it.

Diaphragmatic breathing offers many benefits as a relaxation technique. Once mastered, it's highly efficient and also allows you to carefully regulate how relaxed you are. Simply take the number of breaths required to bring you to the desired anxiety/excitation levels. Sometimes, one or two breaths will be completely sufficient. At other times, more extended use may be needed (for example, pre-game or in the settee area between shots). The technique is portable and "invisible" in that your eyes may stay open, keeping the process totally private.

DIAPHRAGMATIC BREATHING

Inhale through your nose and exhale through your mouth. Fill your lungs completely with every inhalation and empty them completely with every exhalation. Don't hold your breath. Inhale gently until you feel a pleasant fullness in your chest. Then let the air release with a soft whispered sound.

With every inhaled breath, the diaphragm (muscle located at the base of the sternum) should move down, causing the abdomen to move out. The diaphragm controls the breathing process. When you exhale, it moves back up and the abdomen moves back in. For learning purposes, place your hands on your abdomen so that your fingers touch just below the sternum. When you inhale, the fingers should rise; as you exhale, they should return to a flattened position.

Focus your thoughts on the breathing process. If your mind wanders, gently bring it back. Accept such wandering without judgment and simply return your inner gaze to the breathing.*

(If you ever feel lightheaded, breathe normally and then resume.)

It's recommended that you practice ten minutes twice a day during the first week. Practice when you're alert rather than upon awakening or before bed. Furthermore, it's best not to apply this method in stressful situations until you feel fully comfortable with it and have practiced for a few weeks.

Diaphragmatic breathing often feels awkward at first. Within a few days, however, most people find it increasingly pleasant and natural. Other signs of your mastery will include the feelings of physical relaxation and psychological calm described earlier.

During the second week, you may increase the duration of practice to 12 minutes (twice per day). Some then continue increasing by two minutes weekly until reaching 20 minutes (twice per day).

Continuing practice is important. The purpose is not only to acquire and maintain mastery, but also to foster an association between the breathing and a relaxed state. This association is conducive to triggering relaxation with a few breaths in stressful situations (such as competition). With sufficient training and use, shifting to this way of breathing will become second nature, even spontaneous. After six weeks, one practice period per day is the minimum.

Set your watch or use some other alarm so that checking the time is unnecessary.

Diaphragmatic breathing is a valuable skill which can add years and quality to your life as well as pins to your score.

NOTE: Those with asthma are advised to consult with their physician before using this method.

---

* The potential benefits of this refocusing process are considered in our discussion of meditation later in the chapter.

Recall that we recommend including breathing technique in your pre-game and pre-shot routines and as part of the thought stopping process. Even when regularly used in these ways, you can vary the number of breaths based on how anxious or otherwise stimulated you are.

Other Breathing Techniques

Some bowlers count as they breathe. This can help maintain a consistent rhythm and also promote concentration. For instance, you may count to three or four as you inhale and repeat the same count as you exhale.

You can also make relaxing suggestions to yourself. As an example, at the outset of a breathing session you may think "calm in" while you inhale and "tension out" while you exhale. Once you become relaxed, shift to "calm" as you breathe in and "calmer" as you breathe out.

Other breathing systems can be used. No one is the "right way." What matters is finding the method which comfortably works for you.

Progressive Muscle Relaxation (PMR)

This process involves systematically tensing and then releasing muscles throughout the body. In addition to producing an overall relaxed state, PMR training creates awareness of what relaxation is and teaches how to voluntarily control it.

PMR can enable you to readily identify tension in specific muscle groups and then quickly relax them. For example, as you bowl you may become alert to tightening (even if it's subtle) in the shoulder or arm. You can then consciously relax the tightened area. With sufficient PMR practice, you can accomplish this in competition without contracting the muscle. The most advanced levels of PMR training condition tensing muscles to automatically relax without any effort.

A benefit of PMR is robustness in the face of distraction. On occasions when you may find it difficult to focus during other relaxation techniques, PMR can retain its effectiveness. Some reasons for this are the physical activity involved, the external direction (if the script is on tape), and the relatively long duration of the full process.

Numerous variations exist in the PMR format. A script we use is found in the box beginning on the next page. Recommendations for learning the method are also provided.

You have the choice of following a PMR script without any external direction or using an audiotape. The voice on the tape may be your own, your coach's, or anyone whose cadence is slow and rhythmic and

PROGRESSIVE MUSCLE RELAXATION

Keep the following points in mind as you proceed through the script:

- After relaxing each muscle, observe the difference between the sensation of tightening and the sensation of relaxing.

- When a muscle is relaxed, allow the relaxed sensation to flow to surrounding areas.

- If you experience any discomfort upon tightening, reduce the level of tension so there is no discomfort. If discomfort remains, simply bypass the muscle group.

- If you're receiving medical treatment related to any muscle involved in the script, consult your physician before proceeding with PMR.

- As you tighten a muscle, allow all other muscles to remain relaxed.

- Tighten large muscles for eight seconds; small muscles for six seconds. After relaxing a muscle, wait five seconds before the next muscle tightening.

- The total time for the script is approximately 20 minutes.

- Remember to breathe! Breathe in a smooth, easy manner.

- When the script is completed, enjoy the sensation of relaxation throughout your body. Open your eyes when you're ready.

-Script-[15]

Clench your dominant hand, tighter and tighter. Be sure you continue to breathe, allowing the lips to be slightly parted. Exhale through the mouth, whispering "haa." Be sure the rest of the body is relaxed. Observe the sensation of tightening ... Now let go and relax. Observe the contrast in feeling between your hand when it's tensed and when it's relaxed. Observe the difference in the way your right and left hands feel now ...

Clench your other hand, making a tight fist. Observe the sensation of tightening. Be sure you keep breathing and that the rest of the body is relaxed ... Now let go. Observe the feeling of letting go. If your attention wanders to other things, gently bring it back to the sensation in your arm ...

Now clench both hands. Observe the sensation of tightening ... Then let go and relax all over. Enjoy the feeling ...

Stretch out your dominant arm, palm down and fingers extended. Bend your wrist and hand up and back, keeping your arm straight. Note the feeling of tightness ... Now let go and allow your arm to comfortably drop ...

Stretch out your other arm, with palm down and fingers extended. Bend your wrist and hand up and back, holding your arm straight. Feel the tension ... Release your hand and let your arm comfortably fall . . .

(continued)

PROGRESSIVE MUSCLE RELAXATION (continued)

Now extend both arms and bend both hands up and back in the same way. Observe the tightening ... Relax completely and let your arms rest at your side or on your lap ...

Stretch out your dominant arm again, with palm down and fingers extended. This time, bend your wrist and hand down and back, keeping your arm straight. Observe the feeling of tightness ... Now let go and allow your arm to easily drop ...

Stretch out your other arm, palm down and fingers extended. Bend your wrist and hand down and back, with your arm straight. Feel the tension ... Release your hand and allow your arm to easily fall ...

Now extend both arms and bend both hands down and back in the same way ... Release your hands and relax fully with your arms at your side or on your lap. Observe the contrast between tightening and releasing ...

Bend both your elbows and tense the biceps muscle on the top side of your upper arms. Let your hands and fingers be relaxed. Observe the sensation of tightening. Keep breathing. Be sure your neck, your jaw, and the rest of your body are relaxed ... Now relax and let your arms drop either to your side or to your lap. Notice the difference in feeling between tensing and letting go . . .

Extend your arms, palms up. Tense the triceps muscle on the bottom side of your upper arms. Again, keep your hands and fingers relaxed. Continue to breathe smoothly. Observe the sensation of tightening ... Relax your arms at your side or on your lap. Relax all over ...

Notice that your arms feel comfortable and heavy. Feel the relaxation spread up your arms. Notice that your arms feel heavier and heavier as you relax more and more . . .

Frown hard. Be sure the rest of the body is relaxed ... Relax and let go ...

Now wrinkle your eyebrows up toward your scalp. Be sure your tongue, jaw, and neck are loose, and you're not holding your breath. Observe the sensation of tightening ... Relax and let your brow be smooth. Observe the sensation of relaxation ...

Tighten your eyes. Tighten the muscles deep in your eyes as well as the facial muscles around your eyes. Be sure your tongue, your jaw, the back of your neck, and the rest of your body are relaxed ... Relax and keep your eyes gently closed. Observe the sensations of relaxation and how they differ from those of tightening . . .

Now smile, raising the tops of your cheeks as far as possible toward your eyes ... Let go, releasing all tension. Feel the relaxation ...

Clench your jaw and clench your teeth. Study the tension in the jaw. Be sure you keep breathing ... Relax and let go. Slightly part your lips. As you exhale, let the air go out your mouth in a whispered "haa." ...

(continued)

Press your tongue hard against the roof of your mouth. Observe the tension … Relax and let go …

Feel the relaxation in your cheeks, scalp, eyes, face, arms, and hands …

Now tighten your neck by gently tilting your head backwards. Be sure you keep breathing and the rest of the body stays relaxed. Feel the tension in your neck …Relax and let go . . .

Breathe comfortably and let your jaw be relaxed. Bring your chin gradually down toward your chest. Feel the tension in your neck … Relax and let go …

Tilt your head slowly toward your right shoulder. Observe the tension in your neck … Return to your regular posture and relax …

Now tilt your head slowly toward your left shoulder. Again, observe the tension … Resume your normal posture and relax fully …

Raise your shoulders toward your ears. Be sure the neck and the rest of the body are relaxed. Notice the contrast between how your shoulders feel and how the rest of your body feels … Relax and let go …

Let the relaxation flow into your back, neck, throat, jaw, and face. Let it spread and go deeper and deeper. Feel the force of gravity pulling on your body …

Breathe in deeply and hold your breath. Note the tension in your shoulders and chest. Be sure your eyes, your jaw, and the rest of your body are relaxed … Exhale and observe the feeling. Breathe in and out normally. Notice how on each exhaled breath you feel more and more relaxed. Let the chest walls be loose and soft as you breathe out …

Now take another deep breath. Hold your breath. Be sure the neck is relaxed … Exhale. Feel the release of tension …

Let the relaxation spread to your shoulders, neck, back, and arms …

Tighten your stomach as if you were receiving a blow there. Make it solid … Relax and notice the well-being that accompanies your relaxation …

Now suck your stomach in and hold it … Relax and let go …

Note that you can feel the whole lower abdomen move out as you inhale. Notice how exhaling relaxes your shoulders, chest, and stomach. Let go of all the contractions in your body . . .

Arch your back slowly so there's a space between it and the chair, couch, or floor. Feel the tension along your spine and back. Be sure your legs and the rest of your body are relaxed … Relax and let go …

Relax the lower back, upper back, stomach, chest, shoulders, arms, and face. Relax even more …

(continued)

PROGRESSIVE MUSCLE RELAXATION (continued)

Now tighten your buttocks. Be sure your abdomen and the rest of your body are relaxed. Keep breathing ... Relax and let go. Feel how different the sensations of relaxation are from those accompanying the tightening ....

Tighten both thighs and the muscles in back of your upper legs. Observe the tension ... Let go completely and relax ...

Point your toes and feet downward to tighten your calves and the arches of your feet. Be sure you keep breathing ... Relax and let go ...

With your heels stationary, pull up your feet and pull back your toes. Feel the tension along your shins and tops of you feet ... Relax and let go ...

Now let go more and more of each part of your body: Feet relax ... ankles relax ... calves and shins ... keep breathing easily ... knees and thighs ... legs fully relaxed ... buttocks and hips ... feel the heaviness of your lower body ... stomach relax ... waist relax ... lower back ... let go more and more ... upper back relax ... chest relax ... shoulders ... arms ... let relaxation take over ... throat relax ... neck ... jaws and face—all relaxed ...

(Coaches making a tape for athletes unfamiliar with the script's ending can add this final sentence: "When you're ready, take a deep breath, sit up, and open your eyes.")

Our recommended practice schedule for PMR is as follows:

- Once per day for the first two weeks

- Every other day for the next two weeks

- Two or three times per week for maintenance

We regard this as a minimum in order to master the technique and derive the most benefit from its use in competition.

whose tone you find pleasant. Calming background music is optional. Bowlers with whom we work sometimes bring their PMR tape to events. They may listen to most, if not all, of the tape pre-game (typically in their car or in the paddock) or to brief segments between shots. After one month, it's useful to practice at least some of the time without technological assistance. This will help prepare you to apply PMR during a game.

It's common practice for a coach (or sport psychologist) to guide athletes in person through the initial PMR session. After that, "live" sessions are beneficial, yet not essential.

Monitoring

Through PMR training, you'll develop an acute sensitivity to muscular tension. Consequently, you may readily recognize when a muscle becomes tight. At the same time, your concentration on the process of bowling may deflect awareness from physical sensations such as muscle tension. Therefore, to ensure prompt spotting of developing tension, it's advisable to monitor yourself.

Monitoring can be performed in two ways. You can monitor specific muscles or all muscles. Let's look at both these ways.

During PMR sessions, you'll likely become aware of certain muscles which tend to be tight. You may very well already know which muscles tend to tighten in competition (or even pre-game) either from stress or physical demands. You can then monitor these specific muscles.

You can also use a monitoring technique known as "body scanning." This involves quickly directing your attention to muscle groups throughout the body. You may scan your muscles in the order used during full PMR sessions or simply scan up or down your entire body (generally preferred).

There are options as to when you monitor muscle tension. You can be selective or systematic. Armed with your knowledge of pressure points, you can monitor yourself in these particular situations. For instance, monitor a specific muscle or do a body scan before a clutch shot in the tenth frame. Examples of a systematic approach to monitoring would be doing so before each frame or every other frame or between games. You may find it best to combine selective and systematic approaches. Say you're scheduled to do a body scan every third frame. At the same time, you know that your back muscles tend to tighten when you fall behind late in a match. As soon as this competitive situation develops, you monitor your back even if you're ahead of schedule.

Whether it's through spontaneous recognition, specific monitoring, or body scanning, once you know a muscle is tense, immediately relax it. If you become aware of tension in the midst of a body scan, relax the muscle and then continue scanning.

Additional Activities

Regular PMR training teaches you to relax any muscle "at will" (this may not even be necessary if a muscle has relaxed automatically). In other words, the contraction/relaxation involved in the full PMR process isn't required. An additional exercise will hone your readiness in this regard. This involves proceeding step-by-step through each of the muscle groups exactly as you usually do. However, instead of tensing and releasing, simply relax the muscles. Focus on each muscle group for 10 seconds. The entire process lasts some 15 minutes. We suggest starting this exercise after the first month's training is complete at a minimum frequency of twice per week. In order to best prepare for application in competitive conditions, this process should be performed without a guiding tape or background music.

If you're aware of specific muscles tending to tighten, we advise thoroughly stretching them before and after competition as well as during the event as the setting permits. Any muscle which becomes tight while bowling might benefit from gentle stretching at that point. Stretching in general is recommended pre-game and following the event, as well as in training.

PMR's most obvious function is to ready muscles for the demands of performance. Its value goes beyond this. Sufficiently relaxing your muscles can elicit an overall relaxing effect covering multiple physiological and psychological reactions. For instance, your heart rate slows, thoughts become clear, emotions calm. The more your muscles relax, the more overall relaxation will tend to occur. By the end of a PMR session, all your muscles are relaxed. Practicing the PMR procedures prepares you to consciously relax your entire body and, with it, your mind. A final exercise we recommend sharpens this skill. At least once a day, pause in whatever you're doing for about one minute. Focus on your whole body, re-creating the sense of relaxation in all your muscles experienced at the conclusion of a PMR session. Enjoy the feeling of comfort and the psychological calm accompanying it.

Self-Directed Relaxation

PMR is an extremely thorough and certain way to acquire awareness of muscle tension and gain the ability to relax specific muscles as well as your entire body. It also offers the unique potential to enable muscles to automatically relax. The disadvantage of the method is that it's somewhat time-consuming, particularly in the early stages of training.

Self-directed relaxation is a briefer muscle-by-muscle relaxation approach. A script devised by Rainer Martens is found in the box on the next two pages.

The duration of this process is approximately ten minutes. As with PMR, practice will lead to greater effectiveness and efficiency in relaxing muscles individually and together. You'll learn to become more deeply relaxed in less time. Ultimately, you can reach the point where full relaxation is possible within seconds. In fact, the final exercise we

SELF-DIRECTED RELAXATION SCRIPT[16]

Take a deep breath and slowly exhale. Think "relax" (pause). Inhale deeply ... exhale slowly. Now focus all your attention on your head. Feel any tension in your forehead. Just relax the tension in your forehead. Relax ... (pause). Relax even deeper ... and deeper ... and deeper.

Feel any tension in your jaw or other facial muscles. Just relax the tension in these muscles. Feel the tension flow away.

Inhale deeply ... exhale slowly. Feel the relaxation in your facial muscles. Relax ... (pause). Inhale deeply ... exhale slowly (pause). Relax even deeper ... and deeper ... and deeper.

Now feel any tension in your arms, forearms, and hands. Just relax the muscles in your arms. Relax ... (pause).

Feel any tension in your hands, fingers, or arms, and just relax the tension in these muscles. See the tension flow out of your body.

Inhale deeply ... exhale slowly. Feel the relaxation in your arms and hands. Relax ... (pause). Inhale deeply ... exhale slowly (pause). Relax even deeper ... and deeper ... and deeper.

Now focus your attention on your neck and upper back. Feel any tension in the muscles of your neck and upper back. Just relax the tension in these muscles. Relax ... (pause).

See the tension flow out of your body. Inhale deeply ... exhale slowly. Feel the relaxation in these muscles. Relax ... (pause). Inhale deeply ... exhale slowly (pause). Relax even deeper ... and deeper ... and deeper.

Remember to keep your facial muscles relaxed. Keep your arms and hand muscles relaxed. Keep all these muscles relaxed. Inhale deeply ... exhale slowly. Feel the relaxation in all these muscles. Feel the relaxation even deeper ... and deeper ... and deeper.

Now feel any tension in your lower back and stomach muscles. Focus all your attention on these muscles and ask them to relax. Relax these muscles fully. Feel the tension flow away.

Inhale deeply ... exhale slowly. Feel the relaxation in your lower back and stomach muscles. Relax ... (pause). Inhale deeply ... exhale slowly (pause). Relax even deeper ... and deeper ... and deeper.

Now feel any tension in your upper legs, both the front and back. Focus all your attention on these muscles and ask them to relax. Relax these muscles fully. Feel the tension flow away.

Inhale deeply ... exhale slowly. Feel the relaxation in your upper legs. Relax ... (pause). Inhale deeply ... exhale slowly (pause). Relax even deeper ... and deeper ... and deeper.

Remember to keep your facial muscles relaxed. Keep your lower back and stomach muscles relaxed. And keep your upper leg muscles relaxed. Keep all these muscles relaxed. Inhale

(continued)

SELF-DIRECTED RELAXATION SCRIPT (continued)

deeply … exhale slowly (pause). Feel the relaxation in all these muscles. Relax even deeper … and deeper … and deeper.

Now feel any tension in your lower legs and your feet. Focus all your attention on these muscles and ask them to relax. Relax these muscles fully. Feel the tension flow away.

Inhale deeply … exhale slowly. Feel the relaxation in your lower legs and feet. Relax … (pause). Inhale deeply … exhale slowly (pause). Relax even deeper … and deeper … and deeper.

Now relax your entire body. Relax it completely. Feel all the tension flow away from your facial muscles … your arms and hands … your neck and upper back … your lower back and stomach … your upper legs … and your lower legs and feet.

Inhale deeply … exhale slowly. Feel the relaxation in all your body. Relax … (pause). Inhale deeply … exhale slowly (pause). Relax even deeper … and deeper … and deeper.

---

suggested for PMR training can be of comparable benefit here. Pause at least once per day to focus on your entire body, instantly relaxing all muscles and remaining relaxed for one minute.

We recommend the same practice schedule, options for following the script, and muscle-monitoring procedures used for PMR.

Visualization

We've previously covered imagery as a tool for mental practice, routines, positive perspective, and concentration.

Another valuable function of visualization is bringing about relaxation. Techniques such as diaphragmatic breathing and PMR are physically-based processes which work on the principle "Quiet the body to quiet the mind." Visualization is among the methods which go the other way: "Quiet the mind to quiet the body."

What imagery athletes find calming is a matter of individual preference. Scenes of nature and images involving colors commonly comprise the content. A visualization may be original and personal, deriving from your own experience, or it may be created by someone else. We'll shortly provide examples of each type.

Another way in which visualizations vary is whether they are self-directed or guided externally. A guided visualization may be read to you live or recorded. You may, in effect, guide yourself on tape or have your coach or some other suitable person record the script. The guide's voice should be one you find soothing, with the words delivered rhythmically and deliberately. Typically, there is a pause of about five seconds after each relaxing instruction. Calming music in the background is optional.

To obtain full benefit from this tool, it's essential that you learn to self-direct visualizations even if you prefer to be guided and actually listen to tapes most of the time. During competition, it may not be possible or practical to listen to a tape. Since the capacity to immediately relax during an event is vital, you must be prepared to experience the imagery without the aid of technology. Of course, if you were only interested in using visualization for relaxation purposes outside the center or pre-game inside, then a guided visualization would be sufficient.

A calming visualization ("The Blue Sky"), which has benefited many athletes, is found on the following page.

There are an enormous variety of published visualizations from which to choose. The self-help section of any large book store or equivalent on-line site should provide an ample selection of resources. On page 183 we present another visualization adapted from the same source as "The Blue Sky." This particular visualization nicely complements the muscle-relaxing effects of PMR.

You'll now have an opportunity to develop your own personal visualization. *Position yourself comfortably, close your eyes, and take several slow, deep breaths. Envision yourself in an ideal place, a setting where you feel completely safe, comfortable, and at ease. This peaceful spot can be a favorite place that you regularly visit or did as a child, or a location to which you've traveled. Instead of an actual location, the setting may be one you've seen in a movie or on TV or read about or heard described. If you wish, use your imagination to totally create a location. Once you've found your ideal place, use all your senses to fully experience the setting's tranquility. For example, if you're on a beach, envision a rolling blue ocean, puffy white clouds, and sparkling sunlight. Hear the gentle lapping of the waves and the cry of gulls. Feel the warmth of the sun, a cool, light breeze, and the sand beneath you. Perhaps you can smell the scent of the ocean or suntan lotion. Lose yourself in the total serenity of the setting.*

The place you select for this personal visualization is a reflection of your own unique experience. The imagery can be extremely effective since it originates from an inner reality that truly calms you. While settings in nature are most frequent, any place you associate with comfort and tranquility is fine. In order to relax between shots, one

THE BLUE SKY[17]

Picture a beautiful blue sky without any clouds in it ... There are no limits to the blue sky. It stretches endlessly in every direction, never beginning and never ending ... As you picture the clear blue sky, feel that your body is growing lighter and lighter ... Feel that your body has become so light that you have floated up into the clear blue sky ... Feel that you are floating in the sky and that all tension, fatigue, worry, and problems have left you ... Relax your mind and allow your breathing to seek its own level ... Feel yourself floating gently in the clear blue sky which stretches endlessly in every direction, never beginning and never ending ...

As you feel yourself relaxing more and more, picture that your entire body is merging with the blue sky ... Your body is merging with the peace of the blue sky ... Your mind is merging with the tranquility of the blue sky ... Feel that you have actually become the blue sky ... You no longer have a body or a mind. You have become the infinite blue sky that stretches endlessly in every direction, never beginning and never ending ... Feel that you have become the perfect peace and tranquility of the blue sky ... Completely let go and experience total relaxation ...

The potential impact of visualizing is reflected in the following vignette. At the 1995 US National Amateur Bowling Championships in Reno, Nevada, Dr. Lasser conducted a "Relaxation Class." This one hour class, open to athletes and their coaches, families, and friends, along with event officials, covered the basics of stress management. This included a range of relaxation techniques. "The Blue Sky" was recited to class participants with bamboo flute music in the background. One of the athletes in attendance was Lynda Barnes, a former Team USA member coming back from injury.

Barnes went on to qualify third. In the nationally televised championship round, she faced formidable opposition—the first and second qualifiers. To gain the title, she would have to win back-to-back "sudden death" matches. In the heat and dazzle of the lights, in the emotional cauldron that is a championship round, Barnes prevailed. Moments after securing this dramatic victory, she was interviewed by the color commentator. Asked what enabled her to come through when it counted most, Barnes cited the relaxation class. As Dr. Lasser walked up to congratulate her, the national champ smiled broadly and exclaimed, "I am the blue sky."

There's a postscript. Several years later, Barnes won the WIBC Queens Tournament* in Las Vegas. This event, a pro tour stop in which top amateurs also bowl, is one of the most prestigious national competitions. Barnes' message to Dr. Lasser after the win was "Nothing but blue skies."

Note: Barnes captured her second National Amateur title in 2005, earning a position on Team USA for the eighth time.*

* As of 2006, renamed the USBC Queens, presented by Reno Tri-Properties
** Barnes became a Team USA member for a record-equaling ninth time in 2006.

ASSOCIATIVE RELAXATION[18]

Think of the color green for a moment. Imagine that your feet, ankles, legs, knees, and thighs are being bathed in a beautiful green light ... Now relax these parts of your body ... Continue relaxing them until all tension has left ...

Think of the color purple. Imagine that your stomach, abdomen, lower back, and lower ribs are being filled with purple light ... Now consciously relax these areas of your body until they are completely relaxed ...

Visualize your chest, upper torso, back, and ribs. Feel that they are being bathed in a beautiful light-blue light ... Now relax these parts of your body until all stress and tension have left them ...

Feel the area of your shoulders, neck, face, and head. Imagine that they are surrounded with a beautiful golden light ... Now consciously relax these parts of your body until they are completely relaxed ...

After you have completed this process, imagine that your whole body is being bathed in a glowing white light ... Now relax your entire body until all signs of tension have left you ...

After you've practiced this technique, you'll be able to use it to relax specific sections of your body at any time. For example, if you find that your stomach is tense, then imagine that it's being filled with purple light. Your muscles should relax very quickly. If you develop tight shoulders or a tense neck, imagine that this area of your body is being bathed in golden light. If you feel tightness around your chest, then imagine that your chest is being bathed in a light-blue light, and so on. The more you practice, the better and more quickly the technique will work. Eventually you should be able to relax any part of your body within moments of visualizing the color you associated with it.

---

bowler visualized herself on top of a raft in a swimming pool on a warm summer's day. This visualization consistently enabled her to cope with competitive pressure. Another individual, a lifelong baseball fan from New York, had spent countless hours in Yankee Stadium. A sports injury necessitated an MRI. To cope with the tight confines of the machine, he closed his eyes and imagined he was in the upper deck of the Stadium looking towards the spacious outfield. The wide open vista, especially the expanse of sky above the facade, instantly created a sense of calm.

In order to prepare yourself to apply a visualization in competition, we recommend experiencing it once per day for one week, every other day for the second week, and then minimally twice per week thereafter. The duration of a visualization is approximately ten minutes.

As we've indicated, visualization skills tend to improve with practice.

Lynda Barnes: Here competing on PWBA Tour, in 2005 earned four medals at first Women's World Championships and won the World Cup

Since imagery can be so beneficial, give yourself sufficient time to learn the full potential this technique holds for you.

In addition to relaxing imagery, visualization can help you directly cope with pressure-inducing situations through "dissociation." This is discussed later in the next chapter.

Music

Music can tame the savage beast within—for many athletes it's an exceptionally effective means of relaxing. Used systematically, music may prove to be a valuable tool for calming yourself prior to competing as well as during an event.

The key to the effective use of music is to have it all "cued up." What this means is pre-selecting what works for you and being ready to hear it at the instant needed.

Away from the center, at home and in your car, the format and/or type of player can vary considerably. Prior to an event and most often during a game, you can use a walkman, Discman, or iPod. Significantly, some bowlers are able to hear music distinctly in their head and experience it at will. Having this ability guarantees that the music can be heard at any time, even on the lane.

In addition to serene music, which most directly calms you,* other types can also help reduce anxiety. Any music you enjoy and which occupies your attention removes you, to a certain extent, from the pressure of the competitive situation. Music can also uplift and inspire, which may boost confidence and even increase positive feelings about yourself. Music somewhat changes the context from one of testing to one of pleasure. This can lighten the moment. Your personal associations to the music are all your own and may bolster you in any number of ways.

Debbie Kuhn is a former US National Amateur Champion and three-time member of Team USA. Music plays an important part in her mental game as reflected in these remarks: "Music always relaxes me. On just about every shot, I play music in my head. Sometimes it's country, sometimes its mellow, sometimes it's hard rock. Bowling can't be all serious—you can't feel as if somebody's holding a gun to your head."[19]

In common with other relaxation methods, music can be used as needed or be a fixed part of a routine (pre-game or pre-shot). Whatever the intended application, it's crucial to prepare, including mental rehearsal and on-lane practice. A benefit of this technique is that preparation can continue even as you ride to the center. For example, listening to music in your car can calm you while at the same time making the songs more accessible to recall during play.

Another major function of music is energizing. This application is considered in Chapter 16.

Finally, music can be used to control the tempo of your bowling. This is described in our discussion of performance audiotapes (also in Chapter 16).

Humor

Humor isn't commonly thought of as a psychological technique for performance enhancement. However, this form of entertainment, like music, can be a tool for defusing tension generated by competitive situations.

Humor promotes relaxation in several ways. One is physical. When you laugh, there's a release of muscle tension. Laughter brings into play muscles in our head, neck, chest, and abdomen. If laughter is prolonged, its physiological effects in terms of heart rate and blood pressure are similar to moderate exercise. In fact, a Stanford University researcher used the term "stationary jogging" to describe the physical impact. Following laughter, these measures drop below base level and muscles

---

* Recorded sounds of nature such as ocean waves can have the same soothing effect.

are relaxed. The calming effects generated by laughter may also be attributable to factors relating to brain chemistry. In addition, humor relaxes people in some ways comparable to music. That is, humor provides a means of avoiding stress-producing cues and changes the context from one of performance to one of enjoyment. Finally, the content of the humor itself touches our psyches in ways which tend to reduce inner tension.

At home you have the basic media choices of watching, listening to, or reading humorous material. Traveling to the bowl or pre-game inside the center, the second and third options are available (e.g., listening to a comedy album or recorded "bit" from a TV or radio program; reading jokes or looking at cartoons). In addition, memorized material can be recalled. The "dose" of humor is whatever works to relax you to the desired level.

During competition, you may readily listen to a tape, CD, or digital recording; read (for instance, pull out a card with verbal or visual jokes); or recall in the settee area. The recalling of a humorous situation (personal or otherwise) or a joke can occur in a few seconds. Therefore, it's available to relax you at any time, even when standing up on the lane (stand up comedy?). Here's a sample for rapid recall:

SITUATION: Pete Weber. The 1991 US Open. Need we say more? For the few unfamiliar with this classic bit of bowling lore, picture Pete Weber being presented with a beautiful championship trophy—a sculpted eagle sitting on a base. See him proudly hoist the trophy high above his shoulders. See bowling executives standing to Weber's right applaud and TV announcer Chris Schenkel on Weber's left lower his mike to let the moment speak for itself. See the eagle topple off its perch and elude the desperate lunge of one executive to catch it. See the shocked look on everyone's face as the eagle nose-dives to the lane and splinters into countless fragments. This incident is why bowlers, unlike the rest of the population, think "crash landing" instead of "soft landing" when they hear those famous words, "The Eagle has landed."

JOKE: Rodney Dangerfield on how tough his childhood neighborhood was: "You'd see guys bowling overhand."

CARTOON:

TAKE TWO OF THESE AND CALL ME
IN THE MORNING !!!

Speaking of cartoons, one Team USA bowler who eventually joined the pro ranks included a favorite Garfield cartoon in his pre-shot routine whenever he faced a puzzling lane condition. Inevitably he would chuckle and relax.

To prepare humor for pre-game or within-game application, first ready your material. This means selecting what's funny and editing if necessary to fit the time constraints you'll face. Readying material also includes memorizing if its use will involve recall. Then proceed as you would with any psychological tool in terms of the steps to mastery/implementation.

Centering

Centering was introduced as a method for coping with distractions. This technique can also be used for preventing or reducing feelings of pressure. The sense of calm associated with being centered is opposite to the effects of anxiety. A benefit of the centering process is that it can be used at any time. To develop maximum effectiveness, we recommend centering yourself for one minute at least three times per week while in a highly relaxed state induced by a more prolonged technique, such as diaphragmatic breathing. This heightens the potential for centering to produce a relaxing result.

Meditation

Meditating involves the act of contemplation—extended focus on a stimulus that is unchanging, slowly changing, or monotonously repetitive. Techniques of meditation vary from one another essentially based on the object of attention.

In Transcendental Meditation (TM), an Eastern style, the object is a one or two syllable sound without meaning. This is referred to as a "mantra."* TM is the most widely used meditation approach. Robert Benson took the mystery out of meditating. He suggested that with the right conditions (as described in our "Essential Tips" earlier in the chapter), the "Relaxation Response"[20] can be attained with a wide range of stimuli, such as repeating a single word. In fact, a relaxed state can be reached by focusing on experiences involving any of the senses, whether internal (e.g., a mantra) or external (such as a flickering candle). You can even meditate on a feeling. Diaphragmatic breathing actually involves a meditative aspect since you focus your attention on the process. Zen meditation, a less utilized style in the West, involves a rigid sitting posture, carefully controlled breathing, and more active focusing.

In addition to its calming effect, meditation may indirectly increase your concentration skills and have other benefits. Whenever your attention wanders, simply return it to the object of focus. This process of noticing that your attention has drifted and non-judgmentally redirecting it can enhance awareness and attention control as well as self-acceptance.

Twenty minutes is commonly regarded as suitable for reaching a fully relaxed state through meditation. If you meditate regularly (once per day is suggested), it may well be possible to use an abbreviated process pre-game or during competition. With ongoing practice, you become increasingly adept at meditating. At the same time, the object of your attention (word, image, etc.) can become a relaxation trigger. Consequently, you're able to quickly calm yourself by focusing on the internal or external object. As an example, one of the country's top bowlers routinely relaxes between shots by gazing at a person or physical object at a distant part of the center.

Relaxation Switches

Any of the relaxation techniques in this chapter can be used to develop a relaxation cue or "switch." Once you've reached a deeply relaxed state, repeat a word or bring to mind an image involving visual, auditory, or kinesthetic senses. If you do this anchoring for several minutes on a

*Outside of the classic TM format, mantras may be longer and have meaning.

regular basis, the verbal stimulus, or a stimulus of some other type, can then trigger a calming effect.

Words such as "relax," "so calm," "feeling good," and "very, very peaceful"; visual images like clouds, ocean waves, sailing on a warm summer day, and blue or pink colors; pleasant tones, sounds, or music; and reassuringly placing one hand, even briefly, on the opposite hand, arm, or shoulder, all make effective cues. Even completely neutral stimuli, such as a number or letter or meaningless sound, work perfectly well. So long as the cue isn't stimulating, you'll be okay. You may also combine cues such as hearing the surf as you say "relax" to yourself.

There is the option of using your relaxation switch as a reminder, or performance cue, about physical technique. Let's say you've repeated the word "soft" when deeply relaxed after 20 minutes of a calming visualization. In addition to making you feel calmer, this same word (or a variation such as "soft hand") can remind you to keep your hand loose rather than squeezing the ball.

Pre-Competition Techniques

The relaxation methods presented so far can all be readily adapted for use in competition. You may also benefit from other excellent approaches best suited for use during training and pre-game away from the center.

Pairing*

To diminish the level of anxiety you experience in specific competitive situations, try pairing images of that circumstances with relaxation. As with relaxation switches, use any method which effectively calms you.

When you've reached a highly relaxed state, visualize a situation where you typically become tense (e.g., needing a strike to win an individual or team match). Spend 10 to 15 minutes maintaining the deep level of relaxation. If you start to become tense, let go of the imagery until you've regained full relaxation, then continue. Your aim is to sustain the relaxed state for the full time.

To get the most benefit from this approach, it's important to be systematic. The more you do it, the quicker you can progress. As a rule of thumb, we suggest ten consecutive sessions during which you hold the relaxed state the whole time.

If maintaining relaxation proves too difficult, try this method first for a less stressful situation. An alternative approach is to begin by listing

* Technically known as "desensitization."

five to ten competitive circumstances which create anxiety for you, from lowest to highest levels. Then work your way up the scale using our rule of thumb.

The ultimate goal here is to mute the level of anxiety you experience so that it can be readily handled.

Biofeedback

This approach teaches control over physiological states correlated with relaxation. Learning is achieved through immediate and precise feedback about these states provided by electronic technology. Muscle contraction, skin conductance, skin temperature, heart rate, and brain activity are several common indices.

As an example, muscle contraction is measured by the Electromyograph (EMG). When a muscle tenses, bioelectrical impulses travel across the covering myelin sheath. The EMG registers this electrical activity. Higher readings (relative to baseline) indicate increasing tension, lower readings reflect decreasing tension. By measuring activity in the frontalis muscle (forehead), the EMG can assess overall (global) bodily tension. This device can also be used to measure specific muscles for the purpose of learning to relax them individually. Other biofeedback devices safely measure global tension.

In a typical procedure, athletes first receive some form of relaxation training. In subsequent sessions, the individual is instructed to relax as sensors transmit input to the device employed. Auditory and sometimes visual signals, in effect, inform the athlete whether he or she is becoming more or less relaxed. This process enables the person to become aware of subtle internal changes as they occur. In this way, biofeedback enhances the ability to relax using already mastered techniques as well as teaching how to relax at will. While biofeedback is most often administered by a sport psychologist or other trained personnel, portable devices (e.g., heart monitor) are increasingly available.

Autogenic Training

This highly structured method combines meditation, deep relaxation, and self-suggestion. Autogenic training's application in sport psychology has mostly been in Europe, where it has proven very popular. The term "autogenic" means self-origin or self-generation. A progression of six exercise stages is used to induce feelings of heaviness and warmth throughout the body, accompanied by a sense of control.

You begin each autogenic training session by calming yourself in a brief preparation or warm-up phase. As described in the "Essential Tips" section, a comfortable position is assumed and several slow, deep breaths taken.

The process consists of repeating suggestions (phrases) to yourself. Attention is focused on the designated body part. The desired state is one of "passive concentration." This means calming your mind, letting go of daily concerns, and not worrying about the session itself.

Here are the stages and a sample suggestion for each:[21]

Stage 1: Heavy Limbs	"Both my arms are heavy"
Stage 2: Warm Limbs	"My right leg is warm and heavy"
Stage 3: Calm Heart	"My heart is calm and steady"
Stage 4: Slow Breathing	"My breathing is calm and regular"
Stage 5: Warm Abdomen	"My abdomen is warm"
Stage 6: Cool Forehead	"My forehead is cool"

There are multiple suggestions within each stage. For instance, Stages 1 and 2 have several suggestions for the arms and legs. Whatever the sequence of suggestions, the same phrase is typically repeated four or more times. While the format of autogenic training programs (including the wording of suggestions) varies, the basic progression of stages is always the same. Tailoring a program to an individual is possible by adding specific suggestions such as "My upper and lower back are heavy."

It's common for there to be several brief sessions (one to two minute) per day. There may be as many as six of these. Some programs call for increasing session duration (up to 30 minutes) with a corresponding decrease in frequency (down to one or two). Mastery requires up to six months. Autogenic relaxation can then be readily attained. Brief maintenance sessions sustain the relaxation skill.

Self-hypnosis

The most direct use of hypnosis* is for the purpose of relaxation. The induction and deepening phases of the process as described in

---

* Standard hypnosis as well as self-hypnosis

Chapter 7 can enable you to reach a fully relaxed state. You can then develop a relaxation switch by repeating words such as "relax" or "deeply relaxed." Give yourself the suggestion that reciting the cue in competition will create feelings of calm similar to your present state. To fine tune your degree of relaxation control, suggest that saying the cue once will be slightly relaxing; twice, more relaxing; and three times, deeply relaxing.

Physical Methods

Diverse physically active and physically passive approaches can produce relaxing effects. Sports, dance, yoga, t'ai chi, and stretching are among the activities which may bring about an immediate calming impact. If undertaken regularly, the result can be an overall reduction in anxiety and enhanced reserve for coping with stress in competition and elsewhere. Passive methods include massage, warmth (e.g., sauna), and rest.

Diversion

A non-stressful, non-bowling activity that occupies your attention can temporarily reduce anxiety related to competition. In addition, a pleasurable activity of any sort (for instance, a computer game or other entertainment) may very well leave you feeling calmer. Even a brief period of "pure fun" can decrease psychological and physical tension. In fact, such carefree experiences can be part of your training and pre-game routines. So-called "down time" actually contributes to a build-up for maximum performance readiness.

Three Additional Applications

We've presented these relaxation methods to provide you with tools for better handling competitive pressure. There are three other major uses. First, relaxation techniques may enhance visualization for varied applications, such as mental practice (discussed in Chapter 4). Second, these calming methods can help you cope with competitive adversity (Chapter 10). Third, relaxation approaches are important life skills. The most common uses are to cope with anxiety and adversity as well as overall stress reduction. Who among us hasn't felt wound up, anxious, or agitated and wished we could be calmer? Many of the methods in this chapter and the next can be used as needed or on a regular basis. Before and during an exam, presentation, audition, or job interview; between clients; when late for an appointment; or headed home after a rough day—all of these are times when such approaches can be put to good use. As part of a stress management program, they can protect and enhance your physical and psychological health.

Exercises

1. Do you systematically use techniques for coping with competition pressure?

2. If yes, which ones, when do you apply them, and how effective are they?

3. After reading this chapter and initially trying or considering the techniques presented, note how well they match you as an individual: (circle one)

   1=Can't Tell Yet   2=Minimal or No Match
   3=Moderate Match   4=Very Good Match

Diaphragmatic Breathing	1	2	3	4
PMR	1	2	3	4
Self-Directed Relaxation	1	2	3	4
Blue Sky	1	2	3	4
Associative Relaxation	1	2	3	4
Ideal Place	1	2	3	4
Music	1	2	3	4
Humor	1	2	3	4
Centering	1	2	3	4
Meditation	1	2	3	4
Relaxation Switches	1	2	3	4
Pairing	1	2	3	4
Biofeedback	1	2	3	4
Autogenic Training	1	2	3	4
Self-Hypnosis	1	2	3	4
Physical Methods	1	2	3	4
Diversion	1	2	3	4

Note: After mastering/applying these methods over a month's time, we recommend reevaluating the degree of match.

4. Make a list of the pressure points you identified in Chapter 12. Next to each, write the method or methods which you can use to effectively cope.

5. Visualize yourself bowling successfully in each of these situations after applying a coping technique or techniques. Envision yourself reaching your optimum activation level. Repeat each visualization several times.

REVIEW

Coming through in the clutch is an essential of sports excellence. The ability to cope with crucial game situations is necessary for reaching your bowling potential.

To excel in the clutch and other situations of potential pressure calls for mastery of coping methods. In Chapters 13 and 14, we present diverse approaches from which you can fashion an effective strategy.

Behavioral relaxation techniques are mind/body methods which can be used before and during competition to manage anxiety. This chapter covers such approaches. Following tips related to their use, these methods are described:

- Diaphragmatic breathing
- Progressive Muscle Relaxation
- Self-directed relaxation
- Visualization
- Music

- Humor
- Centering
- Meditation
- Relaxation switches

Various relaxation techniques are best suited for training and pre-game use away from the center. Among these are pairing, biofeedback, autogenic training, and self-hypnosis.

In addition to managing competitive anxiety, relaxation techniques have several potential applications related to competition and life in general.

Cara Honeychurch: World Bowling Writers International Hall of Fame, 2000 PWBA Rookie of the Year (tour-best 215.18 average), Australian

——14——

SCORING IN THE CLUTCH: BEYOND RELAXATION

I love having to close the match and throw the ball [in] the clutch.
Robert Smith

Complementing the relaxation techniques described in Chapter 13 are a variety of other approaches for coping with competitive pressure. These are equally important. In fact, they may limit and in certain situations eliminate the need to apply a relaxation method. After discussing these approaches, we close the chapter with recommendations on developing an effective and dynamic strategy for succeeding in the clutch.

Ten Ways to Beat the Heat of Competition

1. Accept Anxiety.

Some degree of anxiety is to be expected in competition. It's perfectly natural for a highly motivated athlete to feel "on edge" to an extent before an event and at various moments, such as in clutch situations, during the contest. Ricky Ward, winner of six PBA Tour titles, put it this way: "If you didn't feel pressure, you wouldn't be human."

Even the greatest performers in sport can experience "butterflies" and other signs of physiological and psychological reactions to competitive circumstances. Bill Russell, Hall of Fame center for the Boston Celtics and one of basketball's all-time greats, reportedly threw up in the locker room at every single game.

A key to coping with pre-game and within-game pressure is recognizing that some signs of anxiety or other forms of excitement come with the territory that is competition. The body instinctively prepares to handle challenges by biological reactions that increase energy, strength, and alertness. Instead of interpreting these changes as something "wrong," think of them as a sign that you're getting ready to excel. In other words, instead of letting the anxiety feed on itself, let it be and just bowl.

Bowling is exciting. So it makes sense that you become excited during competition. However, this doesn't mean that whatever reactions you have are best for performing. This is where knowing yourself is crucial. It may very well be that your butterflies pass when the event gets underway or that a moment's worry in the tenth frame quickly passes. If this doesn't happen, then apply methods in the preceding chapter to the ones here to bring yourself into your range of optimal activation. When you're on the approach, it's time to be primed to execute, not worried, tight, or overly charged-up.

Above left: Ricky Ward: Started PBA career with Rookie of the Year honors.
Above right: Dave Arnold: Career PBA 300 games total 30

2. Focus.

"All you can do when the pressure is on is focus on what you have to do and then get the job done." These words of PBA Tour professional Dave Arnold point to a major tool for succeeding in the clutch. Concentration plays a crucial role in controlling competitive anxiety. If you're acutely focused on the process of bowling, totally immersed in the present moment, then your thoughts won't concern results. Limiting the attention given to outcome and its consequences reduces feelings of pressure. The various techniques already presented can be applied before and during an event to maximize your focus. Adhering to routine is a prime example. Routines, in addition to enhancing concentration, can directly reduce anxiety through the sense of comforting familiarity and control they provide. However, pressure may disrupt your mental and physical routines. This makes maintaining or returning to them a vital step.

3. Stay Positive.

Another key to limiting pressure is a positive perspective. Earlier chapters identified methods to increase confidence, positive ideas, and self-acceptance. Optimism and other thoughts of success are the opposite of the negative outlook (expectations, images, etc.) which generate anxiety. Consistent self-worth dramatically limits what's at stake. Simply put, your value as a person is not. Pressure to prove yourself will also be reduced to the extent your overall skills and bowling potential are trusted. Since it's achievable, equating success with growth directly counters anxiety. Applying the psychological tools which create a positive perspective channels your intensity into eagerness rather than nervousness. This enables you to welcome the challenge.

A prime example of using positive self-talk to coach yourself when the chips are down was provided by Randy Pedersen at the 2002 PBA Pepsi Open. After winning the title (his 13th),* Pedersen remarked, "When I had to strike in the 10th to win, I got focused. I told myself, 'You've done it all week long when you had to—just relax.' I threw a good shot."

4. Dissociate.

"Dissociation" is a long word for a simple process—thinking of something else. This involves momentarily directing your thoughts away from the pressure-producing situation. Where your attention goes is up to you,

* With this victory, Pedersen became the 24th PBA bowler to surpass $1,000,000 in earnings.

just so long as it's not to another anxiety-generating circumstance. Dissociation could be described as a mental "road trip." Replay a scene from a film or TV program. Recall a great vacation. Compose a letter. Plan renovations in your home. Name your ten favorite actors, books, movies, or websites. Solve a math problem. And so on. Although you might be able to mentally "take off" without pre-planning, we advise preparing and practicing as with other techniques.

5 & 6. Engineer and Avoid.

In some situations, you may be able to limit pressure by altering or not attending to a source of anxiety. We refer to the former technique as "engineering" and to the latter approach as "avoidance."

For an example of engineering, let's say that the comments of a teammate, friend, or family member made in a particular clutch circumstance tend to make you nervous. Tactfully asking this person to not make the remark in question can help reduce your anxiety. (assertiveness is covered in Chapter 19).

The unknown can generate anxiety. Familiarizing yourself with a new center prior to the day of bowling* or as soon as you enter it on the day of competition** can increase your comfort level. Planning what you'll do between blocks is another example of this type of engineering (Chapter 15).

An instance of avoidance would be not looking at the score as a match progresses or at a given point in the game. This action contributes to a process orientation and has effectively assisted a great many bowlers in coping with pressures and potential distraction. Of course, if looking at the score doesn't adversely affect you, avoidance of this type is unnecessary.

Just as bowlers have different preferences about how much scoring information is ideal for them during a game, they also vary as to what's best in this regard between games. Overall, strive for immediacy. This means directing attention to the first frame of the next game. Focus on what you can accomplish rather than thinking of what others may do. Instead of being governed by the larger competitive situation, shape that situation by your own performance.

---

*Actions to take in the days before a tournament are cited in Chapter 16.
**Part of your pre-game routine

Randy Pedersen: Color analyst for PBA telecasts on ESPN as well as Tour bowler

7. Be Active.

The advice "Don't just stand there, do something" can be applied to reduce competitive anxiety. For instance, in the settee area, engage in some actions not immediately related to the upcoming shot. Occupy your attention by checking equipment, examining or changing your tape, tending to your hand, squeezing a small bean bag, playing a hand-held computer game, etc. The two pressure-coping tools we describe next are actually activity options.

8. Get Away.

As the situation allows, however briefly, literally walk away from the lanes. Engaging in another activity at the same time can further change your focus and help break the tension. This could be any action, such as stretching, chatting, or drinking a sports beverage. Recall Parker Bohn's splashing water on his face in response to frustration. That could work for pressure situations as well.

Of course, between blocks there can be a more complete change of scene. The opportunity exists to leave the center and engage in an extended diversion (e.g., take in a movie).

9. Communicate.

Conversing is potentially a terrific way to help manage anxiety before or during an event. Talking with your teammates or coach or even fellow competitors might provide useful information regarding ball reaction or any specifics concerning your game. In addition to technical information, communication may convey explicit or implicit support. All of this could ease the perception of pressure by increasing confidence and self-acceptance. Equally important, social contact may be entertaining, playful, or otherwise enjoyable. This type of interaction can take your mind off the performance situation for the moment and point you towards having fun instead of grinding. You may also feel less pressure if you assist other bowlers. This not only shifts your attention to others' performance, it potentially leaves you with a good feeling about what you've done. Communicating with the right person for needed information is of value to all bowlers. Whether interacting for other purposes proves helpful depends very much on your personality. Some bowlers are significantly aided by social contact while others are distracted. Tish Johnson and Tim Criss are professional bowlers who readily interact during competition. In contrast, Brian Voss and Cheryl Daniels personify those who focus best by minimizing contact.

Communication can be very brief. Even a word or two potentially conveys a lot. Communication may be non-verbal as well. If you're inclined to benefit from interacting, eye contact and gestures such as hand slapping can be meaningful.

10. Adopt a Life Perspective.

We've recommended viewing a situation in life perspective as a method to cope with adversity. Considering an event or game circumstance in the context of your entire life is also an effective way to limit competitive anxiety. Take a wide angle view of what you face. Against the backdrop of life and death, love and loss, and the misfortune of others, knocking down pins tends to take on a different meaning. A full look at life can lighten the moment's pressure.

How to Master Skills for Pressure Situations

The last two chapters have introduced you to a wide selection of techniques for reducing anxiety generated in competition. The successful application of these skills requires the same steps recommended throughout the book for mastery of mental game methods.

- Learn the method

- Mentally practice

- Practice on the lanes (include simulation)

- Use in competition (league, then tournaments)

Let's consider an example. First, learn diaphragmatic breathing away from the lanes following our instructions. Next, mentally rehearse your use of this technique. Visualize deep, slow breathing as part of your pre-shot routine. In clutch situations, see yourself increase the number of breaths within your regular pre-shot sequence and also take relaxed breaths on the settee. Envision yourself relaxing to your optimal activation level and executing successfully. When this way of breathing feels comfortable to you, start using it in practice situations—again, within your regular pre-shot sequence and as needed if you sense pressure. Simulate those circumstances which make you excessively anxious and manage your reaction. Finally, apply diaphragmatic breathing in competition, initially in league action and then in tournament events. In mental practice, active practice, and competition, be attuned to your pressure points, pressure indicators, and optimal activation.

Prepare for the wide range of clutch situations and other moments before and during competition when you might experience anxiety. Anticipate these circumstances in mental rehearsal scenarios and on-lane practice simulations. In these scenarios and simulations include some situations where you use back-up techniques as described in the following section.

Here are some other suggestions for preparing to handle clutch circumstances: If you're bowling on a team, bowl first or fifth in order to experience the situations typically carrying the most pressure. If you bowl doubles, bowl second so you'll be the one to throw the strike to win. Play your friends—for dinner, a wager, or just plain bragging rights. Speaking of hotly contested bragging rights, at our Team USA training camps, we've had the men's and women's squads bowl matches against each other. In short, put yourself in clutch and other pressure situations at every chance you get. You'll find yourself becoming used to it. As you learn to handle the pressure, your confidence, score, and enjoyment will soar.

Find Out What Works and Adjust

We suggest trying all these approaches to learn what works for you. Develop a repertoire of responses. Some methods you may use routinely (such as diaphragmatic breathing and communicating) and others in particularly stressful situations (for instance, PMR and dissociating). It is also important to have back-up techniques, methods you can use if what you first try isn't effective. In other words, if your "A" mental game doesn't deliver, go to your "B" or "C" game. Becoming well-rounded and versatile in these ways will significantly—perhaps even dramatically— strengthen your total game.

The key to developing a consistently effective strategy is knowing what method to apply to what degree in what circumstances. Your exact reactions to various situations, how you respond to techniques, and what your optimal level of activation is represent a combination that's all your own. Therefore, the strategy which proves effective in clutch situations and other moments of potential pressure must be one tailored to you. This is the same principle of individuality discussed in relation to concentration and elsewhere.

Be prepared to modify your overall pressure-coping strategy based on how helpful it continues to be. Let your experience guide you to upgrading the psychological tools you're prepared to use. This type of adaptability will enable you to most consistently execute when the chips are down.

The clutch performance in the box which follows shows how psychological skills can be effectively combined.

CLUTCH [3]: COPING WITH PRESSURE IN A 900 SERIES

On February 2, 1997, in Lincoln, Nebraska, Jeremy Sonnenfeld rolled the first sanctioned 900 Series.

As any bowler who has been there knows, after mounting tension, strikes 10 through 12 must be earned in the teeth of enormous stress. Sonnenfeld struck out in the tenth frame three consecutive times and in the third game did it facing the added challenge of an historic world record.

(continued)

Sonnenfeld credits the following for helping him handle the clutch circumstances throughout this remarkable series:

- Breathing for relaxation (in his routine and as needed)

- Pre-shot routine (consistent in form, consistently used)

- Immediacy ("one shot at a time")

- Communicating with teammates, friends, and fans (chatting, hand slapping, etc.)

- Confidence (trusting his skill, leading to fast adjustments)

- Mindset (telling himself to stay calm and focused)

- Self-talk (only positive)

- Self-acceptance (valuing the effort)

- Avoidance (not looking behind the lane at a crucial point)

- Goal setting (realistic and, ironically, non-perfectionistic)

Here's how Sonnenfeld describes his record breaking 10th frame of the third game:

"Now it becomes my turn for the 10th frame. I walk up there, wipe off my ball, wipe off my shoes, pat my heel, and take a deep breath and say, 'Make the best shot you can.' Anybody can throw a great shot and get tapped, leave a 10-pin or a 7-pin. All you can do is make the best shot you possibly can and if things are going your way, if you're on, you'll carry.

"So I got up there in the 10th frame and got the first one. Now everybody's clapping and cheering and I didn't even look back because I knew that would make me a little bit nervous. So I just came back off the approach, waited for my ball to get back, wiped it off, wiped my shoes off, patted my heel and said, 'Just go up there and make another good shot.' So I went up there and got the 11th one.

"Probably the question I'm asked the most is how did I throw the last shot because this is the record breaker right here and this is very emotional and the most pressure that you could have on yourself. I must honestly say that I think the 36th strike was probably one of the easiest of all of them, because I just told myself, 'You've struck 35 times before this. You only have one more to go. No matter what happens this is going to be a pretty incredible thing, so just go up there, trust yourself, and make the best shot that you can.' And I just went up there and I trusted myself and I made a good shot."

Exercises

1. After reading this chapter and initially trying or considering the techniques presented, note how well they match you as an individual: (circle one)

   1=Can't Tell Yet   2=Minimal or No Match

   3=Moderate Match   4=Very Good Match

Accepting Anxiety	1	2	3	4
Focusing	1	2	3	4
Staying Positive	1	2	3	4
Dissociation	1	2	3	4
Engineering	1	2	3	4
Avoidance	1	2	3	4
Being Active	1	2	3	4
Getting Away	1	2	3	4
Communicating	1	2	3	4
Life Perspective	1	2	3	4

   Note: After mastering/applying these methods over a month's time, we recommend reevaluating the degree of match.

2. List the pressure points you identified in Chapter 12. Next to each, note the method or methods from this chapter which can contribute to your bowling well.

3. In each of these situations, picture yourself bowling successfully after applying the coping technique(s) just noted. Envision yourself optimally energized. Repeat each visualization several times.

4. Which method or methods from Chapters 13 and 14 can be included in your standard pre-shot preparation? Visualize using the method(s) during your routine in the settee area and/or at the ball return. Repeat the visualization(s) several times.

5. Which method or methods from Chapters 13 and 14 can contribute to your pre-game preparation? Visualize yourself including the method(s) in your activities outside the center and/or inside the center. Repeat each visualization several times.

6. Which method or methods can you routinely use to cope with pressure during the pre-day period? Visualize the method(s) fitting into your regular training activities.

7. Write a detailed scenario of your succeeding in the clutch. Describe the game circumstances and what you do to stay optimally activated. Note all your reactions as you perform to potential. Include any relevant elements of the scene as it unfolds, such as others who are around. Above all, convey the deep satisfaction and pride you experience as you come through in the clutch.

REVIEW

This chapter presents ten ways to improve your performance in the clutch. These complement the relaxation techniques presented in the last chapter. The approaches covered include accepting anxiety, dissociation, communicating, and life perspective. Methods that enhance concentration and contribute to positive perspective play a vital role in handling competitive pressure.

To ready yourself for competition with the methods covered in Chapters 13 and 14, follow the familiar four-stage mastery process. Then use mental rehearsal and practice simulation to anticipate the range of clutch situations you may face. Develop back-up approaches and upgrade your pressure-coping strategy based on ongoing experience.

The first sanctioned 900 series illustrates the effective use of psychological techniques in clutch situations.

15

DEALING EFFECTIVELY WITH COMPETITION RESULTS

If you do your best, then you can hold your head up, regardless of the competition results.
Pat Rossler

So far we've covered the skills needed to effectively train, prepare on the day of an event, and cope with challenges during competition. This chapter considers the question, How can you deal with competition results—both successes and failures, whether it's a game, a block, qualifying rounds, match play, or a full event (tournament or league session)? Your goal is to deal with the outcome in a way that best prepares you for the next shot in an upcoming game or event.

Coping with Competitive Ups and Downs: A Recap

Methods for handling adversity as well as success during a game were presented in Chapter 10. These same skills can generally be applied to productively process outcomes. Therefore, we suggest you review that chapter now. Here are some highlights:

- Emotional overreactions tend to impair performance and adversely affect teammates.

- A proportionate response to frustrating situations is constructive.

- Accepting a disappointing reality is essential to effectively moving ahead.

- Learn from what's occurred and adapt strategy accordingly.

- After responding, accepting, and adapting, orient towards the future.

- A broad range of actions can enable you to successfully follow the preceding steps.

- In the face of adversity, changing certain beliefs about your performance can change its meaning and assist emotional coping.

- When successful, avoid overexcitement, complacency, the pressure of expectations, and "attitude," which may hinder your efforts.

We'll take you through various post competition circumstances, calling attention to certain noteworthy aspects of an optimal approach. Remember, the RALLY guidelines and multiple methods from the earlier chapter are your framework for coping with all competitive outcomes.

During a Tournament or League Session

After a Game/Match

After a game (tournament or league), allow yourself to experience the fitting emotion and come to terms with the results. Call upon whatever Keys to Resilience may be needed to bring this about. Then adapt to the conditions based on what you've learned. Complete any between-game chores and enter into your pre-shot routine. When you've bowled well, avoid overconfidence and the other potential pitfalls of success. This approach also applies to a game determining the outcome of a match.

After a Block

After a tournament block, we recommend three phases of activity:

1. <u>Deal with results.</u> Every bowler has preferences concerning behaviors such as time to oneself or with whom one communicates. Discover what most effectively enables you to proceed through our suggested coping steps. When you've met with success, remain methodical in analyzing your performance and strategizing. Contributing to team meetings is a priority regardless of outcome.

2. <u>Unwind.</u> There are many effective ways to unwind before you bowl again, both passive and active, from music to communicating (Chapters 13 and 14). Reducing competition stress is essential in preparing for the next block. This is true even when you're pleased with results.

3. <u>Rewind your pre-game/pre-day routine.</u> If you're bowling later in the day, plan to restart your pre-game routine at a designated time. Adhere to your standard pre-day routine if the next block is scheduled for tomorrow.

In the box on the following page, three of the world's best bowlers describe how they process a disappointing block.

After an Event within a Tournament

After an event within a tournament (e.g., a doubles championship), process results essentially as you would after any block. Just bear in mind that the outcome's significance may tend to trigger intense emotions. Consequently, whether faced with adversity or success, select and apply those methods which allow you to smoothly proceed through the three phases of activity.

After Qualifying Rounds/Match Play

Process the results of qualifying rounds as an event within a tournament if you make the cut. Otherwise apply our suggestions for handling the end of a tournament. Treat match play leading to the championship round the same way.

HOW THREE CHAMPIONS COPE WITH A TOUGH BLOCK

Tammy Turner (a.k.a., "The Tamminator") received multiple All-American Honors as well as designation as Amateur Bowler of the Year* and PWBA Rookie of the Year. She earned gold medals in two FIQ events and was a two-time member of Team USA. She has four national pro tour titles and three PWBA regional titles to her credit.

"I'm very introverted. I keep to myself and don't generally talk about it for a couple of hours. It takes me an hour or two to get calm. I boil for awhile. Even when I bowl well, I don't talk about what happened. That's my personality. When I get it together, I realize there are a couple of things I didn't do right. I say to myself, 'So I had a bad block, it's OK now.' A lot of times I talk to other bowlers in a general way about how the lanes played."

Michael Mullin, a former collegiate All-American, has won multiple international titles (team and individual) as well as the US National Amateur Championship. He is a four-time member of Team USA.

"Everybody reacts differently. I'd probably want to be alone for a little bit, maybe 10 or 15 minutes. I'd be trying to cool off and regroup—trying to figure out and understand what didn't go well and looking at what did go well, even if it wasn't a successful day. Then I'd try to make the next day go better. You have to let go of it and look forward to the next day."

Robin Romeo is a member of the USBC Hall of Fame and the Women's Professional Bowling Hall of Fame. The winner of 17 career pro titles, she holds the PWBA records for most consecutive match play appearances and most consecutive cashes. She was the first woman to bowl two 800 series and has rolled seventeen 300 games. She retired from the PWBA national tour in 2001.

"What I'd do after a bad block was try to relax, have a good laugh. I enjoy company. Just being around people and having fun helped me get over frustration. Also, from the first day I went out on tour, after each block, I'd make a call to my parents and let them know how I did.

"While some players like to be off on their own after a tough block, my roommates and I had a rule: You get 15 minutes to stew, but once you get into the car that had to be left behind. It led to being positive. We'd talk about equipment, the lanes, and overall we'd help each other.

"I felt it was just a bad block and wanted to go forward. Afterward, I'd go back to the room and think out what could make the next block better. I'd try to figure out what had really happened—I might have made bad equipment choices or had trouble staying focused. Then I'd listen to music and get pumped for the next block. Other bowlers did different things like nap, call their coach, or go for a walk. But this worked for me."

---

* Voted by the Bowling Writers Association of America (BWAA)

After a Tournament (Including the Championship Round) or League Session

Our discussion of how to best handle the completion of a tournament consists of two parts: First we identify what to do immediately and then what steps to take in the days that follow. The recommendations in this section generally apply also to the completion of a league bowling session.

The Day Your Bowling Ends

After your last ball in a tournament is released, you're faced with many results.* These are your final throw, frame and game, the last block, the end of a round (whether qualifying or championship), and the cumulative outcome of the whole tournament. You're also confronted with the totality of your performance, including earlier outcomes which may now take on a new significance in terms of final pincount and results.

In disappointing circumstances, we first recommend that your coping approach for emotional responding and acceptance be essentially the same as after any block. Like Tammy Turner and Mike Mullin, you may spend some time by yourself. Or like Robin Romeo, your preference may be to immediately interact. When successful, we advise that humility is the best policy. A preliminary review of the tournament is useful from the standpoint of providing fresh information and pointing you towards future growth. Remember the primary goal of being a better bowler at the end of the event than at its beginning. Consider what you did well, what you did better than before, and what made you more aware of skills needing work. Unwinding remains important. If applicable, provide input and support to teammates.

The Following Days

Critique Your Own Performance

The days after an event are an ideal time to fully analyze your performance. The dust of competition has settled, enabling you to carefully zero in on all details of your effort while they remain distinct.

This review of "the game film" is crucial to your bowling development. If you have a coach, this is a vital part of your work together. If not, draw upon feedback from others most familiar with your game, such as teammates or your ball rep.

---

* Due to the need for tabulation and/or other squads which still must bowl, how you stand competitively may not be known right away. However, what faces you is the same even with this delay.

Review any and all aspects of your performance and integrate what you find into your Master Plan. Systematically consider your performance with respect to the physical game, equipment, lane play, the mental game, and conditioning and revise goals accordingly. You want to affirm and build on what you're doing right and target your less advanced areas for development. Aim at making what is weak strong and what is strong stronger.

To accomplish this, you must be unflinching in examining the reality of your performance and the current state of your game. You may be able to convince yourself that your game is stronger than it actually is. You may even temporarily convince others. You will not convince the pins. Part of being mentally tough is having the willingness to look at things the way they are. Take pride in your capacity to do this.

Looking at oneself honestly goes hand-in-hand with willingness to genuinely consider input from others. Both require the ability to tolerate imperfections, large and small. This ability rests on the bedrock of self-acceptance which allows you to feel worthy as a person despite flaws. It's also based on knowing that perfection is more an ideal than reality, that advancing requires awareness of uncovered ground, and that growth is all about adaptation to failure. Honest self-assessment calls for a full picture of yourself, including present level of skills and capacity to raise that level. Value yourself, value your game, and trust your ability to learn.

We respect to the utmost those bowlers hungry to learn the truth about their performance and who then commit themselves to reaching goals based on this. At the same time, we are sensitive to the vulnerabilities of more defensive athletes and work to help them become more open to feedback and self-scrutiny. Even the most open person will tend to close down when confronted with a harsh attitude. Coaches and others providing input are advised to be highly supportive when giving criticism. Athletes need to know that you admire their skills, believe in their potential to grow, and value them as a human being. If at all possible, bowlers should receive their coaching input from individuals who interact in this manner.

In post tournament processing, use whatever technological aids are available. Videotape, Dartfish, and BowlersMap technologies are devices we've covered in the book. Also refer to any logs you've kept, such as those recording ball changes or self-talk.

In a team setting, meetings held on days following an event can serve several main functions. First, complete the type of information pooling and assessing undertaken during the competition. For example, with the picture now complete, what can be said definitively about lane play? What strategy proved most effective given the conditions as they developed? What might have worked better? Second, congratulate, bolster, and, in any other way, offer support to teammates. Third, evaluate how the team did throughout the competition with respect to information sharing and interpersonal support. Fourth, set goals in terms of performance factors, sharing information, and providing support. Regardless of the tournament's results, the chances for improving future performance will be increased to the extent that lessons were learned and a plan developed for their practice and implementation.

Meet the Challenge of Disappointment

If a tournament has been a disappointment, expect some lingering emotional reaction in its aftermath. Consistent with the RALLY approach, strive to react proportionately, accept the reality, learn from your performance, and lean towards future competition. The major risk to future performance is discouragement, which affects motivation to prepare for the next event. Maintaining optimism and an overall positive perspective is vital. Slumps represent a particular challenge in this regard. Our recommendations for coping with them are presented in the box on the following pages. Whether it's one or several disappointing events you encounter, we firmly believe the coping tools covered in this book can enable you to transition to success. The very act of learning to handle adversity adds to your mental toughness. Dedicate yourself to growing, valuing yourself, and loving our great sport.

Meet the Challenge of Success

A sense of success at tournament's end is inherently rewarding and also signifies that you're on the right path for advancing your game. What you must be on the lookout for is complacency. If you're on a streak— the opposite of a slump—the probability of this attitude developing increases. Your game will be affected if the overconfidence results in reduced practice quality or other changes in the training regimen which have led you to succeed. As previously mentioned, if this attitude persists into competition, your performance may suffer due to factors such as lack of edge, inconsistent concentration, and variation from routines.

Success can prove burdensome if it produces feelings of pressure stemming from your own expectations or the expectations of others. This is true after an event as well as during it. In order to get the

BEAT THAT SLUMP!

Slumps are an unpleasant fact of life for bowlers and other athletes. No one is immune to these episodes of sustained adversity. With its potential to depress mood and dampen motivation, slumping can be aptly described as a rough edge in the fabric of sport.

Developing ways to minimize the impact and duration of slumps is crucial to pincount and an important part of the mental game. In a slump, lackluster bowling produces a series of disappointing results. Therefore, the approach for processing outcomes covered in this chapter can be directly applied. However, slumps pose a particular threat to future performance because of the emotional toll they can exact.

Loss of enthusiasm, discouragement, anger, and resultant distraction are some reactions which may disrupt the quality of training, hinder execution in competition, and impair relationships with teammates and others.

We'll now cite a variety of methods to help you conquer slumps. Try them on for size. What this means is weighing the possible usefulness of each recommendation. Apply the most promising methods, monitor effectiveness, and modify their application as needed. Your goal is to fashion a slump-busting strategy stemming from your individual makeup and suited to your game.

Our keys for coping with slumps are of three types: action, attitude, and interpersonal.

ACTION KEYS

Actively strive to overcome the slump: It's common for bowlers to feel helpless, as if the slump had a mind of its own. Instead, aggressively search for ways to bounce back. How you think and what you do can hasten the recovery.

Identify factors which helped break prior slumps: Did you iron out a flaw in your physical game? Perhaps you put in extra practice time. Maybe advice received or a videotape reviewed proved crucial. Was a constructive outlook maintained? Once identified, try to repeat the relevant behavior.

Be systematic in problem solving: In order to evaluate your game, be organized and thorough. Reviewing a skills' checklist can assist you in making a comprehensive assessment. In this way, all areas of the Master Plan will be covered and corrective goals set.

Practice effectively and efficiently: This means engaging in quality practices—attend to the physical game, equipment, playing lanes, the mental game, and conditioning. Use goal setting. Simulate game circumstances. Strive to develop both consistency and versatility. While extra practice may be beneficial (especially if focused on a particular skill), don't overdo it. In the midst of a slump, too much bowling can be mentally and physically fatiguing. That would be counterproductive and could contribute to feelings of despair or burnout.

(continued)

Solidify the basics: Even if a breakdown in fundamentals doesn't appear to be causing the slump, reviewing and practicing the basics can be beneficial. Shoring up skills such as armswing, equipment selection, and concentration-enhancing methods is conducive to optimal performance and can boost your confidence.

Develop your skills: The sense of lost time and opportunity is one of a slump's disheartening aspects. This can be countered, at least partially, by advancing your game in whatever way possible. Add to your arsenal of equipment. Raise your level of physical conditioning. Fine tune your timing. Master a new facet of lane play. Further develop your mental game (see our next suggestion). While your scores may not reflect this development until the slump subsides, the enhancement of skills is real and you may be immediately bolstered by the sense of progress.

Grow the mental game: By honing psychological skills and/or mastering new ones, you can emerge a stronger, more complete bowler after the slump. For instance, your pre-game or pre-shot routine might become more consistent and you could add PMR to your repertoire of relaxation techniques. Learning to more effectively refocus when distracted, upgrading communications skills, or gaining more emotional control in the face of adversity are some other ways your mental game might be strengthened.

Consider a strategic time-out: Sometimes a break helps. If your best efforts haven't yet stemmed the tide, continuing frustration can lead to spiraling stress. Under these circumstances, consider a time-out from competing or, perhaps, even practicing. Let your emotional response determine the length of the break (whether a day, a week, or longer). What you're seeking to do is restore motivation, concentration, energy, and optimism.

Experience competence: Participate in activities where you display competence. Whether these are work-related or recreational, the purpose is to generate positive feelings towards yourself. Relying less on bowling performance for self-acceptance can reduce pressure and so contribute to your comeback.

Apply stress management methods: The intense stress which slumps can generate may adversely impact both psychologically (e.g., anxiety) and physiologically (e.g., headaches). Therefore, the goal of stress reduction is to safeguard/improve health as well as enhance performance. Among the available approaches are regular exercise, relaxation techniques like diaphragmatic breathing, reframing, socializing, time management, and recreation. If life stressors are a significant factor behind the slump (such as work or family issues), learning to cope with them is of prime importance.

ATTITUDE KEYS

Remind yourself that slumps end: Nothing is forever and slumps are no exception to the rule. They are finite. They all end. So will this one. Bearing this in mind enables you to step back

(continued)

BEAT THAT SLUMP! (continued)

from the moment's disappointment. The resultant perspective can redirect you toward optimism and away from the debilitating anxiety and discouragement so common to slumping.

Be positive: Staying positive in outlook fosters energy, effort, and focus. To accomplish this aim, you can call upon any number of methods. These include mindset, thought stopping, affirmations, visualizing (both process-oriented and outcome-oriented), and communicating. Follow our other slump-busting recommendations as well to promote a positive frame of mind.

Stay in the "here and now": A slump exists in your mind's eye and exerts a negative impact on performance (for instance, increased doubts and anxiety and panicky ball changes) only if you're conscious of the past. Instead, focus on the present (immediacy). Regard each event as a fresh start.

Think of great bowlers and their slumps: You're in good company. All Hall of Fame bowlers and other elite athletes have suffered through slumps. Recognizing this can not only provide perspective on a slump's limited duration and lift confidence, it can increase self-acceptance.

Remain clear about your abilities and self-worth: Performance pressure can be minimized if you stay realistic about your ability and maintain a high level of self-regard. Receiving trustworthy feedback and reviewing past successes should help you accurately view skills and potential. You might also note those aspects of performance which have stayed strong during the slump. Valuing your perseverance in a slump and overall efforts and focusing on positive personal attributes are some ways to keep a steady sense of self-regard. Above all, recognize that pinfall has no bearing on your worth as a person.

Have patience: Naturally, you want the slump over yesterday. As an event approaches, the need to regain your usual form may become particularly pressing. However, feeling that the slump must end now or on a particular date will tend to hike frustration and pressure. Avoid setting immediate or future deadlines. Instead, trust your resilience and follow through on these guidelines.

Recall the end of previous slumps: In particular, focus attention on the successes you then enjoyed. This is aimed at reinforcing the belief that your slump will be over and your bowling will equal or surpass its pre-slump level.

Ask yourself, are you really slumping? It's certainly possible to have a rough stretch competitively without bowling poorly. In other words, a losing streak isn't necessarily a slump. Some factors are outside your control. You may simply be out-bowled or not match up to the conditions. How you respond to tough competition or challenging conditions, however, is part of the game. In other words, coping psychologically and adapting your game accordingly are the tasks at hand. Or your form could be affected by injury. Here you're not bowling well,

(continued)

but there's no mystery. Assess whether you're handling the circumstance as well as you might. Finally, in a team situation, you could be bowling well and the team still lose or bowl poorly overall. That's not individual slumping.

INTERPERSONAL KEYS

Receive coaching: It is advisable to work with someone during a slump. This might be an ongoing coach or simply a knowledgeable individual who's already familiar with your game or can readily grasp it. Trusting this person is essential, since you need to be comfortably open and not feel judged when questioned or given feedback. Also, the support you receive can play an important role in overcoming your slump because of its positive emotional impact, raising of self-confidence, and bolstering of self-acceptance.

Obtain prompt feedback: It is crucial to learning and confidence building that you receive prompt input about your performance. Such feedback is an essential responsibility of the person coaching you. Technological aids (such as standard videotaping) can usefully complement direct observation.

Find a coach with a constructive attitude: Unwavering determination, optimism, and enthusiasm can stimulate your motivation and color your outlook. These traits also offer a model for making constructive psychological responses to adversity. Work with someone whose empathy, patience, and openness convey acceptance. A coach who is there for you in this tough time will make it more likely that you will be there for yourself.

Ask your coach to recount his or her own slumps and what it took to overcome them: Here coaching provides a meaningful model to follow. While you ultimately must discover what works for you, some, if not all, of what the coach did may prove effective in your case. This communication also sets a tone for openness in your relationship.

Socialize: Feeling disheartened by a slump, some bowlers withdraw from their regular relationships. However, maintaining social contact is crucial. Communication plays a critical role in managing stress. Unless you express thoughts and feelings, anger and frustration may escalate. This could lead to increasing discouragement and even depression. Socializing can provide grounding in terms of support, realistic input, and steadying of self-esteem.

Assist others: Engage in coaching or other service activities. These can divert your attention from excessive self-scrutiny. They can also produce feelings of accomplishment and heightened self-worth as well as provide social contact.

What about team slumps? These guidelines can generally be applied as well for struggling teams. Keep in mind that team-related skills like as those discussed in Chapters 18 and 19 become centrally important for purposes of assessment and remedy.

most from training and to fully enjoy bowling, you need to be loose, not stressed in this way. You also don't want to carry such pressure into the next competition. Consistent with our recommendations for handling expectations while bowling (Chapter 10), consider taking these actions:

A. If you're concerned about others around you (your coach, for instance), you might check out the reality of their attitude towards your performance and request that communication with you be positive but not laced with specific predictions about results. Above all, you're entitled to an attitude in which your being respected and valued are not on the line when you bowl.

B. More important is recognizing that pressure from expectations is ultimately generated by the meaning you give to your performance and that this perspective is within your control. Confront any belief in which feeling good about yourself as a bowler and person requires performing to a specific level at a specific event. Instead, value your quest for success, your ongoing improvement, strengths in your game (including the mental game), and, above all, your worth as a person.

C. Use thought stopping and any other method needed to limit thoughts and concerns about expectations. Stay in the "here and now" and go about your business of preparing for the next event. Regardless of previous results, your aim is to perform your best when you bowl again. The streak to truly prize is day-in and day-out effort to master and strengthen skills, including successful application in competition. Do that and results will reflect your growth.

Finally, as you head into training, let your demeanor reflect sureness rather than swagger. By being full of confidence instead of full of yourself you'll be genuinely admired instead of just endured.

Transition to Training

With its resetting of goals and renewed commitment to practice, the post tournament stage morphs into training for your next event. You've come full circle. From training through competition and back to training. Rather than a flat circle, visualize an ascending spiral of development. Your skills grow as you train, compete, and train again. In this realistic vision of your sports career potential, rising levels of skill and success lead to increasing satisfaction and the maximum joy bowling can bring.

Exercises

1. Rate the way you cope with a disappointing event segment: (circle one)

   1=Poor   2=Fair   3=Good   4=Very Good

Game/Match	1	2	3	4
Block	1	2	3	4
Event within a Tournament	1	2	3	4
Qualifying Rounds/Match Play	1	2	3	4
Tournament	1	2	3	4
League Session	1	2	3	4

2. If you circled a 1 or 2 for any segment, describe your reactions.

3. For each of these segments, what methods can enable you to more effectively cope with disappointing outcomes? (Draw upon our suggestions in this chapter along with the RALLY guidelines and Keys to Resilience.)

4. If you circled a 3 for any segment, where is there room for improvement? What will you do to improve?

5. Place a check next to each slump-busting key you already use. Then, category-by-category (Action-Attitude-Interpersonal), review the other keys and visualize using them to pull out of a slump.

6. After a successful result, is there a tendency to be overly excited, overconfident, pressured by expectations, or arrogant? If so, after which segment does this occur? Remind yourself of the possible consequences and note what actions you can take.

7. In particular, are you burdened by expectations following a successful tournament? If you are, consider our recommendations and apply them now and/or as needed in the future.

REVIEW

Bowling to your potential requires constructive processing of the outcome of a game, block, tournament, or other competition segment. In Chapter 10, we presented a framework for coping with adversity during a game (the RALLY guidelines and Keys to Resilience) and also considered how to effectively respond to success. Building on these principles, here we offer recommendations for handling results:

- After a game/match
- After a block
- After an event within a tournament
- After qualifying rounds/match play
- After a tournament (including the championship round)
- After a league session

In the discussion of how to effectively respond following an event, special consideration is given to coping with slumps and coping with expectations arising from success.

PART IV

Answers to
Bowlers' Questions

*Life throws you curves and the same is true
when you're bowling.*
Marshall Holman

16

RAISING YOUR GAME: PSYCHING UP TO ZONING IN

Bowling is a very hidden game; you can't see obstacles in front of you or within yourself. To prevail you must read those outer and inner realities and then make the right moves.
Bill Spigner

To raise your overall game to its full potential, you must meet the wide range of competitive challenges posed by the sport. The next two chapters will help gear your mental game to handle some of the very toughest hurdles.

When coaching, teaching, and speaking to the media, we're asked numerous questions about the mental game. These concern an array of topics encompassing the many issues and situations bowlers encounter. Most of these are covered throughout the book. In Chapters 16 and 17, we answer questions referring to challenges not specifically or fully addressed elsewhere.

These challenges are basically of two types: those concerning performance in general and those concerning issues which involve others (such as competitors or crowds). This chapter addresses the first type; the next chapter the second type. The strategies offered typically build on or complement skills covered earlier in the book.

List of Challenges

Here, in order, are the questions we address and the pages where they are covered:

- During competition, my energy level is sometimes low, and that hurts my scoring. Is there anything I can do about that? (p. 227)

- What's the best way to get mentally prepared for more challenging lane conditions? (p. 231)

- If I get off to a slow start, I tend to feel discouraged. Especially if it's the first game. A voice in my head says, "It's gonna be a long night." Often it's hard to shake that attitude, and I know it hurts my performance. What mental game methods can I apply? (p. 232)

- I'm thrown if something unexpected happens. What can I do to handle things that happen out of the blue? (p. 233)

- Sometimes I'm at an event and realize my equipment isn't what I'd really like for the condition. This knocks down my confidence. How can I not let this get to me so much? (p. 234)

- Any time I bowl for money, I start to think about the amount I could win. Is that good or bad? (p. 236)

- There are times when I have a perfect feel for the ball and everything seems easy. When it's not there, I lose confidence. How can I get in that zone more often? (p. 236)

- In the days before a tournament, should I do anything different than usual? (p. 239)

- Can motivational audiotapes improve my bowling performance? (p. 240)

- I'm not enthusiastic about bowling the way I used to be when I was younger. At times it feels like a chore. Can I get the fun back? (p. 243)

- I've known a number of bowlers whose careers have been affected by injury. Is there any way I can guard against this? (p. 246)

- There's a lot of publicity these days about steroids and other drugs which athletes take to improve performance. If a drug is legal, is there anything wrong with that? (p. 249)

- Being a PBA national tour bowler is something I've always planned on. It's never crossed my mind to do anything else. I was doing great, but an injury changed things. I still bowl competitively but the reality is I won't make it as a pro. I feel lost. How can I let go of my dream? (p. 251)

Challenges and Strategies

Q During competition, my energy level is sometimes low, and that hurts my scoring. Is there anything I can do about that?

A You can master techniques for situations where "energizing" or "psyching up" is needed. Lethargy at the start of a match or fatigue at the end of a long day is common. If you're bowling in a tournament, fatigue may be cumulative over several days. Especially in a long event, ongoing pressure and other stressors can take a toll in terms of diminished energy.

An essential step to psyching up is self-monitoring. Your aim is to recognize low energy as soon as possible in order to promptly counter it. This calls for knowing the psychological and physical signs associated with being under-aroused (e.g., distracted thinking, feeling weak, and drooping shoulders). Keeping a log, as described in Chapter 12, can help you become alert to these signs. By knowing what your low energy cues are, a coach can also alert you to their occurrence in competition.

Through reflection and a log, learn the intensity level at which you bowl best. Even if you don't feel tired, at times some psyching up may be needed to lift you to the optimum energy level.

Here are various methods available for energizing.[22] Experiment with them to learn which are most effective for you. As with other techniques, we recommend mental rehearsal and use in practice before applying them in competition. Their application should then be monitored and modified if necessary.

VERBAL CUES: Some words, particularly in combination with imagery, can increase energy. "Psych-up," "power," "blast," and "explode" are examples. To find cues that work for you, try the following: *Recall a competition situation in which you were optimally energized and bowling well. Re-experience your feelings in that moment. Now consider what words, as well as images, capture the sensation of ideal activation.*

VISUAL CUES: See the box on the following page.

SUCCESS IMAGERY: Recall great bowling moments you've had in the past or picture yourself performing tremendously in the present or future. A related technique is to visualize exceptional bowling efforts by others that you've heard or read about, seen in person, or watched on TV.

MUSIC: Up-tempo music (played or recalled) is stimulating and generally effective for increasing energy. Lyrics that inspire may contribute to

activation. To derive maximum benefit from the technique, have at least two up-tempo selections in your repertoire: one moderately fast and the other one even more intense. Use whichever music increases your energy as needed before or during competition. For some bowlers, music associated with a drive to succeed, such as the classic themes/ soundtracks from *Rocky, Top Gun,* and *Chariots of Fire* are especially uplifting and energizing.

PRE-GAME WORKOUT: Bowl several games four to ten hours before competing. An equivalent level of other exercise will also work.

Carolyn Dorin-Ballard during 2001 WIBC Queens Tournament win

VISUALIZE FOR ENERGY

Visualization is a frequently used and highly effective psyching up method.

To experience energizing images, do the following: Breathe easily with your eyes closed. Inhale through your nose and exhale through your mouth. Take a few relaxed breaths and enjoy the calmness. You feel peaceful, yet focused. Your mind is a screen set to experience crystal clear, distinct images.

Now imagine you're a smoothly running machine or an animal of power and grace.

For example, if you're a train, nothing can stop you. If you're a dolphin, you glide through the ocean. If you're a cheetah, you run with dazzling speed. For three minutes, conjure up these types of images and experience them one after the other. Sense the energy, rhythm, movement, and power.

Let these images fade. Once again, your mind is a blank screen. Continue to breathe easily and remain focused.

Next, visualize a series of images and spend one minute experiencing each.

1. You're running on a conveyor belt. There's no sense of exertion.
2. You're wearing high-powered energy shoes.
3. You're enveloped in a sphere of energy. Impulses radiate to your whole body, particularly areas where you're most tired.

When athletes focus on feelings of low energy, these feelings may be magnified. By rapidly shifting attention to energizing images, you avoid the negative focus and give yourself a boost. If possible, link these images to the process of bowling. For instance, see yourself as a cheetah and then see yourself with that power and control on the lane. Similarly, imagine being engulfed by a sphere of energy and then see yourself fully recharged, fresh, and alert when bowling.

STRETCHING/LIGHT EXERCISE: Stretching before and after bowling is always advisable. Combined with a light activity, such as brisk walking or jogging, body temperature rises, muscles become loose, circulation is enhanced, and energy increases. Such low intensity exercise (in contrast to a genuine workout) can suitably occur within an hour of competing.

ACTIVATED BREATHING: Briefly increase your normal breathing rhythm as you imagine energy being inhaled and fatigue being exhaled.

FATIGUE PARKING: Visualize all the fatigue in your body flowing into the ground or, alternatively, into a bucket or cup. This method can be used in conjunction with activated breathing.

ENERGY FROM THE ENVIRONMENT: Draw energy from environmental stimuli. Examples of such stimuli are teammates, other bowlers, spectators, and the American flag. The rolling ball and flying pins can serve this function very well.

ENERGY TRANSFER: Negative emotions such as fear and anger can be redirected towards obtaining performance goals.

GOAL SETTING: Individual and team goals which are both challenging and attainable work best to promote driving motivation.

MINDSET: Direct yourself to start quickly or maintain intensity based on where in the competition you're lethargic or tired.

DISTRACTION: There are various methods for directing your attention away from feelings of limited energy. Among these are music, imagery, social interaction, self-talk, and focusing on distant objects.

COMMUNICATION: Words of inspiration and encouragement, written or spoken, can lift spirits and boost energy. These could come from anyone. Yet, the most meaningful would likely be from those whose knowledge or acceptance you especially value (such as coach, friends, and teammates).

Here's an example of how psyching up methods can be applied:

A highly-regarded professional bowler reported a problem with his starts. As he put it, "I can't get psyched up until I've done a lot of bowling." This would leave him in a hole.

Because of this bowler's talent, he often made up the ground. Yet these slow starts cost him pins and hurt his position in the final standings. In fact, he sought assistance from a sport psychologist after nearly winning a major championship.

The following strategy was developed for this athlete based on his emotional makeup and various preferences:

A. Use mindset. He directed himself to start fast.

B. Engage in pre-competition exercise. He took brisk walks.

C. Listen to music with a fast beat. He had a couple of selections.

D. Visualize. He imagined himself as a hurtling train engine.

E. Transfer anger into intensity. He readily conjured up this emotion by recalling specific life situations.

F. Repeat a motivating phrase in the within-game routine. One phrase was "Bear down now."

Because this package of psychological skills was matched to the bowler, he felt comfortable with it. It increased his confidence and led him to be more optimally energized at the outset of competition.

We want to emphasize that maintaining optimum energy levels is far more than a matter of applying techniques. Of prime importance are regular exercise, good nutrition, adequate sleep, stress management, and overall care of your health. In addition to producing steady energy output, these factors create a reserve which can be drawn upon by psyching up methods. Think of an analogy to a well. If that well is dry, pumping will be to no avail.

Q **What's the best way to get mentally prepared for more challenging lane conditions?**

A Remember that competence is the cornerstone of confidence. So, first and foremost, become skilled in handling all types of conditions. The truth is you can learn to play on any pattern. No matter what your style of bowling, there is a way to solve whatever you encounter. To reach that level of adaptability you need a plan and a strong commitment to follow it. Here are our suggestions:

Find a center that can put down the different lane conditions needed to prepare for competitions, such as the ABC Tournament,* Team USA qualifying tournament, and other sport bowling events. Your aim is to know what to do on oily, medium, and dry conditions and the more challenging sport conditions—to develop a feel for the right angle, equipment, speed, rotation, and loft. Then you need to know what adjustment to make when these conditions change during play. The only way to master this is by putting in time on all types of conditions. Receive input from your coach or teammates to help evaluate your game on each condition the lane technician puts down. Practice with other bowlers to compare ball roll and hooking power. Play some matches to simulate tournament play. Develop an eye for the changes you'll make during competition.

* As of 2006, renamed the USBC Open Championships

To cope with lane conditions, call upon whatever methods exist in your mental game repertoire. We call your attention to a few in particular.

For overall learning, mentally practice bowling on all conditions. Visualize yourself quickly and effectively adjusting as you compete on the various patterns. Use as much detail and as many senses as possible in the imagery. If the pattern in an approaching event is known, mentally rehearse competing on that pattern in the preceding days.

In conjunction with the confidence gained from increasing competence, we recommend this mindset message during *training:* "I can do this. I will do this. I'll learn what to do and when to do it on each and every type of lane condition I'll be playing on." Before *competing,* change the message to "I can do this. I will do this. I'll make every necessary adjustment. I will handle the condition. I will solve it."

Be thoroughly positive in your self-talk before and during competition. Use thought stopping to eliminate any negative ideas or beliefs related to lane conditions.

Adhere to routines. Use relaxation and refocusing methods as needed.

Also keep in mind that other bowlers face the same conditions you do. To the extent that you stay focused, loose, and positive in outlook, you'll hold an edge over competitors who are upset by the pattern. If you master the methods in this book, you can be confident of your ability to maintain these optimal states.

Finally, recall the concept of the lane as a friend who gives you feedback about where to play. In facing any given pattern, you can think of the lane in this way. Let the ball reaction guide you in making the proper adjustments.

Dear Jeff,
In order to strike, move two boards to the right, keep your mark the same, and slightly increase the ball speed.

Yours truly,
The Lane ☺

Mr. Jeff Bowler
Anytown, World

Q **If I get off to a slow start, I tend to feel discouraged. Especially if it's the first game. A voice in my head says, "It's gonna be a long night." Often it's hard to shake that attitude, and I know it hurts my performance. What mental game methods can I apply?**

A Our recommended approach for handling adversity can allow you to effectively cope with slow starts. Apply those Keys to Resilience which enable you to let go of what didn't go right and focus entirely on the shot ahead. Promptly knock out doubting thoughts and any other negative notions. Be sure to have affirmations and process imagery (visualize perfect execution) as part of your regular pre-shot routine. You may very well benefit by using more of these two methods until settling down.

Understanding the basis of your slow start will be extremely useful. Note pre-game and within-game thoughts and feelings in a log to increase your awareness. It's not at all unusual for athletes to be a bit "wired" or have the "jitters" at the outset of an event. You might find that by not making a big deal of it, you can settle down relatively quickly. Apply relaxation techniques to help achieve your optimum level of excitement.

If it turns out that doubts about ability and other forms of negative thinking are fueling anxiety, develop a program for increasing self-confidence and overall positive perspective. Equally important, fashion a full strategy for managing anxiety.

On the other hand, if your slow starts are due to being emotionally "flat," psyching up will likely benefit you. Draw upon our discussion at the outset of this chapter to develop an energizing approach that works for you.

With your coach, review how technical improvements can help your start. Learning to read lanes better and faster and improving equipment selection will translate into stronger starts.

Mentally rehearse your starts. Visualize bowling more effectively at the outset. Also see yourself coping when you start slowly. That means staying determined, upbeat, and immersed in the process of bowling instead of fighting yourself.

In practice, simulate the start of events. Go through the pre-game approach you'll use in competition. Create a scenario where you're off to a slow start. Do whatever it takes to get on track.

Q **I'm thrown if something unexpected happens. What can I do to handle things that happen out of the blue?**

A Unexpected situations affect a lot of bowlers. These include equipment problems, injury to yourself or teammates, mechanical or electronic malfunctions on the lane, loud or provocative comments, and a much stronger performance from a competitor than you expected.* In order to be the master of these situations rather than their victim, we recommend the following:

*This can happen if you underestimate opponents or they give an exceptional—perhaps breakthrough—effort. Always focus totally on your game, on bowling your best, regardless of the competitor. Predictions about opponents, one way or the other, are distracting and not relevant to your performance.

- Let go of any illusion that life events will always unfold in orderly and predictable ways. This will enable you to be briefly surprised rather than stunned by the unexpected.

- When encountering the unexpected, maintain your routines and use your repertoire of mental game skills to stay focused, positive, and loose. In particular, we recommend the RALLY approach for coping with adversity.

- Before an event, tell yourself that you will handle whatever comes your way. Trusting your ability to cope with the unexpected will add to your confidence.

- Mentally rehearse managing unexpected situations successfully, especially the ones which give you the most trouble. Simulate these situations in practice and cope using the methods which best keep you on track.

- Recognize that novel, completely unanticipated circumstances can occur. Simply apply your mastered methods to readily adjust.

- View those unexpected situations also experienced by competitors (e.g., interrupted play) as opportunities. Some, perhaps most, opponents will not ideally adjust, giving you a potential advantage.

- "Anticipate and forget." Assured you can handle whatever comes your way, there's no need to think about possibilities you can't stop anyway. Be fully into what you can control—your own bowling process in the "here and now."

Q **Sometimes I'm at an event and realize my equipment isn't what I'd really like for the condition. This knocks down my confidence. How can I not let this get to me so much?**

A There are three answers to this question. One, improve your equipment arsenal to be prepared for the variety of conditions you may face. Do whatever research you can about the house so you have an idea of what to expect. Two, recognize there are physical adjustments which will

Wendy Macpherson: Bowlers Journal
"Female Bowler of the Decade" for the 90s,
four-time PWBA Player of the Year

enable you to get increased versatility from the equipment you have. Changing wrist/hand position, speed, etc. can result in one particular bowling ball behaving much like another specific ball. Make the right adjustments and your score can be similar to what it would have been with the ideal equipment. You must have an advanced physical game and thorough knowledge of your equipment to be versatile in this way. Three, be mentally disciplined and direct your thinking only to the equipment you'll be using. Concentrate your effort on getting the most from what you have. Short of perfection—and perfection is in short order—this is what we all need to do in all arenas of our life every day. Adhere to your pre-game and pre-shot routines and use thought stopping to eliminate any negative thinking connected to your equipment. We know of a world class bowler who had all his equipment stolen (with his car!) days before a major championship. He totally focused on pulling together what he could and bowled quite effectively. The key for the athlete was directing his energy to the challenge at hand, not what might have been.

Q **Any time I bowl for money, I start to think about the amount I could win. Is that good or bad?**

A We begin our answer with a question: How does that thought make you feel? If you're optimistic about winning money and these thoughts contribute to feeling upbeat, energized, and focused, all well and good. However, if you're worried and distracted, then obviously such thinking is detrimental. For dedicated athletes who love the sport, motivation will be essentially fostered by successful participation and growing skills. While the prospect of earnings (and other external rewards such as fame) adds more incentive, dwelling on these can be costly in terms of pressure and distraction. This can detract from both performance and enjoyment. The key to adapting here is zeroing in on process, narrowing attention to the actions directly at hand, and not thinking about outcomes and consequences. Use attention-enhancing tools to assist your attaining this focus. The great value of a process orientation applies to tour players and elite amateurs who rely on earnings as well as to other bowlers. It's not as if the importance of earnings is forgotten or denied. It's a matter of where your attention is directed before and during competition.

Q **There are times when I have a perfect feel for the ball and everything seems easy. When it's not there I lose confidence. How can I get in that zone more often?**

A When a bowler or other athlete feels that mind and body are one and performs optimally, that's called "flow" or being "in the zone." Essential characteristics[23] are

- Balance between the challenge involved and the athlete's skill;

- Merging of actions and awareness—there is an awareness of actions, but no sense of that very awareness—a unified feeling of mind and body, a sense of effortlessness and spontaneity;

- Clear goals;

- Feedback that is immediate and unambiguous;

- Focusing total attention on the activity;

- Sense of control;

- Loss of self-consciousness—no self-doubt or concern about performance;

- Time transformation (slowing or accelerating depending on the athlete and event); and

- Feelings of enjoyment/exhilaration/perfection.

Here's how PBA Tour player Ken Yokobosky describes what it's like to bowl in the zone:

> Everything becomes much clearer. I'm more aware of my body and what it's doing at each point—my armswing, my release, and so on. I can feel everything a lot more acutely and I'm able to make very subtle adjustments because everything is firing properly. I just seem to execute everything much more easily. It's much more natural. I don't have to think—that's the bottom line. You can put it in overdrive. I think autopilot is the best way to describe it. The computer has all the directions in it and you hit the autopilot button. I'm aware of what's going on around me, but not concerned. I'm just into myself, it's a calm intensity. When you're out of the zone, that intensity isn't so calm. I can see people bowling, but it doesn't affect me. Everything goes into a kind of day-dream-type state. When I'm going to the line, I hear no sound whatsoever, I completely lose sound as I'm making my approach and letting go of the ball. I pick it up again when the ball is halfway down the lane.[24]

Both physical and psychological characteristics of being in the zone are listed in the box on the next page. See how they contrast to the feelings associated with underachievement due to choking.

While there's no formula for attaining flow, we can point you in the right direction. Mastering mental game skills is crucial to getting there or at least in the neighborhood. Specifically, research[25] suggests several ways to create the ideal circumstances for flow:

IN THE ZONE[26]

PHYSICAL FEELINGS		PSYCHOLOGICAL FEELINGS	
The Zone	**Choking**	**The Zone**	**Choking**
Loose	Tight	Controlled	Beaten
Relaxed	Tense	Confident	Scared
Solid	Shaky	Powerful	Weak
Balanced	Unsteady	Commanding	Dominated
Strong	Weak	Calm	Upset
Light	Heavy	Tranquil	Panicked
Energetic	Tired	Peaceful	Worried
Effortless	Hard	Easy	Rushed
Fluid	Choppy	Clear	Confused
Smooth	Awkward	Focused	Overlooked

- Seek competitive situations where a balance exists between skills and challenges. This is crucial for motivation and confidence. A level of challenge which requires you to "stretch" is best.

- Call upon various approaches to build confidence. These include control of self-talk (and thought stopping), practice simulation, and attention to goals.

- Employ pre-competition plans and game plans. This involves routines and goals that are clear, specific, process-oriented, and obtainable.

- Use feedback effectively. Look to multiple sources to monitor progress and adjust goals. Learn to productively process negative feedback.

- Develop open communication with your coach.

- Try to maximize team cohesion.

- Acquire and consistently apply attention-enhancing techniques. Stay process-focused and in the present moment.

- Know your ideal energy level. Apply relaxation methods to help achieve this.

- Be physically conditioned through optimal training.

- Recognize that you have a choice in how you respond to disappointing or frustrating situations.

- Seek to derive the most enjoyment from bowling. Concentrate on mastery of the sport rather than rewards external to it. Take pleasure in the details of bowling and the challenge it offers.

Since you can't count on achieving a full flow state, it's essential to perform your best at all other times. "Feel" is elusive. There are days when it just won't be there. If that "feel" you associate with being in the zone isn't present, don't let this throw you off stride. Rely on other senses (i.e., watch the ball reaction and make the necessary adjustments). If you line up properly on the lane, use the right piece of equipment, match speed, release, and loft to the condition, and you wind up getting pretty good results, just keep doing what you're doing. Don't question it. Like a major league pitcher, you can often win without your best "stuff." Stay with your routines and keep a positive attitude, using affirmations, thought stopping, etc. as needed. You might still get that ideal feeling and, most importantly, bowl great whether or not you do. Most importantly, it's the hallmark of a winning bowler to strive all-out and to stay focused even if external or internal conditions aren't ideal. On any given day, make realizing your potential the goal.

Q **In the days before a tournament, should I do anything different than usual?**

A We call the program of activities leading to the day of competition "pre-day" routine. Throughout training, it's vital to establish a regimen of practice, league play, conditioning, and mental rehearsal. Devote the time necessary to acquire new mental game skills. Adequate sleep, sound health practices, injury management if needed, leading a balanced life, and general stress reduction also figure into the preparation for successful bowling. In the week before an event, you want to be especially diligent about adequate rest. You may modify your workout schedule so that muscles aren't tired when the tournament begins. Reviewing/revising goals for the event, increasing frequency of mental practice (e.g., three times per day), and increasing use of relaxation methods are suggested. If you have one, regularly listening to a performance tape is recommended.

Scouting the center is a good idea. This leaves you with less to figure out logistically and creates familiarity with the competition environment. Both can reduce pre-day and pre-game stress. In addition, knowing the center lends itself to more realistic, detailed mental practice.

When the event is out of town, give yourself enough time at the location so you're recovered from the trip and acclimated to the setting. If you've crossed several time zones, take steps to limit jet lag. Ideally, this would mean arriving one day in advance for each time zone shift. More likely, what's practical is making strategic changes in your diet and sleep pattern to reset your circadian rhythms ("body clock").

Plan where you'll be eating the night before competition and pre-game meal(s). Set up transportation to the center. In hotels, carefully arrange wake-up calls and use an additional alarm (bring your own travel alarm).

Spending time with teammates in the days before competition can increase rapport and enhance communication. The support lends itself to increased confidence and lower anxiety. Teammates also may benefit from shared information about conditions, equipment, transportation, etc.

Having relaxed fun the day prior to a tournament is great for stress reduction. It's also conducive to getting a good night's sleep.

While these pre-day activities/adjustments are important, it's essential not to make fundamental changes—e.g., in diet (no new foods!), equipment, and warm-up routine.

Q **Can motivational audiotapes improve my bowling performance?**

A Personalized performance audiotapes* designed to fit your competitive makeup can boost your readiness to bowl. These tapes may be used in the training period (especially as an event approaches), pre-game (before arriving at the center and inside), and even between shots. They are aimed at solidifying skills and priming you for an optimal effort, much the way mental practice, mindset, and affirmations do. The words can remind you of keys in your physical or mental game or any other aspect of performance, suggest an attitude conducive to bowling well, and offer encouragement. Think of such tapes as taking a coach on the road.

The recorded voice can be your own or someone who knows your game and inspires confidence, such as your coach or a sport psychologist. It's very common for music to be part of the tape. This

* Our use of the term "audiotape" here is generic, referring to any recorded format.

can be heard before and/or after the message or continuously in the background. The choice is entirely a matter of personal preference. Some bowlers prefer calming music and some more up-tempo sounds. Just be sure the music doesn't distract from the words.

It makes good sense to collaborate with your coach due to his or her knowledge and influence. Not all coaches are attuned to this technique. The coach must appreciate the value of a tape, grasp the principles and methods involved, and be open to learning. There's a skill to creating an effective tape. Practice is required. What is essential is a give and take between coach and bowler. The coach needs to feel comfortable with—actually welcome—any suggestions for change in response to a recording or a script that's been produced. This cooperation process may actually contribute to the coach-athlete relationship.

The following suggestions for making tapes more effective are based on a USOC framework.[27]

- Working from a script is best. Be organized and detailed and include all you want to communicate.

- Concentrate on your strengths. References can be made to your physical game, equipment knowledge and arsenal, adaptability to conditions, mental game skills, and fitness.

- Add realism and power to the tape by including details of a setting. Use sensory information. Describe the center and who's there (e.g., family and friends), even including facial expressions if you like. Note the crashing of pins, fan chatter, and other sounds. Cite physical sensations from the feeling of the ball to your feet on the approach to the air temperature. You might even include the smell of food. Focus on the positive, like the looseness of your muscles and expressions of support you receive.

Tapes are a completely individual matter and so vary widely in structure. The USOC recommends four phases. These recommendations, adapted for the purposes of this book, can serve as a guideline. These are described in the box on the following page.

A performance tape, like other mental game tools, may well be modified based on actual experience. Even before applying it in competition, its use in practice is advised in order to get the kinks out regarding cues, content, pacing, music, etc.

PERFORMANCE AUDIOTAPE PHASES

The first phase is relaxation. This is intended to create a receptive state of mind. Diaphragmatic breathing or a guided visualization can be used.

Second is the pre-event phase. Simulate a highly positive pre-event state of mind and physical state. For outside the center, you could go through the mindset script cited in Chapter 5. Then for pre-game within the center, you might say, "As you notice your competition, you feel calm and confident. You feel good about your preparation and as you take in your environment, you know you'll have a good performance."

Phase number three is the event. Initially you're instructed to visualize the start, feeling calm, powerful, and in control. Focus on perhaps two or three performance keys (e.g., "your armswing is smooth and free") and visualize performing them perfectly. The tape then informs you that should any negative thoughts occur, use thought stopping, and then continue, totally immersed in the process of bowling. After experiencing a successful effort, you're told to observe how good it feels to be performing well. The taped voice encourages you to use all senses and experience the various sensations accompanying the recognition of success. Next you receive instructions to remain both calm and alert and to make ongoing adjustments. Directions to be confident, but not overconfident, and to know that this approach works conclude the phase.

Fourth is the post-event phase. Following imagery of bowling successfully, you're instructed to savor the moment—to take in the environment and sense what success feels like. Finally you're told to take a few deep breaths and become increasingly alert as you gradually exit the visualizing process. You should now feel calm. Use a relaxation technique to achieve this if you're overly excited.

As your skills develop and perhaps new keys emerge, appropriate changes can enable you to get maximum benefit from a tape. For particular competitions you may want to create an event-specific tape with detail about time and place. Based on expected conditions, you can incorporate keys related to specific lane adjustments. Verbal and music changes keep a tape fresh, contributing to its impact.

Recall that you can benefit from two other types of audiotapes mentioned in this book. PMR tapes can be used throughout training and also on the day of competition. The soothing tone of the speaker, especially if there's music in the background, can serve to relax apart from the active process itself. Tapes that are entirely music can be calming or stimulate to different degrees and used pre-day, pre-game, or within-game. Music tapes are so versatile that you can even select a beat based on the lane condition in order to control your tempo. On a dry condition, bowling with a faster tempo will generate more energy. Rock n' roll or another hot sound is conducive to this. On heavy oil, where you're looking to just roll the ball, an easy beat may help slow your tempo. On lanes that are medium, use music with a somewhat moderate beat to achieve a moderate tempo. Recall that you can listen to tapes at home, in your car, and/or in the center.

You might also benefit from a personalized videotape. Some tapes are primarily inspirational, with footage of yourself bowling successfully, set to great music, containing whatever images and sounds you want on there (from movie clips to bowling greats). Videotapes can also closely mirror the audiotape structure, using images to complement the spoken word.

Q **I'm not enthusiastic about bowling the way I used to be when I was younger. At times it feels like a chore. Can I get the fun back?**

A Because you've obviously had a passion for bowling and are asking the question, the chances are you can. The first key to enjoying the sport again would be to determine exactly what has eroded your motivation. The second will be for you to consider some actions, including possible change in attitude and behavior.

A variety of psychological and physiological reactions can be associated with loss of motivation and what's popularly referred to as "burnout." There's actually a continuum of symptom severity from frustrating/unpleasant to profoundly disturbing and even health threatening.

Psychological indicators of motivational issues include

- Minimal enthusiasm,
- Must push oneself to bowl,
- Anxiety,
- Irritability/anger,
- Cynicism and pessimism,
- Depression,
- Insomnia,
- Loss of appetite, and
- Overreacting to disappointment.

Among possible physical symptoms are

- Tiredness,
- More health problems (e.g., particularly headaches, digestive disorders, and body aches),
- Increased injuries,
- Hypertension,
- Weight loss,
- Elevated heart rate at rest/slower recovery after exercise, and
- Shortness of breath.

What are the causes of this? Ongoing excessive stress (distress) in one form or another can ultimately dampen motivation. Possible sources of such distress include physical pain, continuing dissatisfaction over performance (especially without expectation of future success), intense pressure related to competition (including finances), unpleasant interpersonal situations (e.g., with coach, teammates, or administrators), boring and/or excessive training, and illness or exhaustion.

Stressors outside of bowling can affect motivation in several ways. One is a direct effect through mood. For example, loss of interest in formerly pleasurable activities can result from depression. A second way is by hampering performance (e.g., through distraction) and contributing to the other stresses we've mentioned.

Actions which can limit or prevent the various causes of distress are safeguards of motivation. These are what we generally recommend to bowlers:

- Take steps to prevent and manage injuries (our suggestions are presented in response to the next question).

- With the assistance of a coach, evaluate your game, develop a Master Plan, and commit yourself to reaching realistic and challenging goals. Use the methods presented throughout this book to facilitate your growth.

- A positive perspective is essential. Increase your confidence and self-acceptance. Guard against perfectionism, which sets you up for stress and frustration.

- Learn to cope with competition pressures. This includes use of relaxation techniques.

- Focus on your bowling when you bowl, not extrinsic rewards such as prize money.

- Develop your communications skills, including assertiveness.

- Engage in quality practices.

- Manage the stress of daily living by using a variety of strategies. These include a healthy lifestyle and leading a balanced life encompassing achievement, interpersonal, and recreational activities. Our upcoming discussion of controlling injuries cites other coping actions.

- If bowling isn't enjoyable and feels overwhelming, take a break (e.g., for several weeks) or simply reduce how much you compete and practice.

- Consult a sport psychologist or other mental health professional if the symptoms are unremitting and affect the quality of your life as well as those around you. If events and/or your behavior external to bowling are of concern, then at least a consultation is warranted.

Our safeguards can also remotivate. Motivation can usually be rekindled if the distress is relieved. Then the underlying love of the game will eventually reassert itself.

With respect to your question in particular, ask what has changed since you enjoyed the sport. That may help you see which recommended action

Tommy Jones: 2002 PBA Rookie of the Year, his four titles in 2004-2005 topped the Tour

may be helpful. The sense of satisfaction and fun that bowling brings usually flows from a feeling of success and growth. Establish goals that reflect your realistic potential at this time. In other words, strive to do what's within your control and leave everything else alone. Find ways to develop strengths in your game that you may not have had before, such as in the mental game or in your choice of equipment. Feel genuinely good about who you are and you may very well soon feel good again about bowling.

Q **I've known a number of bowlers whose careers have been affected by injury. Is there any way I can guard against this?**

A Your awareness of the importance that injuries hold and your decision to be proactive are a big plus. Denial is a major factor increasing risk of occurrence and impact. When discussing the subject of injury, there are really two major considerations: prevention and recovery. Let's look at both.[28]

Bowling injuries usually result from microtraumas which emerge over time. Excess physical stress produced by practice and competition eventually creates damage to a specific area. The most common injury in the sport (other than blisters) is probably "bowler's thumb" (a callous resulting in nerve compression and multiple symptoms). Other typical bowling injuries include muscle strain of the fingers, hand, and wrist; carpal tunnel syndrome, tennis elbow; and rotator cuff and back injuries.

There are seven actions which can prevent most injuries in bowling:

1. Adhere to an aerobic workout program to stay in shape.

2. Protect parts of the body prone to injury by strength training.

3. Practice correct bowling form.

4. Be sure that all equipment is fitted to the anatomy of your hand.

5. Follow a sound nutritional regimen.

6. Get adequate rest.

7. Stretch before and after practicing, competing, and working out. Warm up before you first stretch.

Since bowler's thumb is so common, here are specific steps to prevent it:

- Bevel thumb-hole edges, especially the palm side.

- Notice the release. Excessive strain on the thumb will occur if it doesn't release smoothly and naturally at the bottom of the armswing. Smoother thumb release can be promoted by redrilling the thumb hole with more reverse pitch and left-side lateral pitch.

- Use lotions and ointments to help prevent the formation of calluses. Apply these at night or several hours before bowling.

- Shave off a callus which starts to develop at the base of the thumb. Pharmacies sell callous shavers with straightforward instructions.

Studies have found that higher levels of life stress are associated with greater severity or frequency of sports injuries. Generalized muscle tension and disruption of attention are thought to be the most likely stress response changes affecting the occurrence of such injuries. Increased muscle tension directly affects bowlers since it can produce fatigue, reduced flexibility, lowered motor coordination, and decreased muscle efficiency. This increases risk for sprains, strains, and other musculoskeletal problems.

The risk-producing impact of life stresses can be reduced by various coping actions. Among these are sufficient sleep, good nutrition, exercise and a range of stress-reducing skills such as time management techniques, behavioral relaxation methods (e.g., diaphragmatic breathing), and thinking-related tools. These tools include thought stopping, reframing, and other approaches which build confidence and enhance self-esteem. Social support is a fundamental coping resource. Being part of a social network contributes to life balance and cushions the impact of daily hassles and life events.

If you suffer an injury, the immediate action to take is assessment. Your teammates and coach may provide very useful information and if the injury is relatively minor, this could be sufficient. Trainers and/or physicians should be consulted if an acute injury is sufficiently painful and unresponsive to basic first aid, or if it's obvious or suspected severity merits prompt professional examination and care.

We know bowlers to be tough customers who deal matter-of-factly with pain and tolerate injuries remarkably well. However, we strongly advise you to learn the difference between an injury which isn't significant and one which will be aggravated or become chronic if not addressed.

Use common sense in managing less serious or minor, nagging injuries. Some rest might be called for. Or you might need to temporarily modify your bowling schedule if this has been aggravating an existing condition. Certain adjustments in form or equipment might reduce physical demands.

Should the injury merit medical attention, it's essential to find a physician with the relevant expertise and experience. For instance, while orthopedists treat a host of injuries, some see more athletes than others. Also, some orthopedists specialize in knees, others in arm/shoulders or wrist/hands or the back. Seek a doctor who looks at you as a whole person and who is comfortable answering your questions.

We also recommend that an injured athlete be accompanied by a teammate, coach, family member, or friend during an initial medical consultation, at the minimum. In addition to obvious physical assistance if needed, this is to help manage anxiety and avoid possible depression. Also, due to anxiety, pain, and other factors, information is often not fully grasped or retained by the patient at a consultation. The person or persons accompanying the athlete can ask questions and remember/record all the physician says. It can be psychologically helpful if at least one accompanying person is the coach or a teammate if applicable. This signals that the bowler is valued and that the link to active bowling and team remains strong.

If you'll be working with a trainer, physical therapist, chiropractor, or other medical personnel, make sure you feel comfortable with the individual or individuals as well as trust their skills. Feeling relaxed and expecting improvement is conducive to getting the most from treatment. It's also very important that the professionals involved in your rehabilitation communicate with one another and with your coach and/or family as may be appropriate. Create a "comeback team." You'll benefit from the coordinated effort and the sense of support. If injured, learn about the specific nature of the injury and the expected recovery process.

Find out how you can participate in the rehabilitation, from preparing for a medical process to doing physical therapy exercises to cross training.

Various psychological skills have facilitated recovery from sports injuries. Setting short-term goals can contribute to feelings of progress and focus your activities. Relaxation methods in general increase blood flow and decrease muscle tension. Biofeedback can directly lower blood pressure. Positive self-talk and imagery of your recovering and comeback can lift mood and raise energy. Managing pain through rehabilitative activities as well as distracting actions (e.g., listening to music) reduces a major source of stress. Other stress management techniques combined with the above approaches may help your immune system and hasten recovery.

Staying involved with the sport during a recovery period is highly recommended. Not only can you enjoy the game and relationships with fellow bowlers, you can actively participate through feedback and support. If you're on a team, your teammates and coach will appreciate your assistance and presence. Even though you're not bowling, you are able to learn through observing and talking to your coach and other bowlers, acquiring information about equipment, and developing your mental game. You may even improve your fitness through working out and focusing on nutrition.

When an injury occurs, emotional distress is expected. Once the assessment is made and the path to recovery clear, set your sights on the comeback. Process the adversity as you would any disappointment and move ahead with determination and pride in your capacity to cope.

In contrast to this constructive attitude, ongoing anger can hinder recovery. Missing rehabilitation appointments, not following through on medical advice, and denying the severity of an injury will also interfere with the process of regaining health.

It is crucial for bowlers returning after a significant injury and substantial time away to be very patient. Timing, rhythm, and form need to be regained. Physical game and equipment modifications may be called for. You must also get back into the flow of making rapid adjustments. Handling the various demands and stresses of a competitive environment will take some time. Be grateful to be bowling once again. Allow yourself the room to fully come back and you'll regain your edge faster.

Q There's a lot of publicity these days about steroids and other drugs which athletes take to improve performance. If a drug is legal, is there anything wrong with that?

A Many substances used to enhance performance are already illegal and others may be declared so.* Beyond the issue of their legality, anabolic steroids and other performance enhancing drugs are very problematic for several reasons. First, they are detrimental to health and most have addictive properties. As far as we're concerned, that is sufficient reason to never use them. Second, they create an uneven playing field. In today's brave new world, where values often seem topsy-turvy and grey is a primary color, we believe sports should be a life arena where fair is still fair and foul is still foul. Third, bowling is a family sport and best served by the presence and image of wholesome athletes competing in clean, modern centers. Fourth, team, league, and governing organization rules may prohibit their use. The United States Anti-Doping Agency** publishes a full list of prohibited substances ("I.O.C. Prohibited Classes of Substances and Prohibited Methods of Doping").[29]

We also offer a few words of caution about so-called recreational drugs. Alcohol and other mood-altering substances may be outright illegal or illegal in certain circumstances (e.g., driving while intoxicated). As with performance enhancers, these substances may be prohibited by teams and other organizations or their use may be restricted. Some substances pose a health risk with even minimal use. With others, risk comes with excessive or inappropriate use. Alcohol, for example, can be readily abused and lead to serious problems, such as addiction, overdosing, and destructive behavior. We are not saying never have a drink. We are saying be responsible for the sake of others as well as yourself.

The pressures, demands, and overall stresses in bowling and other competitive sports are many. While the exact reasons may be complex and varied, athletes initially turn to substances in order to cope in some fashion with these and/or larger life issues. Hopefully the application of principles and tools presented in this book for use in sports and life generally can add significantly to your coping resources. Among these principles is seeking assistance as needed for any aspect of bowling and life outside of bowling.

We advise consulting a mental health/substance abuse professional if

- You're using a substance to enhance performance;

---

* The Anabolic Steroid Control Act of 2004 significantly expanded the list of controlled substances in the US.
** The agency phone number is 719-785-2000 and its website is usantidoping.org. A pharmacist is available for specific inquiries at 800-233-0393.

- You wish to cut down or stop using a substance and are unable to do so;

- You rely on alcohol or another substance to handle emotions;

- You're using increasing amounts of a substance or can't control the amount you use once you start;

- You suspect or believe or have been told by others you respect that use of a substance is adversely affecting you or places you at risk; and

- You're using a substance that is illegal and/or violates team or organization rules.

This list is not inclusive. It simply suggests circumstances where substance use is directly or indirectly detrimental to you, others, and the sport.

Q Being a PBA national tour bowler is something I've always planned on. It's never crossed my mind to do anything else. I was doing great, but an injury changed things. I still bowl competitively but the reality is I won't make it as a pro. I feel lost. How can I let go of my dream?

A Although the injury has apparently diminished your bowling skills, we assume you're physically recovered otherwise. We're glad that's the case. Just like it's essential to have A, B, and C games in bowling, it's essential to have A, B, and C dreams. That's true for all of us. Unless you have access to a very special script, there is no certainty about how life's events will unfold. Sure, there are probabilities and it's absolutely reasonable and important to set goals accordingly and strive all-out to reach them. Yet, part of taking care of yourself is developing other options. We all have various skills and definite potential to take more than one career path. If supporting yourself as a pro bowler is not in the cards, you may still earn a living (full or part-time) in the sport in some capacity. Beyond this, many of the strengths which contributed to your bowling success, such as discipline, handling adversity, and making sound decisions under pressure, can be applied to other endeavors. Aspects of your athleticism such as hand-eye coordination might also be of value in what you do.

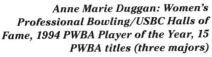

Anne Marie Duggan: Women's Professional Bowling/USBC Halls of Fame, 1994 PWBA Player of the Year, 15 PWBA titles (three majors)

Your challenges now are to find a new career direction, design a game plan to realize success, and then go for it. If you meet these challenges with your characteristic determination, you'll be fine. Speak to as many people as you like to help you find a match between your aptitude and interests. Then map a Master Plan and be great in whatever you do.

Simultaneously, you're also challenged to value yourself apart from being a professional bowler. It's not uncommon with talented people who have a single-minded purpose to identify themselves solely with that pursuit. Not only do you have talents and professional potential outside of the tour, who you are as a person goes beyond any particular profession. Keep in mind the words of bowling great Anne Marie Duggan: "I'm more than just my bowling." Do whatever it takes to expand your sense of yourself (self-image) and to accept the whole person you discover (self-worth). Recall our discussion of how important self-acceptance is.

Allow yourself time to find a new career direction and to adjust. You've suffered a major life disappointment and need to experience the emotions appropriate to that. Accepting the reality and moving on is a process. Call upon the type of actions discussed in Chapter 10. Most crucial is having a support network and expressing yourself to those you trust. What will help immeasurably is keeping bowling in your life. Whether or not bowling is a source of income, keep it a source of joy. Reset your goals and be passionate about your participation. If the sport is in you, nothing can take it away.

Exercises

1. Note those general performance challenges which are relevant to you.

2. Describe how each challenge has affected you or could affect you in the future.

3. Review the recommendations concerning those relevant challenges. After each review, place the suggested methods in one of three columns: "Currently Use," "Implement Immediately," and "Take Steps to Implement."

4. What steps will you take to implement each method in the third column?

5. Visualize yourself successfully handling each significant challenge.

REVIEW

In this chapter, we respond to questions about a range of key challenges faced by bowlers. Strategies are recommended for the following issues:

- Increasing your energy
- Handling the more testing lane conditions
- Overcoming slow starts
- Adjusting to unexpected occurrences
- Responding to equipment shortcomings
- Focusing on process instead of prize money
- Bowling in and out of the zone
- Following routines prior to the day of competition
- Benefiting from performance audiotapes
- Regaining motivation
- Coping with injuries
- Staying clear of substance misuse and abuse
- Making a career shift

17

CONQUERING PSYCH-OUTS AND OTHER INTERPERSONAL CHALLENGES

You can't control what other people do. All you can control is yourself.
Tammy Turner

Some of the most challenging situations faced by bowlers involve other people, such as competitors, fans, or family. In this chapter, we present strategies for tackling such crucial challenges. As in Chapter 16, the information is provided in response to questions. A concluding question about spirituality represents a special challenge.

List of Challenges

What follows are the questions we address, in sequence (with page numbers indicated):

- How can I be successful in match play? (p. 257)

- I don't bowl as well in front of big crowds. What can I do? (p. 260)

- I know my family has the best intentions, but when they come to see me bowl, they give advice I don't need, and it distracts me. I don't want to hurt their feelings. What can I say to them? (p. 261)

- I've just entered a league with better bowlers than I'm used to competing against. I feel a bit intimidated and tense. How can I cope? (p. 262)

- Competitors sometimes psych me out. What's a good way to handle this? (p. 263)

- I put a lot of work into my bowling. It upsets me when a bowler whose physical game is less than perfect carries better than me. I dwell on it and my game suffers. Can you suggest something? (p. 265)

- I'm a left-handed bowler. It bothers me a lot when I bowl great in a tournament and hear comments about the lefties having an unfair advantage. What can I do to not let this get to me? (p. 266)

- I worry about media interviews and sometimes feel distracted by their very presence at events. What do you suggest? (p. 267)

- I coach a high school team. Apart from bowling, I feel an obligation to support these kids in any way possible. If I suspect drug use or other serious problems, what should I do? (p. 272, *Coaching Corner* section)

A Special Challenge

- I am a deeply spiritual person. I also care deeply about my bowling. Is there a way to relate these two parts of my life? (p. 274)

Challenges and Strategies

Q How can I be successful in match play?

A A good place to start is realizing the following:

1. <u>Success means bowling your best. It doesn't require beating any given opponent or winning any given number of matches.</u>

Until bowling becomes a contact sport, you can't control the number of pins your opponent knocks down. It's counterproductive to set goals over which you have no control. Your own game is under your control. Strive for peak performance. That's an exhilarating challenge you can reach.

If you consistently bowl to your potential, you'll win your fitting share of matches. As your overall skills improve, your likelihood of winning will likewise improve.

This perspective directs your attention and energy towards the business of bowling and away from the distractions of opponents and outcome. It also enables you to feel good about your game regardless of what competitors do. Not depending on how others perform in order to value your own effort is liberating and reduces pressure. This is a positive factor which can contribute to your bowling well.

This approach towards succeeding is completely compatible with a will to win. Wanting to beat every opponent and win every match is at the core of competing. The irony is that for most bowlers, striving for success in the manner we describe is the most effective way to finish on top. The eye of the tiger is best focused on your own game.

As with all aspects of performance, every individual is unique and there are most definitely athletes who compete best with a different outlook. In our experience, most bowlers at all levels will win more in the long run with the attitude we've described.

2. <u>There is no mystery to bowling well in match play. The skills that result in quality efforts in qualifying rounds or in other formats are identical to the ones needed for match play excellence. By working hard at improving these skills, you're placing yourself in position to score well at all times, including match play.</u>

Your first challenge in match play and at other times is getting lined up. You're trying to figure out the right combination of angle, ball, speed, release, and loft. Consistently match-up and you'll play at a high level. Your second challenge is to make this game plan a reality (i.e., to execute).

To meet both challenges, you need to be loose and alert, focused and positive. On the approach, in particular, you want to maintain a consistent emotional level. If your emotions change, your motion changes too. This will affect ball direction and power. Use the mental game techniques presented throughout this book to help attain these optimal performance states.

Earl Anthony: 1970s' Bowler of the Decade, six-time PBA Player of the Year, bowling's first millionaire, PBA/USBC Halls of Fame

3. <u>The demands of match play coupled with its high caliber of competition make the mental game more important than ever.</u>

Match play is, in essence, a series of shootouts with progressively more at stake. This places a premium on the ability to handle clutch situations and to cope with the ups and downs of competition outcome. The full range of psychological methods covered in relation to these dual challenges comes into play here.

In match play, you may encounter more spectators, greater emotion on the part of competitors, and increased media attention. Overall, there tends to be more potential distractions. Call upon the methods you've learned to maintain concentration and refocus as needed.

Be prepared to flexibly apply the mental game techniques you've mastered. For example, to counter potential pressure, you might increase the number of deep breaths in the settee area or on the wood. Or you may want to add a second calming method. Perhaps you'll need to use thought stopping and reframing more often in the face of disappointment or centering and a verbal cue to neutralize distractions. You may communicate more with your coach or with teammates for information and/or support. To be resourceful in this way, you need a repertoire of skills and the capacity to adapt their application to the psychological demands of the competitive situation.

At the level of match play following qualifying rounds, bowlers are all extremely skilled. With so little separating competitors, a mental game advantage could well translate into the winning margin.

4. <u>Play the lane, not the person.</u>

We've heard players say, "I don't like that person. I really want to beat him (or her)." Regardless of your feelings about an individual, we advise you to not get caught up in such emotions while bowling. Personal reactions on the lanes can drain energy, be distracting, and upset emotional equilibrium. That gives an advantage to the very person you so want to defeat. Instead, go about the business of bowling with an undivided mind. This principle also applies to team situations. Teammates who are overtly distracted in this way can adversely affect one another. Teams will do best when they "stay at home," devoting all energy and attention to communicating and knocking down pins. There's room for added incentive based on who their opponent is. However, the personal stuff is something to consider before and after you bowl, not during.

5. If you're struggling, assessment is essential.

If the level of your bowling during match play is lower than at other times, seek feedback from your coach or other trusted observers. Your understanding may be increased by using videotape or another technology and by recalling your match play bowling through visualization.

Are you obviously doing something different in any aspect of your game? Be sure to check for consistency in routines. Are you tense or worried or displaying other signs of elevated anxiety? See if you can identify specific situations where you have difficulty. For instance, you may start slowly, struggle after a loss, or miss spares when a match is on the line. A log might help you identify your thoughts and feelings throughout a match. You can then develop a mental game strategy to tackle the issues affecting your performance.

In addition to these considerations, we suggest the following actions to improve your performance in match play:

- Follow the guideline for between-game routine presented in Chapter 15.

- Imagine yourself in match play during daily mental rehearsal. Visualize successfully performing in a range of scenarios aided by the flexible application of psychological methods.

- During practice sessions, simulate match play and actually use your mental game skills.

- Think of match play in an event as part of a long chain of matches stretching into the future. This outlook tends to reduce the pressure of having to win immediately.

These are ways to improve match play performance. Of course, some bowlers typically thrive in match play. They generally respond to the clutch situations and competitive drama with heightened concentration and optimum efforts. Yet even athletes who regularly rise to the occasion falter at times. The ideas presented here can be of value in minimizing both the occurrence and depth of such drop-offs in performance.

Q **I don't bowl as well in front of big crowds. What can I do?**

A Mastering and applying concentration methods and relaxation techniques should prove very helpful. Strive to devote full attention to the bowling process. Quickly refocus if any aspects of spectator behavior momentarily distract you. Three types of visualizing we've described—bubble imagery, peripheral blurring, and tunnel vision—can be particularly useful. Make use of any technique presented in Chapters 13 and 14 that cancels the jarring or anxiety-producing impact of fans at your events. Common sense calls for avoidance by not looking at the stands and possibly blocking out sounds through listening to music or recalling it. Keep your mind actively occupied by process imagery and/or dissociative thoughts. Adherence to routines is fundamental to focusing and limiting anxiety, including those worries generated by perceived or expected fan reaction. Supportive communication with teammates or your coach may be extremely valuable in terms of directing attention away from spectators as well as boosting confidence and positive regard for yourself.

If concern about others' approval is at the core of your reaction to spectators, maintaining a positive perspective will defuse the discomfort. Apply our instructions about how to attain this perspective. The methods for handling others' expectations can also be put to good use. Confidence and ideas of success leave no room for thoughts about disapproving fans. Disempower crowd influence by steadfast self-acceptance and unwavering belief in your abilities. While it's nice to receive applause, the reaction of onlookers—positive or negative—in no way determines your skills, talent, and potential and, above all, has zero to do with your self-worth.

Whether your concern is noise or disapproval, the methods we've cited can allow you to keep crowds in their place, which is in the stands. The lanes are your home base, your territory. When you bowl, that process is what you are about. Let all else fade from consciousness. Strive for immediacy. Be totally immersed in the activity you enjoy so much.

Crowds affect athletes very differently. While some feel self-conscious, even intimidated, others may draw energy from spectators and become more focused and motivated. Only time will tell whether you come to experience spectator presence in a positive light. What you can do now, and all you need to accomplish, is neutralizing crowds as a factor in how you perform.

Q **I know my family has the best intentions, but when they come to see me bowl, they give advice I don't need, and it distracts me. I don't want to hurt their feelings. What can I say to them?**

A In the context of competition, family and friends may very well be a supportive and overall positive factor for bowlers. In addition to any useful knowledge they impart, their emotional backing can bolster spirits, boost confidence, enhance self-acceptance, and reduce stress. Yet this isn't always the case. Unfortunately, friends or family can also be sources of stress. This is true whether they're present during competition or just discussing bowling with you away from the center. Common issues include harsh criticism; conditional support; excessive, demanding, or inaccurate advice; controlling behavior; extreme distress over disappointing outcomes; competitiveness; and envy.

The key for athletes is thinking, feeling, and acting independently while respecting others' feelings and perspective. Well-developed communication skills are essential for minimizing conflict and maximizing behavior that is helpful and uplifting. The goal is to draw what is positive from the relationship for the good of both your bowling and ongoing contact. Because our needs with family (including your spouse) and with friends are so intense, the issues cited are potentially disturbing and disruptive. Constructive communication can lead to more favorable interaction, if not complete resolution, of the issues from the athlete's point of view.

The next two chapters can be of great value in dealing with these situations. Families are a team and so are friends. When it comes to tools for communication and respect, the spirit as well as the specifics are the same whether your teammates are on the lanes or in the home.

Concerning youth bowlers in particular, the sections in Chapter 20 dealing with the coaching of young bowlers and family relationships provide relevant recommendations.

When advice offered is counterproductive, as in the question asked, it's necessary to confront the person and the situation in a constructive way. Be quite appreciative of the intent to help. Yet make clear that your concentration is broken when the advice is offered during competition. If you're being coached, indicate that it's essential for you to follow only the coach's input. A chat between your coach and family members may be most helpful in clearly establishing these boundaries. For youth bowlers, it's of primary importance that parents and coach have an open line of communication. The coach must explain how contradictory information will confuse the athlete and potentially undermine the coach-athlete relationship. Excess information, even if accurate, can be overwhelming. This doesn't mean that family members can't be very involved and offer useful feedback. It does mean that family will serve their bowler's interests by following the coach's guidelines with respect to input.

Q **I've just entered a league with better bowlers than I'm used to competing against. I feel a bit intimidated and tense. How can I cope?**

A To improve your skills and reduce anxiety, we suggest viewing this as a terrific learning opportunity. If your ultimate goal is to become the best bowler you can be, then bowling at a higher level of competition is an invaluable part of that learning process. Carefully observe what more advanced bowlers are doing and soon enough your game will be strengthened by adding what they know to what you know. Watch the way their feet move and their overall delivery, note the various releases, and observe adjustments as the lanes break down. You may observe when you're not competing as well as between shots. If you observe between shots, be sure to allow sufficient time for refocusing so you're fully prepared for your next shot. This means going through your standard pre-shot routine.

Goal setting should prove very helpful. Formulate a clear idea of steps in your skill development consistent with a Master Plan. This will enable you to work on attainable goals and feel satisfied and rewarded as you progress. Awareness of skill-related goals also emphasizes your bowling process. This emphasis has important implications:

First, consider yourself successful if you're becoming a better bowler and performing at what is realistically your present potential. Making these your expectations should substantially reduce competitive pressure.

Second, a process orientation, especially when combined with a "here and now" approach (i.e., immediacy), is conducive to good concentration and managing anxiety.

As far as optimal performance is concerned, the challenge is the same regardless of the level of competition: The elements are you, the ball, the lane, and the pins. Use your mental game skills to be focused, loose, and positive about your game and yourself. While you can learn from more advanced bowlers, when it comes to your actually bowling, they don't enter the picture. What does count are your performance and growth. These are under your control. Empower yourself and you won't be intimidated. Use relaxation methods as needed to contribute to being calm. PMR in particular may help if muscles are tight (also try stretching).

As you gain experience and skill, your confidence will increase along with your comfort. Congratulations for the step forward!

Q **Competitors sometimes psych me out. What's a good way to handle this?**

A There are an endless number of things competitors can do, both subtle and heavy-handed, to interfere with an opponent's bowling. Psych-out ploys can be aimed at distracting, upsetting, undermining confidence, and/or disrupting rhythm.

The top bowlers effectively block these moves. The lanes pose enough of a challenge—you simply can't afford to let others get into your head. We'll first alert you to some examples of what goes on in order to increase your awareness. Then recommendations will be provided concerning what it takes to combat these actions.

Comments about an opponent's physical game, or any aspect of play, may lead to self-consciousness. This is true even if they're positive. Calling attention to armswing, tempo, release, etc. could break the effortless groove and absence of thinking on the approach that characterizes good bowling. On that approach, your aim is to be externally focused on the target and line. Remember, the computer is loaded, just press print and go. Thinking about what you're doing is like throwing a wrench into finely meshing gears. If the comments are negative, they potentially create doubts that are doubly distracting and increase anxiety.

Observations that don't directly involve the bowler can also undercut. Seemingly innocent remarks such as "the approach is sticky today" or "the lanes are real dry" could be intended to set off thinking and concerns (whether or not they're accurate or misinformed). Obviously there's no limit to comments which can be made about equipment, ball reaction, scores, the standings, prize money, or outside events. All have the potential to distract and some may cause negative thinking.

Other tactics can be more blatant. These include slowing/delaying play in order to change an opponent's rhythm, creating a commotion through physical gestures and loudness, making provocative comments, and being belligerent. Become riled-up by these and other psych-out maneuvers and you'll play right into your opponent's hands.

The bad news is that there are so many potential psych-out tactics. The good news is that you can defend against each and actually turn them to your advantage.

First and foremost, bear in mind that bowling comes down to you and the lane. The core of the game is making adjustments to get lined up. Nothing anyone says or does can hold you back if you stay dialed-in—unless you let them. So you're in control of how you perform. It's up to you to solve the condition and execute. Use mindset to reinforce the reality of your being in charge of your bowling. Tell yourself that you (and your team, if applicable) will successfully reap the benefits of your hard work and dedication and that no one will knock you off your game.

To maintain concentration, lock into focus and refocus if need be, using whatever methods you've mastered for this purpose. These can include adhering to pre-shot routine, immediacy, process orientation, thought stopping, and visualizing. Imagery of a bubble shielding you from distractions can be readily used here.

Remain positive in outlook. Keep your attitude optimistic, self-talk positive, and self-acceptance high.

Instead of emotionally heating up, stay cool and calm. To do this, sustain concentration and a positive outlook; apply relaxation techniques; and maintain a consistent sense of self-worth. Also utilize whichever Keys to Resilience are helpful. Reframing is one of these and we offer a suggestion in this regard shortly.

If you're sufficiently prepared and disciplined, no psych-out attempt can get to you. You'll simply disregard them or psychologically swat them away.

More than that, once you become aware of a psych-out attempt, turn it to your advantage through reframing.

Think of psych-outs as a sign of respect for your ability, even an act of some desperation. The need to psych you out shows that on some level opponents don't believe they can win just on ability. And, consider this: So long as competitors are thinking about you, they're neglecting their game. Finally, by remaining unfazed and bowling well, you create frustration. These thoughts can actually increase your confidence.

We neither teach nor condone psyching-out tactics. They run counter to sportsmanship. We hope that, above all, you take pride in your skills and truly value those achievements that are a result of your excellence, not your opponent's failure.

Q **I put a lot of work into my bowling. It upsets me when I see a bowler whose physical game is less than perfect carry better. I dwell on it and my game suffers. Can you suggest something?**

A Carry results from a combination of dynamic factors affecting the ball's impact. These include axis tilt, rotation, RPMs, velocity, entry angle, and breakpoint. These can all be controlled by your actions (e.g., angle at which you project the ball, tempo, hand/wrist action, and loft) and equipment selection. If you want to improve your carry, identify what skills need to be developed and work on your game. Get the coaching to help you accomplish this. The key is taking responsibility for your performance. Instead of bemoaning what you can't do, learn how to do it. You'll immediately benefit from this change in attitude. In the words of Coach Edwards, "Keeping the right frame of mind can give you a feeling of control instead of feeling like a victim of fate or bad luck."[30]

Also, bear in mind that while another bowler might carry more on a given occasion or in a given house, the true measures of bowling excellence are versatility and repeatability. Aim for the ability to consistently make fast, effective adjustments on *all* conditions.

You'll perform better and enjoy yourself more if you focus on the process of bowling—your own bowling. Measure success by the development of your game and performing to your potential. Any other measure of success is unfair to you. How well or poorly others bowl isn't relevant to these main goals. Bowl with immediacy. Stick to routines. Limit looking at other bowlers to those times when you can genuinely pick up something about ball reaction. Use thought stopping if your thinking concerns anyone's game but your own. Do these things and you'll compete better and continue to grow. We hope you can fully value your terrific motivation, the progress you make, and your participation in a wonderful sport.

Q I'm a left-handed bowler. It bothers me a lot when I bowl great in a tournament and hear comments about the lefties having an unfair advantage. What can I do to not let this get to me?

A Start by grounding yourself in the truth that achievement in sports means handling the conditions whatever they are. Whether it's poker or bowling, you've got to play the hand you're dealt. That's the challenge. You deserve to feel proud about your effort if you play to your potential, if you meet the challenge.

You can't control the conditions one way or the other (we believe in the long run that conditions, like "breaks," even out), so it's pointless and counterproductive to let that affect you. Those grumbling about unfairness are looking for excuses when they should be looking for answers. They would be far better served by focusing on their own game and how to cope with the lanes, no matter what they present. It's actually to your competitive advantage if opponents complain, since that suggests they're distracted, lacking confidence, and frustrated.

Here and generally, don't give others the power to bring you down by their negative reactions. It would be irrational to let what they say have some bearing on how you feel about your game and yourself. Stay positive in your perspective. Trust those you respect and slough off remarks from those who haven't earned it.

If complaints about unfair conditions are intended to psychologically undermine you during or after play, handle them like other psych-out attempts (see our previous recommendations on that topic). Overall, use whatever methods are needed to stay focused, optimally energized, and positive.

Here's how one of bowling's greats, Parker Bohn III, fielded an interview question[31] about coping with this issue:

Lasser:

As a southpaw, you've no doubt heard your share of comments through the years with respect to the lefty-righty controversy. How do you deal with that?

Bohn:

One of the mystiques in our sport is, "They gave it to the lefties." It's part of our sport, whether there are no lefties in the finals or many. I think it's pretty sad that you can't give a guy like Mike Aulby credit or Eric Forkel or Jason Couch or myself. It's never, "Gee, Mike Aulby bowled great this week," or "Eric Forkel bowled great this week," or "Parker Bohn bowled great this week." It's always, "Oh, they gave you something to play on." We're just as human as Walter Ray, Brian Voss, Amleto Monacelli, or Doug Kent. It's just a shame.

Whoever wins a tournament, the very next week, one of the first things I do is congratulate him. I'm going to do that. It's part of me. It's always been within me.

People can say whatever they want to say. How do I deal with it? I let if fall by the wayside. I'm going to go out and try to win every dollar I can. And by golly, however it comes to me, I want it to come in leaps and bounds. So, have at it, because when I walk out of the center, I don't have to deal with you and my life goes on. Yet, I want people to understand that I can be a friend to anyone, whether they're right-handed or left-handed.

Above left: Amleto Monacelli—PBA Hall of Fame, twice PBA Player of the Year, ranked 4th best Venezuelan athlete of 20th century. Above right: Eric Forkel—21 career PBA perfect games, Tour titles include a PBA National Championship

Q I worry about media interviews and sometimes feel distracted by their very presence at events. What do you suggest?

A Readiness to deal with the media is increasingly important for bowling athletes. Most all competitive bowlers will encounter coverage in one form or another. Local and regional publications abound, with every center receiving them. They report local tournaments and league action. High school and collegiate programs are proliferating and these are covered. Elite amateur and professional tournaments are regularly reported in the print and electronic media.

Let's all remember, if reporters are writing or talking about you and our sport, it's a huge positive. You owe it to yourself, teammates, and bowling to be prepared to do a good job if you're interviewed. Just how do you do this? We think it's very simple:

Be honest. Be sincere and specific. Answer any questions with direct, concise replies.

Take your time. Don't blurt out an answer even if you're in a hurry. If your time is limited, tell the reporter that "Now isn't a good time for me. Can we talk at another time?"

Practice. A great way to do this is listening to others being interviewed and answering the questions to yourself in your own terms. You can also actively practice the interview process with your coach, teammates, parents, or a good friend. Practicing in front of a mirror is good preparation, whether for a speech or an interview. Mentally rehearsing interviews is also recommended.

Listen. Listen to the questions very carefully and if you don't understand one, ask that it be rephrased. Under no circumstances should you make up an answer. It's not necessary to answer every question. Just be honest and say, "I really don't have an answer for that. I've never really thought about it before."

There is no reason to feel intimidated by the media. We think you'll find that most media professionals have good intentions. After all, their job is to get a story and they need you to help them. We estimate that some 95% of the media are fair and friendly. Just relax and trust them and you'll see that most journalists accurately report what you're willing to share with them. In this regard, never convey any thought you don't want printed or aired. You're not protected by saying, "This is off the record."

Even though media personnel make an honest effort to get the facts right in covering you and the sport, they can make mistakes like anyone else, and they're in the business of selling newspapers or magazines or getting ratings or website hits. If a person burns you, go to that individual, talk to them, call them, get to the bottom of the reason for the misquote or misinterpretation or negative slant. Instead of totally ignoring a bad interview, try to gain a proper understanding. You may get a retraction or even a new article if you can demonstrate a need to right the wrong.

During or after an interview, if a change you seek concerning an inaccuracy is not made, move on down the road. Maintain a businesslike attitude. Refrain from barbed exchanges. Even if you're gifted enough to win a debate with savvy media pros, battling the power of the pen places you in a no-win situation.

Reporters are looking for an interesting angle. It can involve your performance, personality, politics, or who knows what else. So be alert. Take your time. And enjoy the interview.

You'll often know who is going to conduct the interview. Find out about that person's style and reputation from your coach, teammates, or others. Get more than one opinion if possible, especially if the interviewer is completely unknown to you. Regardless, in the end you'll be fine in dealing with the media if you say what you mean and mean what you say.

Before interviewing, you may use diaphragmatic breathing or another relaxation method to calm yourself. Stay positive in your thinking, applying thought stopping as needed. You can even develop a full pre-interview routine including an affirmation (e.g., "I enjoy all my interviews" or "I'm articulate and interview great") and visualization (imagine yourself calmly and effectively responding to questions and feeling very satisfied about the process). Recalling prior interviews that went very well can help boost confidence. Limit pressure by centering yourself and staying in touch with your essential self-worth, which in no way dependends on the interview.

Ease and skill with interviewing very much tend to increase with experience. Allow yourself the room to grow. If you're not expecting perfection, you'll be calmer and more effective.

Proper preparation for interviewing can lead to less advance anxiety as well as greater comfort, even enjoyment, during the interview itself.

In the box on the following two pages are a variety of suggestions provided by the USOC.

INTERVIEW TIPS[32]

- Feel free to ask reporters whom they represent. If you can tie in a local angle, you'll make a friend for life.

- Ask for the reporter's name. Try to remember it. The next time you see that individual, say "hi." You don't have to be best friends, but recognition is a courtesy.

- You have the right to know how long an interview will last, it's general content, the setting, and if you will be alone.

- Don't go down a road you don't want to travel. Feel free to say, "I'd rather not go into that" or "I don't feel comfortable talking about that."

- Don't be patronizing to the interviewer. Repeated comments such as "Well, Larry, that's a very good question," could be taken that way.

- Don't start answers with, "Well …" Simply reply to the question.

- You can finish an interview with, "Are there any questions I can clear up?" It's a good way to end on the right foot and eliminate any misunderstanding.

- There are times when you may have to get in front of a group of media and recount how you lost a big match. Take it in stride, but get your thoughts together. Step back and ready your mind. This is the time to stamp yourself as a class act. How you behave when you lose may be more important than your actions when you win.

Concerning newspapers, magazines, and websites:

- Don't treat the media like your best friend, telling all your deep dark secrets. Keep a friendly yet professional distance. Cooperate, but don't bare your soul unless you want to read about it in the morning paper.

- If you get a call at home and aren't ready to talk, ask the caller if he or she could call you back in 10 minutes. Or call back. Sometimes you're just not ready for an interview. Get your mind prepared and then return the call.

- If the reporter is taking notes, give that person time to write. Don't talk too fast. At least pause from time to time to let the interviewer catch up. Many times reporters use a tape recorder. This is no cause for concern. In fact, this is to your benefit because there's far less chance of being misquoted.

Concerning television:

- Make yourself presentable.

- TV wants short, concise answers. No monologues or rambling replies. Talk like you would in a normal conversation. When you need to stop … stop. Don't just talk for the sake of talking.

(continued)

- If you have a suggestion about questions, tell the interviewer. Many times TV reporters have several stories to do and a limited time to do them in and might appreciate the help.

- Make every question count, and feel free to redirect a less than informed question.

- Don't fall for the "Mike Wallace" pause at the end of your answer. That's where the most ill-prepared answers come from. Answer you questions and then stop. If the interviewer keeps looking at you, just look back. They can't sit there forever.

- If you're being interviewed in the studio, don't keep looking at the monitor. Keep your eyes on the interviewer.

Concerning radio:

- This is a very relaxing medium because it's usually in a non-formal setting and the possibility of being misquoted is virtually zero. The radio interview is more like a conversation. Answers don't have to be as short as those for television and you won't need to pause as in newspaper interviews. Give good, solid answers and don't ramble.

Concerning press conferences:

- You'll find this format at major events nationally and internationally. You'll be at a podium with a microphone and questions will come from the audience.

- Be sure to speak into the microphones. This may mean passing the microphone back and forth between several people, but it's necessary.

- Don't be worried about pauses between questions. People are writing. Be patient.

- If there's a pause at the beginning and questions don't come quickly, just give some of your thoughts. Start talking about your event. You can stress whatever you want.

- Usually after a formal press conference, many of the media will approach you for follow-up interviews. Because the mike isn't on, be sure to talk loud enough for all to hear in this part of the session. Those in the back of the group will appreciate it. Ask them if they can hear you. If not, make an effort to speak up.

- Prior to starting a formal interview before a group, compose yourself and prepare mentally. If you're not emotionally ready, delay the interview for a minute or two until you are.

As for the second type of media-related stress—anxiety about their presence during competition—we suggest several actions. Treat media presence, whether it be cameras, newspaper reporters, or broadcasters, as you would any potential distraction. Apply techniques like adhering to routine, mindset, and immediacy to lock into focus. Should your thoughts wander to media, refocus through methods such as thought stopping and visualizing as well as returning to your routine and repeating other attention-enhancing actions. "Tunnel vision" is a particularly useful visualization for both maintaining and

Chris Schenkel: "Voice" of PBA for 36 years on ABC, four-time Sportscaster of the Year, seen here interviewing Harry "Tiger" Smith

regaining focus when encountering the media. Being clear that your value as a person is not contingent on outside approval can greatly temper this type of stress.

· T H E   C O A C H I N G   C O R N E R ·

Q. I coach a high school team. Apart from bowling, I feel an obligation to support these kids in any way possible. If I suspect drug use or other serious problems, what should I do?

A. Three clinical conditions—substance abuse, depression, and eating disorders—create dysfunction and are potentially life-threatening. They each call for prompt professional intervention. Most immediately, assessment by a mental health professional is needed. Should any of these conditions be diagnosed, treatment by the appropriate specialist would follow. Treatment might well include involvement in a structured program.

If you suspect any of these conditions,* promptly communicate your concerns to parents. We also advise consulting with someone whose judgment you respect, such as a fellow

(continued)

---

* To help you recognize and better understand the conditions, we recommend several websites: kidshealth.org, NCAA.org/health-safety, and MayoClinic.com each covers a range of conditions; anred.com and espn.go.com/special/s/drug-sandsports/ provide athlete-related information specific to eating disorders and substance abuse respectively.

coach and/or a qualified professional. Maintain your student's confidentiality as much as possible.

Confidentiality is at the core of trusting relationships. If there's to be genuine openness about personal matters, it's essential. We recommend that a commitment be made to this principle right at the outset of coaching. At the same time, it's honest and appropriate to let the students know of specific circumstances where you'll be compelled to disclose information communicated to you. Circumstances concerning serious health issues (such as those discussed here) qualify in this regard.

As a respected and influential adult, coaches are parent figures to their students and can provide guidance through support and information. We encourage coaches to get to know their bowlers as people and to let them know the door is always open. This approach can enable coaches to learn a great deal about their athletes' lives. For the most part, this will be meaningful without indicating risk. If a red flag does go up, coaches can tactfully inquire about the issue so as to be as informed, supportive, and helpful as possible.

There are any number of ways to contact mental health professionals for the purposes of assessment and/or treatment. High school guidance counselors and other support personnel undoubtedly know of community resources. Colleges provide counseling centers for their students. State psychological associations and other professional organizations offer referrals to the public. Insurance companies have their own provider panels. There is unquestionably an advantage for athletes to work with someone who knows sports and can fully understand their experience. This is especially true if the key stressors are sports-related and if the impact is detrimental to sports participation. The USOC has a nationwide directory of qualified sport psychology specialists. University athletic departments may also know of sport psychologists in the area. The most important thing is finding a caring and competent professional regardless of discipline or background in sports.

Issues calling for professional attention are any which represent significant dysfunction in an athlete's life or pose risk to health or overall well-being. A coach is an ally to the family. Expressing concern to parents, while being sensitive to confidentiality issues, is part of that role.

Coaches can play a vital role in prevention. Measures with respect to substance abuse include communication about dangers and unethical behavior, establishing/enforcing team policy, teaching stress management skills, and readiness to spot personal difficulties in the athlete's life. For eating disorders, education is the key to prevention. Educational resources include videos, written matter, and game techniques. Bringing in a nutritionist is very useful. For both substance abuse and eating disorders, having a former team member speak

(continued)

```
•  T H E   C O A C H I N G   C O R N E R  •
               (continued)
```

about his or her experience can make a significant impact. Concerning depression, coaches can encourage/advise athletes to speak to an adult they trust if they're experiencing emotional distress. For these and all other life issues, developing a bond with your bowlers characterized by truthfulness and acceptance is centrally important.

By collaborating with other adults assisting an athlete, coaches can be an integral part of the recovery process. More important than conveying specific information is providing a sense of steadfast commitment. In a team situation, ensuring that the bowler continues to feel a part of the squad, even if there's a break in participation, is conducive to coming back personally and competitively.

As a coach, you're on the front lines of an athlete's personal development. You can do a lot.

A Special Challenge

Q I am a deeply spiritual person. I also care deeply about my bowling. Is there a way to relate these two parts of my life?

A We know many bowlers who speak of both the power and inner peace they derive from their spirituality. We're not referring to the religion bowlers sometimes get after 11 strikes, but to enduring beliefs. Genuine spirituality is transcendent, a tent over all you do. Whatever the exact nature of your outlook or faith, it no doubt provides strength and comfort and can help keep you centered when confronting challenges of all types in life, including those in sports. Spirituality offers perspective so that mundane, moment-to-moment events, including how you perform when bowling, neither weigh too heavily on nor, conversely, overinflate your ego. If you're religious,* knowing that your relationship to a higher power is constant (irrespective of pincount and other changeable aspects of living) can provide both security and support, promote emotional equilibrium, and keep self-esteem high. The actual experiencing of that special relationship or another core of spirituality can be positively energizing and bolster spirits.

Due to these reasons, your focus and effectiveness may very well be enhanced by spiritual awareness before, during, and after challenging endeavors. Spiritual preparation lends itself to your bowling at your

* The term "spirituality" can also apply to transcendent experience apart from religion.

best. Above all, by contributing to purpose and fulfillment, spirituality is conducive to your feeling enriched by the activities of life and celebrating them.

Exercises

1. Which challenges concerning others are relevant to you?

2. Indicate how each has impacted or could impact you in the future.

3. Review the recommended ways to cope with these relevant challenges. Following each review, place the suggested methods in one of these columns: "Currently Use," "Implement Immediately," and "Take Steps to Implement."

4. Cite the steps you'll take to implement those methods listed in the last column.

5. Use visualization to experience your meeting each significant challenge.

REVIEW

In Q & A format, strategies are offered for issues and situations concerning others (e.g., competitors). These are the challenges we address:

- Achieving success in match play
- Bowling in front of crowds
- Confronting family and friends about advice
- Stepping up to a higher level of competition
- Handling psych-out attempts
- Coping when other bowlers carry better
- Responding to the media
- Dealing with the lefty-righty controversy
- Becoming aware of problem signs in youth bowlers

A special challenge is that of integrating bowling and spirituality.

TEAM AND FAMILY

P A R T V

Tips for Athletes, Coaches, and Parents

Friendships, family, and teams all give me that same terrific feeling.
Lynda Barnes

18

KEYS TO SHARING INFORMATION IN TEAM PLAY

Team communication is a very, very vital thing.
Brad Angelo

There is nothing sweeter than a victory shared with teammates. Opportunity for team participation exists at every level of competition. Local leagues, high school and collegiate play, sponsored tournaments, and elite international events all require effective teamwork. Team triumphs result from attributes beyond the bowlers' individual skills. In the next two chapters, we identify the critical keys to team success. Information sharing and interpersonal support are essential to optimum team performance. Our discussion of these essentials emphasizes the qualities of communication and respect. This chapter covers the sharing of information. Support among team members is the topic of Chapter 19.

Importance of Information Sharing

Bowling involves an ongoing series of decisions that concern all facets of the game. Since accurate information is essential to productive decision making, obtaining it is an absolute priority. Team play introduces complexities to the competitive situation, yet presents opportunity for increased knowledge through communication. The saying "two heads are better than one" is generally true with the major exception being when the heads are butting. Being in sync with respect to information sharing is required for team success.

In the following pages, we consider several areas crucial to effectively conveying information on a team. These are awareness of, and respect for, individual preferences; a coach's overall role and collaboration with bowlers; and communication related to ball reaction.

Individual Preferences

Respect your teammates' individual preferences regarding communication of information. During competition, some bowlers will welcome input about lane play. This input could be in the form of an observation or a suggestion. However, other bowlers feel differently and don't want such input. Some teammates may also be open to feedback about a fact of their physical game (such as starting to rush). Take the time to learn what type of information each of your teammates may want from you and how they want it communicated. You might deduce this by listening to the feedback they give others or by their reactions to what you say to them. However, the surest way to learn is to directly ask. For example, one bowler may be receptive to a suggestion at any time while another may only want information when he or she requests it. On the flip side, some athletes aren't comfortable providing input during competition or will do so only if asked. Let your teammates and coach know your preferences with respect to receiving and providing information.

Such preferences concerning the communication of information can be taken into account in determining a lineup. Placing players who are comfortable giving and receiving information back-to-back is a factor adding to the team's strength and reducing the potential for conflict.

Ball Reaction/Lane Play

During competition it is vital that teammates communicate information about what they see happening regarding ball reaction on the lanes.

· T H E   C O A C H I N G   C O R N E R   ·

The Coach's Role

Coaches can help bring about optimum information sharing by emphasizing its importance and teaching the value of learning and respecting the communication preferences of teammates. Encouraging information exchanges in practice and in meetings and providing instructive feedback about the quality of communication are ways to enhance the informing process. Coaches also teach by example. Their own communication to bowlers provides a model of how to successfully convey information.

Helping athletes with decision making is most effective when coaches recognize certain preferences their athletes may have concerning collaboration.

Collaboration

We've found some distinct differences in bowlers as to how much they generally like to collaborate when making decisions.

- Some bowlers like to be presented with advice in a definite manner ("Now's the time to move two boards").

- Some bowlers like to be presented with recommendations in the form of suggestions ("You might consider a two board move").

- Some bowlers like to problem solve through the give and take of discussion (e.g., discussing possible equipment changes).

- Some bowlers like to have options presented with the decision left to them ("You could move five and three left or change to your ball that goes longer").

- Some bowlers like to have a challenge identified with the entire decision making process left to them ("There's a lot of carrydown—how do you want to handle it?").

For all these types of collaboration, the amount of detail involved in the communication is also a matter of individual preference as well as the constraints of time. In the heat of the battle, the time available for a decision making collaboration may be a few seconds. Limits of time aside, some bowlers are comfortable with options presented without explanation. Others may want to know the thinking behind the choices.

Here's a tip that might help you gauge a particular bowler's preference concerning information-sharing detail. We've found that bowlers often fit into one of two broad categories when it comes to responding to lane conditions:

- Some bowlers rely on what they experience as intuition or "gut" reaction. They go by "feel" and don't consciously analyze. Because these athletes tend to shoot first and ask

(continued)

```
•  T H E    C O A C H I N G    C O R N E R  •
```

The Coach's Role (continued)

(or answer!) questions later, we've nicknamed them "gunslingers."

- Some bowlers are analytic. They seek to gather facts and reach conclusions by careful reasoning. Their piecing together of clues to solve an on-lane mystery has earned them the label of "detectives."

- In general, "detective"-style bowlers will want more explanation than will "gunslinger" types. However, bowlers may not fit clearly into one category or another, and every athlete is unique. Therefore, we always recommend explicit discussion in order to identify preferences.

It is essential that coach and bowlers be synchronized in all aspects of information sharing. Part of the coach's responsibility is to discuss this with the athlete as well as learn from their interactions. In turn, it's an athlete's responsibility to the team to convey his or her preferences to coach and teammates.

This information can enable your team to keep one step ahead of its adversaries. For instance, in a five person team competition, after an individual throws a shot, there will be nine bowlers on that particular lane before he or she bowls again. Naturally, the quantity of balls thrown will factor into changing conditions. Receiving timely information may lead to a move (or other strategic shift) before throwing the next shot. If teammates are watching closely, they may be in a position to provide input leading to a critical adjustment.

In doubles and trios events, the number of balls rolled between your turns isn't as great. However, the value of information sharing remains the same. Since the changes may be more subtle and there's less opportunity to observe the ball reaction in others' play, prompt and accurate information sharing can certainly produce an advantage.

Reading lanes is no easy matter at any level of competition, even without the effects of carrydown and other change factors. Teammates may very well benefit from one another's insights at any given moment. In addition to within-game communication, teamwork calls for information sharing during the warm-up and between games, as well as between blocks. Team meetings after a block (including practice blocks) allow for

INFORMATION SHARING AT A WORLD CHAMPIONSHIP

The following exchanges are excerpted from a team meeting held by the Team USA men's squad during the opening days of the 1999 World Championships (FIQ World Tournament in Abu Dahbi, UAE*). Participants were Palmer Fallgren (head coach), John Gaines, Bill Hoffman, Tony Manna Jr., and Vernon Peterson.

FALLGREN: Okay, I've been hearing some good information about the lanes. Let's figure out what we'll do.

HOFFMAN: I think we should just briefly talk about our ball surface and what we try to see on the lane.

MANNA: I used that green ball. I thought the green ball was going to give me a different look. The Pit Boss. It gave me too much skid to be effective. But it really gave me a good picture of the lane.

HOFFMAN: When you got to tighter pairs, what was your move?

MANNA: Moved left and slowed down

HOFFMAN: What did you do with your hand then?

MANNA: Had a softer, slower hand action.

HOFFMAN: So, the less you hit the ball sometimes, the more it arcs.

MANNA: Yeah, I think the quieter everything is, the more roll into the pocket you get.

FALLGREN: That's what I think. You get more roll, which equates to smoother, stronger movement towards the pocket.

GAINES: None of us wants our ball to hook too strongly. You need to not make it hook that violently

FALLGREN: That's why Kelly**, if you look at her ball roll—she had very little axis tilt and less rotation—used a big, even rolling ball. That's not a big hooking ball. It's just right. It was nice to see a good match-up like that, with a Navy Quantum proactive.

HOFFMAN: Every bowler in the top 10 used a proactive ball. I think that's really important.

FALLGREN: You can't get a reactive ball to roll early enough because it simply won't get over what's there. Then if you really throw it good, you leave all kinds of corner pins because it just gets too much hook too late.

MANNA: On this pattern, where it needs to roll, I'm using a ball where the pin is closer to my axis. I first tried cover stock, but I either burned up too soon or went too long. That's why I went to this.

(continued)

INFORMATION SHARING AT A WORLD CHAMPIONSHIP (continued)

HOFFMAN: The other thing is, you always had room to the left of your target, period.

GAINES: I had tons of room left. I didn't even need to throw it good, just OK. I let the ball feed to the right. If it got there, it was OK. I didn't have to throw it there.

FALLGREN: And that's what happened a lot to some of the players that we're going to deal with—they're throwing it to the right instead of feeding it to the right.

GAINES: A lot of players are trying to make it hook.

HOFFMAN: It already exists, just let it happen.

FALLGREN: And Vernon, I've watched you bowl where the back ends get that reaction. Here it seems to be different. Lay back a little, put a little less on the shot.

GAINES: 'Cause they're not breaking down.

PETERSON: The nine o'clock squad never broke down.

HOFFMAN: When we get to trios and teams, we each want to have the ball we believe we can use for six straight games. Because if the lane isn't breaking down, why are we changing balls?

FALLGREN: This conversation makes sense because Kegel's*** doing the lanes the same. They've got eight or nine people down there making sure that's happening every time. And I don't see 600 new bowling balls coming out the next day because everyone is using one or two balls right now. So it's probably going to stay the same. There may be very little change.

HOFFMAN: Every one of the top scorers is throwing a ball that arcs and rolls very smoothly. Whatever ball does that for you is the one you want to use. Then if your ball does something weird, think about whatever adjustment you need, not quickly changing the ball.

FALLGREN: That's what Kelly and I did. When it got to where it was tighter, we went this way a little bit and when it hooked more, we went that way a little bit.

GAINES: Except the low end. I think the low end, you can move left.

MANNA: Lanes nine and ten didn't let you do that. Then when I moved to the bottom six, I bounced.

FALLGREN: We're all on the same page here.

* United Arab Emirates
** Kelly Kulick of Team USA, who earlier set a world record in the women's singles event.
*** The Kegel Company was conditioning the lanes for the World Championships.

a thorough analysis of what worked and what didn't work. This pooling of information enables your team to develop a strategy for the next block which takes into account the variables affecting ball reaction. A good example of information sharing is found in the transcript on the previous two pages.

In this productive dialogue, coach and athletes provide one another with essential information regarding lane play. Learning takes place through inquiry and response as well as the offering of observations and conclusions. The participants listen closely to what is said and provide relevant examples, statements of agreement and clarification, and added information. In this way, the topics of equipment, angles, releases, and lane breakdown are fully covered, enabling a consensus strategy to emerge. The input of each team member is welcomed and respected. The tone is "all business" (focused on performance), the style cooperative. The result is a game plan built on the solid base of shared experience and insight.

Nowhere is excellent communication better demonstrated than in the opening exchange. Hoffman asks Manna a series of questions about lane play to which he readily responds. This interaction leads them to conclude that a less active, slower release will create more ball roll and an arcing line to the pocket. Fallgren concurs and summarizes, "You get more roll, which equates to smoother, stronger movement towards the pocket." Building on that point, Gaines observes that attempting to aggressively hook the ball would be a mistake. In turn, this leads to consideration of equipment and other aspects of strategy. This sequence is a prime example of team members productively sharing information.

Exercises

1. Are you receptive to input from teammates about lane play?

2. Cite any other aspects of your game where you welcome input.

3. Would you like teammates to wait for you to ask or is it okay if information is presented spontaneously?

4. Have you let teammates know your preferences about receiving information? If not, then convey it.

5. Do you know your teammates' preferences? If not, seek to learn them.

6. If you're a coach, is there anything more you can do to bring about optimum information sharing?

7. If you're a coach, see if you can match a bowler to each of the seven bullets describing types of collaboration.

8. As a bowler, note which of these collaboration styles describes you. Does your coach know this? If not, then discuss it.

9. Rate how productively you and your teammates communicate information about ball reaction during competition: (circle one)

   Not at All   Minimally   Moderately   Extremely

10. Can you recall a discussion among teammates that illustrates effective information sharing?

11. Describe what elements of effective communicating can be added to improve the quality of information sharing on your team.

12. What can you do to help bring this about?

REVIEW

Optimum teamwork calls for effective information sharing. Adhering to principles of communication and respecting team members' individuality are centrally important.

Take into account the preferences of your teammates concerning what information they expect and how they wish to receive it. Similarly, let them know your preferences.

The coach plays a vital role in promoting effective information sharing. It is essential that coaches recognize their athletes' preferences concerning decision-making collaboration.

Providing input to teammates about ball reaction can be crucial for both the speed and appropriateness of adjustments to lane conditions. Information may be usefully shared in tournaments before and after as well as during play.

19

BUILDING A WINNER THROUGH TEAM SUPPORT

What first enabled my team to reach national championship caliber was an in-depth effort to apply the principles of teamwork learned by studying sport psychology.
Gordon Vadakin

There's a story about a wealthy man who was asked to name the most important aspect of business. He replied, "You know I own all the buildings downtown and I'm going to give them to you, but I'm taking the people with me. Now what do you have but a bunch of empty buildings?" The message from this successful businessman: Learn to deal with people and I'll show you a successful person. People are what make it all happen.

What's true for business also applies to the success of a bowling team. The acronym T.E.A.M., "Together Each Accomplishes More," only works if teammates are, in fact, working as a unit. Under the stress of competition, teams either pull together or are pulled apart. Chapters 18 and 19 each focus on a key to team cohesion. The last chapter identified how to improve information sharing. In this chapter, we discuss interpersonal support—how to strengthen relationships among team members.

Value of Interpersonal Support

Support among teammates—a positive attitude characterized by encouragement, trust, and good will—can be constructive in many ways. The benefits include

- Bolstering confidence;

- Enhancing self-worth;

- Providing inspiration, an emotional boost;

- Increasing motivation by giving a purpose beyond oneself;

- Producing shared responsibility, reducing pressure; and

- Decreasing isolation and other stress.

Feeling supported by teammates, the sense of acceptance and bonding, is comparable to being part of a family. The feelings of belonging and respect can help you cope with the stresses of competition and perform to your potential.

Team USA huddles

Here are three recommendations for increasing interpersonal support on a team: improve communication skills, enhance respect for individual differences, and engage in team actions. Each will be examined in turn.

After a discussion of coaching factors, the chapter concludes with an overview of what makes a good teammate and a consideration of leadership.

Communication Skills

Maintaining harmonious relationships on teams (and elsewhere) calls for good listening skills and the ability to resolve conflicts.

Develop Your Capacity to Listen

If you want to be a good teammate, be a good listener. The ability to genuinely listen is essential to supportive social contact. Sustained concentration, intent to learn, and a non-defensive attitude are crucial to being truly receptive to what others say.

Read the following list of characteristics, which commonly interfere with effective listening. To what degree do they characterize your style? In order to improve your listening skills, strive to develop consistent interest, attention, and openness when you communicate.

LISTENING LIMITATIONS AND SOLUTIONS[33]

1. You listen only to those parts of a message that you easily understand.
   Solution: Try to grasp all aspects of a communication.

2. You often miss the main point because you're focusing on details or specific facts.
   Solution: Look for the essential meaning in a message.

3. You concentrate more on the speaker's appearance/delivery than on the message itself.
   Solution: Attend to the content of the message rather than the messenger.

4. You become readily distracted (e.g., by common sounds).
   Solution: Strive to maintain attention and immediately refocus if distracted.

5. You pretend to give the speaker full attention when your thoughts are elsewhere.
   Solution: Commit yourself to full focus on the speaker's words. Consider interacting (e.g., ask questions) to increase your engagement. If necessary and possible, continue at another time.

6. When a topic bores you or causes discomfort, you change the subject.
   Solution: Instead of readily avoiding an unexciting or unpleasant topic, seek to learn something.

7. You tend to quickly disagree with what's said and then focus attention on developing your arguments.
   Solution: Identify areas of agreement as well as disagreement and attempt to dialogue instead of debate.

8. If a person starts to present a problem, you almost immediately shift your concentration to advice you can offer.
   Solution: Listen to a complete statement of the problem and be fully empathic before possibly offering advice.

9. You instantly start defending yourself if a person states something which you take as criticism.
   Solution: Hear the whole message, non-defensively consider any truth in it, and strive to benefit from the information.

10. You act supportive, but in fact you're not genuinely involved.
    Solution: Be genuinely supportive.

Be Empathic

At the heart of supportive relationships is the quality of empathy. It is the essence of effective listening. A classic description of empathy was provided by the renowned psychologist, Carl Rogers: to actively see another person's way of looking at the world, including emotional reactions, as if one were the person. On a team, empathy builds trust between teammates and between coach and athletes. It also has been identified as a condition which facilitates personal growth.

An empathic attitude can be expressed by numerous behaviors. Some of these are

- Consistent eye contact;

- Nodding your head to convey understanding;

- Leaning in towards the speaker;

- Facial expressions indicating involvement and comprehension;

- Rephrasing what's been said to reflect your grasp;

- Statements of agreement, support, and sympathy, if called for;

- Parallel examples from your own life; and

- Questions for clarification or related information.

External behaviors like the ones just listed convey empathy. Yet true empathy is more than an outward sign—it is a way of experiencing another. Consequently, when teammates speak to you, strive to genuinely "be there" for them. This means paying strict attention and seeking to grasp the meaning their experience has for them based on their way of viewing things. Try to suspend all judgment. In effect, enter the world of your teammate and know that person from the inside out.

Here's an exercise for increasing the ability of team members to convey empathy while actively building trust and acceptance among the entire team:

1. *As an introduction, the first three paragraphs above are read or paraphrased.*

2. *Team members pair off and sit facing one another.*

3. *One athlete in each pair speaks for a designated amount of time (typically, four or five minutes) about something meaningful in his or her life. The content can relate to bowling or any other area so long as it doesn't concern conflict with the teammate. The other athlete listens in a manner consistent with the introduction. Note that giving advice is not part of the exercise.*

4. *Then, for a brief amount of time (typically one or two minutes), the speaker provides constructive feedback to the listener about the empathic quality of the listening. This should address the level to which the listener was "tuned-in," note particular actions which conveyed this, and describe any moments when the listener didn't seem in touch with the speaker's experience. It is essential that this feedback be nonjudgmental and reflect appreciation for the effort and attention given by the listener.*

5. *The speaker/listener roles are reversed for each pair and steps three and four are repeated.*

6. *Each athlete pairs off with another teammate and goes through the process again (steps two through five).*

7. *This procedure is repeated until all team members have been paired, if time allows.*

8. *In a group discussion, the team processes their experience. Athletes can tell what it felt like to be in both roles and how their own actions, comfort level, mood, attitude towards teammates, and self-regard may have evolved during the exercise. The key consideration is what each person learned about himself or herself.*

We've found that teams enjoy this exercise immensely. In fact, once the athletes start talking to one another, they don't want to stop! With each new pairing, teammates usually grow more and more comfortable. By the end of the exercise, team members commonly report feeling more confident about their listening skills, supported and validated in their experience, and closer to teammates. For some, this experience is profound and opens the door to more satisfying communication in their lives generally.

Participation from start to finish must be voluntary. Instructions need to make this clear and allow anyone to discontinue should that individual feel uncomfortable.

This exercise can be periodically repeated to further build empathic skills and team relationships.

Be Expressive

Being available to teammates as an empathic listener is an effective way

Team Netherlands celebrates following 1995 FIQ title match with Team Sweden

to contribute to support building. Expressing yourself to an empathic teammate can be an equally important means of contributing to cohesion.

Honest, open expression of your thoughts and feelings is the necessary counterpart to empathic listening. As in the empathy exercise (which is also expressiveness training), rapport and support are boosted when an empathic teammate is presented with a personally meaningful communication. Disclosing genuine feelings to a teammate with good listening skills can enable you to feel understood and accepted. In turn, the listening teammate will feel trusted and valued. Typically this results in both of you feeling good about yourselves and closer as teammates.

When one human being is genuinely open with another, it tends to free the other to also be open. This doesn't happen immediately every time; however, it's a phenomenon very worth noting because of its team-wide implications. By honestly letting teammates know you, they're more likely to allow you into their world. The ripple effect can ultimately help make an entire team personally tighter and mentally tougher.

In describing this straightforward approach to communication, we have in mind predominantly situations other than those where a direct conflict between teammates is addressed. When there is such a conflict, effective communication calls for a more specific strategy, albeit one which still involves the spirit and principles already discussed. We will now consider how you can cope with potentially divisive circumstances.

Learn to Confront Constructively

Some instances of conflict are to be expected in any social system, whether it involves co-workers, friends, family, or teammates. A team's cohesion and performance can be significantly affected by how such situations are handled.

Team members may clash over bowling circumstances (such as behavior on the lanes) or non-bowling ones (e.g., critical comments made to another person). People are not always on the same page in terms of goals, reactions, courtesy, expectations, and, overall, how they perceive things. That's human nature. The stress of competition unquestionably contributes to the potential for conflict. Feelings are easily hurt and tension can often develop. This is true even on a team that generally has good cohesion. The ability to minimize the duration and intensity of conflict is instrumental to team success.

We recommend a method of constructively confronting others, which readily reduces or resolves most conflicts. This is so important that Team USA practices its application during our training camp week at the Olympic Training Center. As you'll see, the process involves a collaboration between teammates. Here's how it works:

The process of *constructive confrontation* involves a step-by-step dialogue between the person who confronts and the one who is confronted. In the directions that follow, the confronting person is "Bowler A," the person confronted is "Bowler B."

STEP 1

Bowler A: Request time to talk and state your purpose in positive terms.

Bowler B: Indicate willingness to talk and state your own positive goal.

STEP 2

Bowler A: Non-provocatively express how you genuinely feel in response to a specific situation and why.

Bowler B: Respond to the other person's distress/concern and offer explanation/support/validation.

STEP 3

Bowler A: Specify any changes you would like to occur and, if necessary, follow-up actions.

Bowler B: Give the other's request serious consideration and explain your reasoning.

STEP 4

> Bowler A: Acknowledge constructive responses.
>
> Bowler B: Acknowledge the effort to communicate.

STEP 5

> Bowler B: Make any requests of your own.
>
> Bowler A: Respond to any requests made to you.

The following example (fictional) illustrates how this method might actually be put into practice:

Situation: Tim is upset. He was told by a teammate that another team member, Carl, was making disparaging comments about him, including remarks concerning his weight.

STEP 1

> Tim: Carl, I'd like to find some time when we can talk. Something's bothering me and I want us to discuss it, so we can be on the same page. That would be best for the team and best for us, too.
>
> Carl: That's fine. Now's as good a time as any. I want to hear what you have to say. I have some things on my mind also. It'll be best all around if we deal with it.

STEP 2

> Tim: I heard from someone I trust that you've been putting me down to guys on the team. Saying things about my weight and other stuff. I can't understand it. I thought we got along well and I think I've been a good teammate to you. I feel angry, but mostly shocked. I feel hurt. It feels like you betrayed me.
>
> Carl: I didn't mean to hurt you, but I've been upset myself. In fact, it really ticks me off that you're late to practice. If we're going to win, we've all got to be here. It also bothered me a lot last week when you gave me this look when I missed that 10-pin in the ninth. I felt bad enough.

STEP 3

Tim: Now this whole thing makes more sense. It's still painful to think about what happened, but I understand why you've been upset. We could talk about that, but in the future come to me directly if there's something you don't like. We can deal with it man to man.

Carl: That's cool. I'll do that. It's got to go both ways though.

STEP 4

Tim: That's fair. I feel good about your listening and being honest with me here.

Carl: I'm glad you wanted to talk. It gave us a chance to deal with things so we can be in a good place.

STEP 5

Carl: My turn. I'd like you to be on time for practice and I could do without any weird look if I ever happen to blow another 10-pin.

Tim: The problem is my job doesn't let me out when I'd like. Coach knows this, but I guess I should've explained it to the team. I'll speak to my boss again to see if I can get out earlier. Maybe make up the time. You're right—it's important we're all at practice. About that 10-pin. No problem because I'm sure you won't miss another. But you've got to know that look wasn't meant to knock you. You're usually so steady, I was just kind of shocked.

Carl: That's good to know, I feel better about it. One other thing. I mean this in a constructive way. You're a great bowler but you'd be even better if you were in better condition.

Tim: You're right. That's something I need to do. I only wish you'd have told me up front.

Carl: I apologize for that. Hey, some of us work out together. You could join us.

Tim: I'd like to. I'll try and schedule it.

Carl: Later.

Tim: On the lanes.

As you can see, the effectiveness of this approach calls for a willingness to cooperate in the process. Being upset with teammates can lead to withdrawal or aggressiveness. Instead of such defensiveness and hostility, constructive confrontation involves mutual disclosure of vulnerability, perceptions, and needs. Motivation to engage in this very different way of relating comes from commitment to the team as well as belief in the conflict-resolving effect.

Steps 1 through 5 provide a framework for resolving conflict. The order of the steps is secondary in importance to the type of personal information which is ultimately shared and the constructive spirit of the dialogue. Clearly, the communication may be considerably longer and involve multiple conversations.

Relationships will be strengthened if conflicts are dealt with in a straightforward and constructive manner. Not only are issues resolved, but respect for teammates is increased if each experiences the other as honest, understanding, and responsive. Even if differences remain, so long as there is integrity in the style of confrontation, trust and support are likely to increase.

Constructive confrontation can be effective in all team relationships, including those involving coaches. While a coach must assert authority appropriate to each situation, the basic principles of this interactive approach to conflict resolution remain the same for athletes and coaches alike.

Practicing Confrontation. At our training camps, athletes practice constructive confrontation by role playing in various situations involving conflict. Five hypothetical scenarios are listed below.

SITUATION 1: Athlete Confronts Athlete

During league competition, a player is being noisy and disruptive. (Alternate scenario: A bowler isn't following the one lane courtesy rule.)

SITUATION 2: Athlete Confronts Athlete

Without calling, someone on your league team doesn't show up one evening. This prevents you from getting a substitute and leads to a penalty.

SITUATION 3: Athlete Confronts Athlete

At a competition, your roommate has been coming in late and waking you as he or she gets ready for bed. You've also been distracted by this teammate's outbursts on the lanes at moments of frustration and sulking at other times.

SITUATION 4: Athlete Confronts Coach

During a team meeting, your coach announces the lineup for the next day. You learn you won't be in that lineup. This is a shock since you felt you were bowling well. You've also been upset with the relatively limited amount of time the coach has spent observing you bowl and providing feedback throughout the event. It seems to you that your teammates, especially one player, have been receiving more coaching.

SITUATION 5: Coach Confronts Athlete

You're concerned about the behavior and attitude of a bowler. Prior to the competition, the athlete didn't practice to the extent you expected despite pledging to do so. At this event, he or she hasn't adhered to the team dress code. The bowler hasn't responded to your recommendations during matches and, at times, seems irritated when you offer them. All the above represent change from behavior at past events.

For each situation, teammates pair off and choose roles. There is a ten minute dialogue following the guidelines for constructive confrontation. Each team member then gives his or her partner feedback about the effectiveness of the confrontation (typically, two to three minutes). This is followed by a discussion involving the whole team. We next proceed to

Duos from Thailand, Finland, and Singapore receive gold, silver, and bronze medals at 13th World Championships

another situation and the process is repeated. For the different situations, pairings may remain the same although switching pairs adds freshness to the exercise and can make the scenarios seem more real since a new person is playing a new role.

In a variation of this exercise, partners dialogue and then switch roles before moving to the next situation. Placing yourself in another's shoes helps increase the ability to understand a frame of reference different from your own.

These training exercises are held in one room with the full team present. For actual situations, find a setting which guarantees privacy. Meeting just before or after practice often conveniently serves this purpose for coaches and athletes.

Managing Conflict: Three Keys

We call your attention to three aspects of communication that can limit conflict and increase cooperation.

1. Be direct and immediate. Deal directly with a team-mate if there's a conflict. Complaining to others may place them in an awkward position, create secrecy and alliances, sow seeds of dissension, and further compli-cate matters if the teammate in question learns about it. Instead, speak to the person with whom there's an issue as soon as possible. Hurt feelings tend to linger and may lead to a rift. If you constructively confront, the air can be cleared and the relationship turned in a positive direction. However, it's quite okay to con-sult someone you trust if you're seeking feedback and suggestions about how to handle a situation. If you're doing that, it's a good idea to make it clear that the con-versation is confidential. Should a teammate complain to you about another team member (coach included), offer whatever feedback might be helpful and, above all, encourage the teammate to deal directly with that person.

2. Seek a facilitator if needed. If attempts to dialogue don't resolve a significant conflict, consider enlisting an objective third party to facilitate. This may be a trusted teammate, assuming the person is comfort-able in that role. Part of a coach's responsibility is to assist in this way if called upon and sometimes to

volunteer or even step in if there's an obvious need. Sport psychologists are trained to fulfill this function. Facilitating calls for even-handedness, honesty, empathy for both parties, a capacity to clarify issues, and an ability to identify common ground. A primary goal of facilitating in a dispute between teammates is guiding them through the process of constructive confrontation. A coach is positioned to make clear what's in the team's best interest in the way of a resolution.

3. <u>Assert yourself.</u> We're referring to the willingness to express what you want from another. Constructively confronting a teammate when there's a conflict is one way of doing this. Asking and declining are other essential ways of being genuine about your needs.

   If there's good will between teammates, making a request should be non-stressful. Whether it's seeking advice about equipment or a ride to the bowl, if you ask for what you want forthrightly and non-demandingly, the other person can then make a good faith effort to meet your request. Hopefully, you'll get the response you're seeking. But remember, you can feel good about being genuine whether or not your request is met.

   Saying "no" to someone is often dreaded and avoided. Anxiety about rejection, angering the person, or feeling guilty are some reasons for the reluctance. A highly effective way of reducing the other person's disappointment is to sandwich the "no" around positive remarks. In a sense, your response becomes a yes-no-yes. For example, if a teammate asks to borrow money and you're really not in a position to lend that day, you might say, "No problem, but I'm short today, any other day would be fine." Being straightforward is essential. If you never lend money, don't pretend otherwise. You could say, "Please don't take this personally, but I never lend money, to anyone. I trust you, it's just my policy." (By the way, the same "positive book-ending" approach also works to make criticism more palatable: "Your swing and footwork look great. I think you'd get more control, though, by slowing everything down. That should be an easy adjustment for you.")

No matter how tactful you are, there will be times that the other person reacts defensively when you say "no." At such moments, it's important to be clear that you're entitled to express yourself, and that it's constructive to be honest in a relationship. Remember, your worth as a person does not depend on others' reactions. Remind yourself that you did your best. You might also consider constructively confronting the teammate concerning his or her response.

Respecting Individual Differences

While people naturally have characteristics in common, everyone is ultimately unique. Being able to understand and accept differences is an interpersonal skill necessary for cohesion in any social unit and is a prime ingredient for team unity.

First and foremost, respect for differences means nondiscrimination in attitude, as well as in behavior, with regard to ethnic background, religious persuasion, sexual orientation, gender, and age. It is essential that a coach make this clear and team rules spell it out. Any issues that emerge need to be addressed with sensitivity and resoluteness. There is room on a team for striving to open mind and heart, but not for unyielding intolerance.

Notwithstanding issues of prejudice that may arise, the day-to-day challenges for most team members will be to accept personality traits in others that differ from their own. In fact, fundamental to being a good teammate (in league and all other contexts) is accepting differences. This does not mean liking everyone equally. It does mean providing the same support you expect to be given. It means figuring out how to best deal with team members based on understanding who they are as individuals. Again, it is a coach's job to make clear what constitutes being a good teammate and emphasizing that various differences in attitude and behavior outside of that (e.g., whether someone is talkative or quiet, adventurous or cautious) are not valid grounds for non-acceptance.

MBTI® Personality Inventory: An Aid to Team Building *

* The MBTI® theory, preferences, and general biases are modified and reproduced by special permission of the Publisher, CPP, Inc., Mountain View, CA 94043 from *Introduction To Type®* 6th Edition by Isabel Briggs Myers. Copyright 1985 by Peter B. Myers and Katharine D. Myers. All rights reserved. Further reproduction is prohibited without the Publisher's written consent. Myers-Briggs Type Indicator, MBTI, Myers-Briggs, and Introduction to Type are trademarks or registered trademarks of the Myers-Briggs Type Indicator Trust in the United States and other countries. The consideration of team implications and applications is original.

In order to increase understanding and acceptance of personality differences, we find the model provided by the Myers-Briggs Type Indicator® (MBTI®) personality inventory very helpful. This questionnaire is the most widely used device for understanding normal personality differences. The MBTI® instrument has many applications. Our use is for increasing appreciation of individual differences as part of team building.

The MBTI® instrument distinguishes between people with respect to

1. Where they prefer to focus their attention and get energy;

2. The way they prefer to take in information;

3. The way they prefer to make decisions; and

4. How they orient themselves to the external world.

According to the theory behind this device, we all have a natural preference for one of two opposites on each of the four areas above (e.g., for focusing attention, the opposites are "Introversion" and "Extraversion"). At different times, you use both preferences but not both at once and not with equal confidence (in most instances). Generally speaking, you perform best as well as feeling your most energetic, natural, and competent when using your preferred methods.

These preferences combined lead to different kinds of people having behaviors, skills, and attitudes that differ. Each combination, or "type," has particular strengths and also probable limitations. There are no right or wrong preferences or types.

We will now cite characteristics for each pole on each of the four personality areas ("dichotomies") tapped by the MBTI® instrument. The purpose is to increase your awareness of how people differ and to consider the implications on a team level. For each preference, there exists a tendency towards a particular bias about the opposite preference. As you read the descriptions, consider which pole of the dichotomy you're closest to and also consider the ways you regard those who are closest to the other pole. In particular, picture how the differing personality types might behave in a team context and identify particular teammates if you can. This will enable you to better understand and accept teammates.

Bear in mind that the common meanings of some terms don't apply here. Preferring Extraversion doesn't mean that a person is talkative. Preferring Introversion doesn't mean that a person is shy or inhibited. A preference for Feeling doesn't mean that the person is emotional, nor does a preference for Judging or Perceiving mean that an individual is judgmental or perceptive, respectively.

MBTI® PREFERENCES

I. <u>Focusing Attention and Getting Energy</u>

<u>EXTRAVERSION:</u> People who prefer Extraversion like to focus on the outer world of people and activity. They direct their energy and attention outward and receive energy from interacting with people and from taking action.

These characteristics are associated with people preferring Extraversion:

- Attuned to external environment
- Prefer to communicate by talking
- Work out ideas by talking them through
- Learn best through doing or discussing
- Have broad interests
- Sociable and expressive
- Readily take initiative in work and relationships

<u>INTROVERSION:</u> People who prefer Introversion like to focus on their own inner world of ideas and experiences. They direct their energy and attention inward and receive energy from reflecting on their thoughts, memories, and feelings.

These characteristics are associated with people preferring Introversion:

- Drawn to their inner world
- Prefer to communicate in writing
- Work out ideas by reflecting on them
- Learn best by reflection, mental "practice"
- Focus in depth on their interests
- Private and contained
- Take initiative when the situation or issue is very important to them

Which of these two preferences do you think you have when bowling? How about at work? At home?

In a team setting, one way athletes might differ concerns social contact after a match. Whereas Extraverted types would tend to seek out teammates and talk about matters,

Introverted types might well prefer to be on their own and think about things themselves. Under these circumstances, Extraverted athletes might believe the Introverted teammates don't like them, don't want to process the outcome or share information, and don't care about the team. This wouldn't be at all the reality. Personal caring, the desire to process performance, and team commitment are the same for Introverted athletes. Only the style differs. Introverted athletes, on the other hand, might perceive their Extraverted teammates as pushy, impulsive, and shallow. Instead, the Extraverted types are simply being spontaneous and earnest in expressing their desire to have team members process the match together.

In general, Extraverted types might believe Introverted types are uninterested or withholding information when they are processing internally. Introverted types might think Extraverted types are uncertain, indecisive, or inconsistent when they are processing decisions out loud.

II. Taking in Information

SENSING: People who prefer Sensing like to take in information that is real and tangible— what is actually happening. They are observant about the specifics of what is going on around them and are especially attuned to practical realities.

These characteristics are associated with people who prefer Sensing:

- Oriented to present realities
- Factual and concrete
- Focus on what is real and actual
- Observe and remember specifics
- Build carefully and thoroughly toward conclusions
- Understand ideas and theories through practical applications
- Trust experience

INTUITION: People who prefer Intuition like to take in information by seeing the big picture, focusing on the relationships and connections between facts. They want to grasp patterns and are especially attuned to seeing new possibilities.

These characteristics are associated with people preferring Intuition:

- Oriented to future possibilities
- Imaginative and verbally creative
- Focus on the patterns and meanings in data
- Remember specifics when they relate to a pattern
- Move quickly to conclusions, follow hunches

- Want to clarify ideas and theories before putting them into practice

- Trust inspiration

Which of these two preferences do you think you have when bowling? When you're working? When home?

In a team setting, athletes who prefer Sensing might adapt strategy slowly based on the information as it comes in. Intuitive types would likely see an overall pattern faster and more readily try a creative approach. Consequently, Intuitive teammates might think Sensing teammates are underreacting when, in fact, they are being methodical. From the perspective of Sensing athletes, their Intuition-preferring teammates could seem illogical and reacting too fast. Instead, they are trusting the "big picture" they see and their hunches.

In general, a common bias that those with a Sensing preference may have towards those with a preference for Intuition is thinking that the latter type are changing topics or avoiding, whereas they are actually generating possibilities. Conversely, individuals preferring Intuition might regard Sensing types as unimaginative when they are raising realistic, practical concerns.

III. Making Decisions

THINKING: People who prefer to use Thinking in decision making like to look at the logical consequences of a choice or action. They want to mentally remove themselves from a situation to examine the pros and cons objectively. They are energized by critiquing and analyzing to identify what's wrong with something so they can solve the problem. Their goal is to find a standard or principle that will apply in all similar situations.

These characteristics are associated with people who prefer Thinking:

- Analytical

- Use cause-and-effect reasoning

- Solve problems with logic

- Strive for an objective standard of truth

- Reasonable

- Can be "tough-minded"

- Fair, want everyone treated equally

FEELING: People who prefer to use Feeling in decision making like to consider what is important to them and to others involved. They mentally place themselves into the situation to identify with everyone so they can make decisions based on their values about honoring people. They are energized by appreciating and supporting others and look for qualities to praise. Their goal is to create harmony and treat each person as a unique individual.

These characteristics are associated with people who prefer Feeling:

- Empathetic
- Guided by personal values
- Assess impacts of decisions on people
- Strive for harmony and positive interactions
- Compassionate
- May appear "tenderhearted"
- Fair, want everyone treated as an individual

Which of these two preferences do you think you have when bowling? At work? At home?

In a team setting, Thinking teammates might provide critical feedback in a blunt way, even in front of others, without considering how that teammate may feel. Feeling teammates tend to carefully give input, weighing the impact on the other person. Feeling team members might believe that the Thinking teammates don't care about them, whereas they're actually trying to be helpful in their accustomed style. In contrast, Thinking athletes could regard Feeling teammates as "tip toeing" on certain matters when those teammates are just trying to maintain team cohesion.

In general, Thinking types might believe Feeling types are over-personalizing when they focus on applying their values. Feeling types could believe Thinking types are harsh and cold when they take a detached problem-solving approach.

IV. Dealing with the Outer World

JUDGING: People who prefer to use their Judging process in the outer world like to live in a planned, orderly way, seeking to regulate and manage their lives. They want to make decisions, come to closure, and move on. Their lives tend to be structured and organized, and they like to have things settled. Sticking to a plan and schedule is very important to them, and they are energized by getting things done.

These characteristics are associated with people who prefer Judging:

- Scheduled
- Organize their lives
- Systematic
- Methodical
- Make short- and long-term plans
- Like to have things decided
- Try to avoid last-minute stresses

PERCEIVING: People who prefer to use their Perceiving process in the outer world like to live in a flexible, spontaneous way, seeking to experience and understand life, rather than control it. Detailed plans and final decisions feel confining to them; they prefer to stay open to new information and last-minute options. They are energized by their resourcefulness in adapting to the demands of the moment.

These characteristics are associated with people who prefer Perceiving:

- Spontaneous

- Flexible

- Casual

- Open-ended

- Adapt, change course

- Like things loose and open to change

- Feel energized by last-minute pressures

Which of the two preferences do you think you have when bowling? When working? When home?

In a team setting, Judging teammates might well prefer an exact schedule of team activities at a competition, whereas Perceiving team members would likely want considerably more flexibility in how time is spent. As a result, Judging team members might see the Perceiving teammates as not taking the event seriously enough, whereas the Perceiving athletes are more comfortable and tend to function best when structure is open-ended. On the other hand, Perceiving team members could feel stifled by Judging teammates when these Judging athletes seek to minimize the stress caused by uncertainty.

In general, those with a Judging preference might regard those with a Perceiving preference as unreliable or procrastinating when, in fact, they are attempting to keep options open. Perceiving persons could very well believe Judging persons are rigid and controlling when what they are being is structured and scheduling.

How to Use the MBTI® Model for Understanding Individual Differences. We can suggest several ways for a team to make use of the concepts just described:

> 1. *Team members simply read the descriptions of types and, as previously recommended, consider the following: Which characteristics apply to them? Which apply to their teammates? How are such characteristics displayed during practice, during competition, and elsewhere? Have they misread or undervalued teammates because of these normal personality differences?*

2. These principles are discussed in a team meeting. This would also be an excellent opportunity for the coach to speak about respect for individual differences in general.

3. Based on the descriptions of personality preferences or on actual results from completing the questionnaire—available to qualified personnel*—team members can cluster into groups representing opposite poles, beginning with focus of attention (Extraverted types and Introverted types). Discussion of the implications of their differences can take place while clustered in this way. Next, the team can cluster into two groups concerning how they take in information and discuss the implications. This process of clustering and re-clustering continues until all four areas are covered. This exercise allows teammates to directly, even dramatically, see how they're both similar and different from others on the team; enables them to grasp the complexity of personality; and makes apparent the team's diversity. Teams seem to enjoy this exercise and become tighter as a unit.

Administration and interpretation of the questionnaire by a sport psychologist meeting with the team would be the best way to derive benefit from the MBTI® instrument. If that's not feasible, we advise the team's coach to consult a sport psychologist or other qualified professional in advance of any exercise or meeting.

The MBTI® personality inventory is a finely tuned instrument and permits more exact and detailed descriptions of individuals based on their combination of preferences. (Group exercises can be designed for these exact descriptions.) This detailed level of interpretation requires a qualified trainer. We've simply suggested several straightforward ways of increasing self-understanding, appreciating individual differences, and avoiding negative stereotyping.

---

* For more than 50 years, the Myers-Briggs Type Indicator® (MBTI®) personality inventory has helped millions of people throughout the world gain a deeper understanding of themselves by giving them a powerful tool for improving how they communicate, learn, and work with others. For more information on the MBTI® instrument, contact: CPP, Inc., 1055 Joaquin Road, Suite 200, Mountain View, CA 94043, 800-624-1765, www.cpp.com.

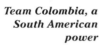

Team Colombia, a South American power

Differences as a Strength

It's much easier to accept individual differences if you view them as potentially adding to your team's strength. Not only does individuality make life generally, and a "clubhouse" in particular, more stimulating and potentially looser, diversity means there is a range of resources to draw upon. The key is to accommodate and cooperate so that the most constructive aspects of each team member can be used for the full team's benefit. As an example, the creativity and flexibility of some athletes may be most valuable in certain situations, while the highly disciplined, organized approach of other athletes proves most useful at other times. In this way, personalities complement one another and the whole emerges stronger than individuals apart.

Individuality in Routine and Total Game

Teammates' routines prior to, during, and following competition differ in ways both large and small. This is understandable, since routines may consist of many elements and are tailored to the individual. Individuality extends from the way bowlers train to the way outcomes are processed. In fact, the entire array of mental game techniques comprises a package unique to each bowler. Support your teammates by respecting their routines and other aspects of performance and style which may differ from you own. In turn, be sure teammates are sufficiently aware of your routines so that they may be respected.

Team Actions

A variety of actions undertaken by the whole team can contribute to a sense of cohesion. Four examples are practice drills, team meetings, bonding sessions, and group activities.

Practice Drills

In addition to developing specific competition skills, practice drills can promote communication and camaraderie. Two drills we use with Team USA to accomplish these aims are found on the following page:

PRACTICE DRILLS

DRILL 1

In team practice sessions, it is important to work on skills. Drills can help make these sessions more focused. For instance, each day do a 7 - 10 workout. Shoot ten 10-pin shots and ten 7-pin shots off a full rack and record progress. Doing this drill identifies who on the team is strong in spare shooting and who is not. It encourages conversation about different techniques for spare shooting. The interest stimulated is so great that the spare shooting often goes beyond the scheduled ten shots just to test new ideas. This is great stuff for team building. Following the skill drill, it is important that players get the opportunity to work on their techniques in order to develop stronger, more versatile games. When players spend time working on adjustments on the lane, such as angles, ball selection, speed, release, and loft, it encourages conversation. Those with more experience can help newer team members and often a newer player brings in fresh insight and an enthusiasm that's inspiring.

DRILL 2

Spice up practice with a game allowing for a doubles competition using a different scoring system. The Swedish team introduced this merciless but fun scoring to us and it's ideal for starting conversation. Here are the rules:

	Elite	Average	Beginner
Pocket and Strike	2 points	3 points	4 points
Pocket and Spare	1 point	2 points	3 points
Out of Pocket and Strike or Spare	0 points	1 point	2 points
Pocket and Missed Spare	-1 point	0 points	1 point
Out of Pocket and Missed Spare	-2 points	-1 point	0 points
Missed Single Pin Spare	-3 points	-2 points	-1 point

A score in the double digits is a good one. Twenty is a perfect score for ten frames. Because the scoring is so unusual and challenging, it adds a twist that typically stimulates interest and talking. It also promotes skill development by focusing on the process of getting to the pocket and converting spares.

Team Meetings

Team meetings can be extremely valuable to a team's overall development and immediate match readiness. The information-sharing function of a meeting was illustrated in the transcript presented in the last chapter. Team meetings represent an opportunity to both learn and to bond. Pooling information, setting team goals, discussing communication expectations, and offering supportive comments are ways that cohesion can be strengthened. These four processes are among the areas we suggest as possible topics to be covered in a meeting (see opposite page). A coach or other team leader can bear these in mind when planning a productive team session.

Conflicts that involve and impact the entire team can be addressed; for example, if there's an issue regarding attendance at practice, attitude during competition, or veterans' treatment of younger players. Other conflicts are best handled on a private basis.

Bonding Sessions

During the annual team USA training camp, a team-bonding meeting is held. Athletes and coaches alike talk from the heart about their experience in the camp, in competition, and in life generally. Dreams and disappointments, emotional highs and lows concerning relationships and bowling careers are shared. At times, virtually all in the room are in tears as someone talks about a searing life experience, such as the loss of a loved one.

As elite athletes who have all dedicated themselves and endured substantial sacrifices to make Team USA, there is a commonality of experience. Yet every team member's path to this point is unique and everybody tells their story in a way that's fully their own. Through honesty, empathy, and encouragement, the meeting nurtures an evolving sense of team family and cohesiveness. At the end, we form a circle and say to one another, "I'm your teammate and I'm here for you no matter what." These sessions contribute to a bond that holds firm in the fire of competition.

Verbal participation in these meetings is completely voluntary. People express themselves when they feel ready.

For a meeting of this type to be successful, there needs to be an experienced leader who is comfortable facilitating group process. The leader sets the tone and provides guidance during any moments of distraction or conflict.

· T H E   C O A C H I N G   C O R N E R ·

Coaching Tips for Team Meetings

Regardless of which topics are covered (a meeting just prior to a match will be more focused in its content than a general team meeting at some other time), encouraging input from all team members is key to making the meeting productive. Speak concisely with energy and convey resolve.

- Present essential information. Lineups, pre-event practice schedules, equipment considerations, and lane conditions are obvious areas to be covered.

- Review what took place in a completed match and devise a strategy based on pooled information.

- Call for teamwork. This encompasses communication of technical information and personal support.

- Cite/discuss team goals. Recall that focusing on the performance process (rather than outcome) is generally most effective, since this involves something the athlete can control.

- Place an upcoming event in the context of growth. This involves noting its significance in terms of team goals as well as individual improvement.

- Voice the expectation of an all-out effort. This is part of instilling the determination essential to championship performance.

- Convey optimism, loyalty, and pride. A coach's confidence, commitment, and valuing mean a great deal.

- Provide praise. Applaud hard work, attitude, and progress as well as successful execution.

- Expand the athlete's perspective. A sense of larger purpose and enhanced support may be produced by reference to God, country, or school.

- Encourage/reward sportsmanship. Fostering sports dignity and overall character is an ethical responsibility for coaches and athletes.

- Welcome feedback on any aspects of the team's functioning and forthrightly address issues raised. Promise to follow through on questions which can't be immediately answered or issues not immediately resolved.

- Address any conflicts directly affecting the entire team.

- Cover team rules as needed (e.g., clarify displaying of logos on uniforms or policy about tobacco use).

- Consider administrative matters (such as obtaining gear, scheduling events, or eligibility requirements).

- Remind your athletes to have fun. Enjoyment derives from the excitement of vigorously competing and striving with teammates as well as from successfully reaching goals.

Team USA 2005: Both men's and women's teams were victorious at American Zone Championships in Costa Rica

All three authors have been present at many bonding sessions, and we can attest that every year this is a special and unifying time for Team USA. Your team can be strengthened through similar meetings.

Group Activities

Shared experiences help cement team bonds. As you compete together, both the victories and defeats become a common history linking teammates. Working together in training towards the same goal further fosters the spirit of team.

Activities unrelated to competition are also a way of bringing a team closer. Attending an event is one example, such as a going to a comedy club or movie. Another would be a trip like the one Team USA took to the Football Hall of Fame in Canton, Ohio, prior to leaving for the 1994 Pan Am Games. A bit more exotic was an activity undertaken by the USA Junior Olympic Team. At the 2002 World Youth Tournament in Thailand, the entire squad took elephant rides at a rescue park.

Nothing beats spending time together in order for teammates to get to know and understand each other. Traveling, eating meals, or just hanging out all provide opportunities to do this. This aspect of team building encompasses activities as a whole group as well as any other contact, whether it concerns bowling or is purely social.

Coaching considerations related to interpersonal support are covered on the following two pages.

·   T H E   C O A C H I N G   C O R N E R   ·

Coaching Considerations

<u>Coach-Athlete Support</u>

The principles of interpersonal support we've discussed apply to all team members—coaches and athletes alike. In the Team USA program, both coaches and bowlers participate in education and exercises meant to improve communication skills, increase respect for individual differences, and build team cohesion in other ways.

While there is certainly a distinction in authority and team roles, on a humanistic level all members of a team are equals. Everyone has the same worth as a human being. We are dedicated to the athletic and personal development of the persons we coach and respect their feelings and rights. In keeping with this, we fully adhere to the *USOC Coaching Ethics Code.*[34]

We use and believe in a cooperative style of coaching. Yes, the coach is in charge and establishes and enforces team rules and ensures there is structure and order. Yet the athletes participate in various types of decision making and are accorded the respect due independent, serious-minded individuals. Obviously, the amount of structure and moment-to-moment oversight provided by a coach needs to vary depending on the age and maturity of the players.

We recognize that some coaches are more command style (authoritarian) in their approach and that certain athletes may very well benefit and even prefer it. After all, preference in coaches is an individual matter and athletes have different personalities and needs. However, the command style is not our style, and we believe that most bowlers will benefit most from a more mutually supportive relationship in which give and take on all levels is welcomed.

We strive to develop trust. The door is always open for an athlete to discuss any subject— personal as well as bowling-related. If there's an issue with a coach, we welcome the athlete's coming to us to deal with it. And we will, of course, go to a bowler or bowlers about issues that affect us and/or the team as a whole. We make these two-way expectations clear to the team at the start of training and at other times.

We know it can be intimidating for athletes to confront a coach. Therefore, we do all we can to get the message across: You can come to us. We are here for you.

Athletes respect their coaches by following team rules and meeting requirements as they arise (e.g., presence at teammates' matches, aspects of interaction with media, various behaviors during competition, etc.). Respect, as well as optimum learning and performance, call for an athlete to carefully consider a coach's input and make a good faith effort to try suggestions. To maximize the effectiveness of coaching, bowlers need to be honest in terms of asking questions, expressing feelings, and making requests.

(continued)

· T H E   C O A C H I N G   C O R N E R ·

Coaching Considerations (continued)

Because coaches are in a position of authority, athletes may lose sight of them as a real person. Given this tendency, whether athletes are fully aware of their coach's humanity will depend a great deal on how genuine and emotionally accessible the coach is. However it comes about, bowlers interacting with their coach in supportive ways will strengthen their relationship and the team. To that end, the interpersonal skills presented in this chapter can be effectively applied by athletes in relating to their coaches.

The Coach's Role

Coaches can promote support among team members in the following ways:

1. Train. Provide education through input to individuals and the whole team. Use structured exercises, such as those we've described. Undertake team actions. Finally, consider enlisting a sport psychology consultant for a team-building session.

2. Intervene. Facilitate conflict resolution as needed. You may be asked for assistance or you may step in based on your awareness of a problem.

3. Model. Athletes may very well learn more by what you do than by what you say. A coach's stature creates the opportunity to exert influence directly through behavior. There will be a tendency to emulate and then integrate your deeds into their own style. So, with respect to all aspects of teamwork, Walk it, coach, just don't talk it.

4. Encourage. Make clear to your bowlers the importance of support to their success and your expectations in terms of communication, respect for individual differences, etc.

Train. Intervene. Model. Encourage. Our unequivocal advice to coaches: Take the T-I-M-E to build support.

Most of what we've covered here applies to all coach-athlete relationships, team or otherwise. As noted in the Introduction, when selecting an individual coach, you should discuss all aspects of the relationship which are important to you. You are entrusting someone with a substantial role in your athletic development. In addition to inspiring and guiding, you deserve a teacher with whom you feel at ease and who unmistakably is responsive in a supportive way. You might ask yourself in the bluntest terms: If I fall on my face (and we all do—that's how we learn), will I be given the front or the back of this coach's hand?

Parents should be guided by the same standards when selecting a coach for their child. The coach may well play a major role in the child's life. It is necessary that he or she be a person of maturity and sensitivity who, through teaching, attitude, and role modeling, will help shape the youngster's development. It is vital that parents find a coach who treats them, as well as their child, in a supportive, communicative manner. The coach is a parental figure, and it is essential that he or she be in sync with the parents, so that the child receives consistent, coordinated guidance and continuous support. (In Chapter 20, we cover the coaching of young athletes, including age-related considerations.)

What it Takes to be a Good Teammate

The essence of being a good teammate is doing all within your power to advance the team towards its potential and achieving its goals. Here are the principles:

1. Learn how best to transmit relevant information to your teammates and let them know what's best for you.

2. Be considerate in the sense of being aware of teammates' feelings and need for support and treat them in the way you would like to be treated. Ask to be supported in kind.

3. Interact with your coach in accordance with the above and with the respect he or she is due.

4. Adhere to team rules.

5. Offer input and ideas that contribute to the team. Value team members doing the same, even if you don't agree.

6. Be attentive and engaged in team meetings.

7. Do all you can to realize your potential. This encompasses all aspects of training and preparation. Developing your mental game is central to this fundamental goal.

8. In order to be your best, lead a healthy lifestyle. Balance career/academic, social, and recreational/relaxation needs.

9. When not competing, root for teammates at their matches.

10. Respect the routines of your teammates.

11. Respect teammates' individual preferences in how they process results.

12. Regard criticism as an opportunity to improve. It's information you may or may not use. If the feedback is offered in a judgmental or otherwise harsh manner, constructively confront your teammate. If it's offered in a thoroughly positive way, thank your teammate.

13. Accept a lineup position you don't like or exclusion from a lineup with grace. Then give teammates whatever information and support help them perform. Your attitude can set a tone for the whole squad.

14. If you're a potential substitute, be ready.

15. Applaud the success of team members even if you compete in tournaments. Do not begrudge teammates who are given more attention, even if you feel equally deserving.

16. Accept the reality that for the good of the team, as circumstances dictate, your coach may spend more time during a tournament with other teammates.

17. If a team member receives the designation of captain or another role you desire, move past the disappointment and fully support that teammate.

18. Before, during, and after an event, do all you can to build up your teammates' confidence, self-regard, and sense of being valued as a team member.

19. Refrain from speaking in any disparaging way (including hearsay) about teammates to other teammates. Ask yourself, would they want this information revealed or gossiped about? Do you want to be talked about behind your back?

20. Conduct yourself in public in a manner that reflects positively on the team.

21. Be media-wise generally and maintain a team focus during interviews.

22. Always display sportsmanship.

23. Be a person of integrity. Ethical behavior contributes to feeling good about yourself, inspires trust and admiration, and casts the team in a positive light.

24. Manage your emotions, especially before or during competition, so that teammates aren't distracted or upset.

25. Compete flat out!

How many of these behaviors now characterize you? To contribute most to your team, dedicate yourself to following all of them.

Leadership

Concerning leadership, the core question we ask is how can an individual influence the actions of others to enhance team performance? This aim may be achieved in several ways.

All bowlers can positively impact their teammates simply by what they do. Adherence to the principles of being a good teammate provides a model for others. Setting an example is implicit leadership. It can teach, remind, and reinforce behaviors contributing to team goals. Interviewed on "Meet the Press," Muhammed Ali once observed, "A picture is worth a thousand words. An action is worth a thousand pictures." We regard every team member as a leader whose actions reverberate throughout the squad.

Influence may be exerted more explicitly. Actively, consistently, and enthusiastically advising and inquiring, cheering, comforting, rallying, confronting, and facilitating are classic leadership actions. Serving as a liaison to coaches, officials, and administrators are other functions associated with leading. Taking on extra responsibilities representing the team at public events and exhibition matches, engaging in administrative tasks, and interacting with the media are further instances of leadership.

Whether implicit or explicit leadership, the level of impact will depend on several factors. The bowler's skills and achievements, work ethic, team seniority, relationship with teammates, and respect for the coach all lend themselves to creating influence. While we can't identify a one-to-one correspondence between an exact personality and effective leadership, experience tells us the following: Confidence and determination combined with excellent communications skills, respect for individuality, and perceived mental toughness are most important. When it comes to explicit leadership, what must come through is an unswerving motivation to lead for the sake of team objectives, not personal power. Clichéd as it may sound, it is the leader's heart that counts most.

Teams have the option of officially designating a leader (i.e., captain or co-captains). On a coachless team, more often than not, one bowler undertakes administrative/organizing responsibilities. In this circumstance, the title of captain is, most of all, a sign of respect.

Wichita State University: Winner of women's team title at 2005 Intercollegiate Bowling Championships

Coaches may also designate or, preferably, have their team choose a captain. This can serve two major purposes. First, the title represents an honor earned. It calls attention to the qualities of being a good teammate and the specific attributes of leadership displayed by the bowler. The athlete is rewarded and the importance of these behaviors is reinforced. Some on the team may then aspire to become a captain in the future. Second, a captain may be given specific duties. Examples are overseeing practices, communicating with the coach on behalf of the players, and speaking to the press as the team representative. In this case, the title conveys authority and the coach's expectation that the captain's directions in the specified areas will be heeded.

Whether a captaincy is useful depends on the coach, the athletes, and the circumstances. For instance, coaches may differ in terms of how they delegate authority and in their prior experiences with captains. A team of veterans may not need a clear leader, whereas a young team might very well benefit from a designated captain. To assume the mantle of captaincy, there must be an athlete suitable to the role. As a final example, in a situation when a coach can't be present during part or all of an event (for instance, due to the tournament format), a designated leader may prove especially valuable.

Conclusion

If you bowl on a team or coach one, understanding and applying the principles of team building are essential to success. As you can see, making the maximum contributions to your team and having all teammates do the same is a multi-task challenge. It is a challenge well worth meeting since the result is the unique satisfaction provided by high quality team play.

Exercises

1. Identify (by numbers 1-10) any listening limitations you have.

2. Read the solution for each and then visualize yourself applying it.

3. How empathic are you with teammates? (circle one)

   Not at All   Minimally   Moderately   Highly

4. Make an effort to apply empathic actions and attitudes in your next two communications, then reevaluate. Continue in this way until you rate yourself "highly."

5. If possible, do the empathy exercise with teammates.

6. How expressive are you with empathic teammates? (circle one)

   Not At All   Minimally   Moderately   Highly

7. Try being more genuine and open with others who are empathic. Periodically reevaluate until you consider yourself moderately or highly expressive.

8. Write a five-step dialogue for each of the practice confrontation situations.

9. Think of specific situations which have actually arisen with teammates or others. Write a five-step dialogue for each.

10. If possible, practice constructive confrontation scenarios with teammates.

11. Evaluate how good you are at using these actions to limit conflict/increase cooperation: (circle one)

    1=Not at All   2=Slightly   3=Moderately   4=Very

Being Direct	1	2	3	4
Seeking Feedback	1	2	3	4
Offering Feedback	1	2	3	4
Encouraging Directness	1	2	3	4
Using a Facilitator	1	2	3	4
Making a Request	1	2	3	4
Saying "No"	1	2	3	4
Coping with Defensiveness	1	2	3	4

    Dedicate yourself to making full use of all as the need arises.

12. If possible, have your team use the MBTI® Model in some way to increase understanding/acceptance of individual differences.

13. Do you fully respect your teammates' individuality when it comes to routines? How about other aspects of their performance/style?

14. Which of the team actions is it possible to engage in? What can you do to bring this about?

15. If you're a coach, place a check next to those team meeting tips you already use. Place a double check next to those you'll apply in the future.

16. Cite the ways a coach can be supportive in relating to athletes.

17. As an athlete, how can you contribute to your coach's supportiveness and effectiveness?

18. Are the T-I-M-E actions for promoting support used on your team?

19. Are there ways you can be a better teammate? Write the number of any principles (1-25) which you'll now start to apply.

20. As a bowler, note how you exert leadership on your team. Can you do more?

21. If you're a coach, how do you utilize the leadership potential of your athletes? Is there more you can do?

REVIEW

Support is essential to team unity and conducive to success. We cite three major ways to build it:

1. Improve communication skills. Enhance the capacity to listen and the ability to resolve and limit conflicts.

2. Increase respect for individual differences. Nondiscrimination, an understanding and appreciation of normal personality differences, and recognition that such differences can increase team strength are aspects of this respect.

3. Undertake team actions. Drills, meetings, bonding sessions, and group activities can all contribute to cohesion.

We believe a coach-athlete relationship characterized by cooperation and trust will best serve the team. A coach has multiple options for boosting support among team members.

Being a good teammate involves a series of unselfish and cooperative behaviors. These encompass all the principles covered in this chapter.

Leadership can be exerted implicitly or explicitly. Leadership needs vary from team to team.

Team building is a challenge well worth meeting.

Team USA men's squad with Coach Edwards after winning gold at 2004 World Tenpin Team cup (Netherlands)

20

BOWLING: THE FAMILY SPORT

When I express frustration, my mom will cheer me up.
Kelly Kulick

Every game I bowl on TV and every shot I throw, I know my dad is with me.
Pete Weber

My dad told me to take one shot at a time.
Walter Ray Williams

Bowling is a sport for all ages, both historically and chronologically. Its history dates back to ancient times. Its door is open to youth and adults of both genders, spanning the spectrum from childhood to senior years. In this final chapter, attention turns to the most important team of all: family. We consider the all-inclusive family dimension of the sport, first focusing on the participation of youth bowlers and their interaction with adults, as well as on skill development for seniors. Factors concerning women's participation are then cited. Bowling provides a recreational opportunity for the family as a unit, and we end with reference to this shared experience.

The information in the pages ahead is directly relevant to coaching. Parents can also benefit from the knowledge, especially those sections earmarked for them. If you're an athlete in a specific category discussed, consider how you can apply our suggestions. Teammates of such bowlers may also find it useful to be aware of the performance factors identified. Finally, bowling families will learn ways to derive the most from the time together on the lanes.

Youth Bowlers

Young bowlers are characterized by their appetite for learning, keen attention to simple details, and animated ways of expressing enjoyment. For many youngsters, bowling is a favored activity. It allows them to be energetic and playful and to experiment with different ideas and approaches as they socialize. It is important to help them enjoy the game and, in the process, capture their minds with all of bowling's fascinations.

Above left: Dick Weber—Three-time PBA Bowler of the Year, PBA and USBC Halls of Fame, chosen century's best in 1999 poll. Above right: Like father, like son— PBA Hall of Famer Pete Weber today ranks second all-time in PBA major titles and career earnings.

From the adult's perspective, it is vital to notice that youth bowlers aren't little adults, they're kids: small, energetic, and eager to learn. And as big people helping small people, coaches and parents need to understand some areas of special concern.

Different Strokes . . .

For many youths, developing their own style is part of the fun of bowling. Helping young bowlers develop good fundamentals is also very important, so it's sometimes a challenge to combine the unique styles with good fundamentals.

For instance, at times children look like they race to the foul line, but if their balance and posture are good, the foot tempo may not be a problem. In fact, with lighter weight individuals, the only way to develop good ball speed is to have energetic foot tempo. Unfortunately, many adults will discourage or simply not allow this, which causes friction between coach and student. A receptive and flexible approach is essential for coaching this age group.

Another specific case is the youngster who likes to see the ball hook. This youth may throw the ball slower so it will hook more. A particular young boy Coach Edwards worked with provides a good illustration. When he was about ten years old, the boy was already a talented young bowler. He was on the small side and really liked to make the ball hook. Even when encouraged to move faster so the ball rolled with more speed (and he, indeed, struck more), he still wanted to go slower and create hook. Consequently, Coach Edwards helped him with other things and dropped the idea of having the boy move faster. Years later, this young man now has great ball speed and one of the strongest hooking shots on the lanes. Even when young, he knew he loved to hook it and just had to grow into the great player he is today. Fortunately, he was encouraged as a young player and not discouraged because he didn't choose to embrace everything he was told.

It is always important to initially help youths with what they want to do, not with what you think they should do. As you gain their trust, they'll recognize that your advice will enable them to score higher.

League Activity

In youth bowling, most of the coaching happens during Saturday morning league. This is probably the most difficult time to help youngsters. Their scores are showing on the monitor and if you give them a new idea and they make a bad shot, you're the "bad guy." In this situation, it's probably best to help only when the player asks specifically or is bowling so poorly that any new thought would help, or when you have an especially strong coach/player relationship.

The other option is to see if the bowler can stay a little while after bowling to work on some "new things." When league play ends, you can turn on the lanes and not keep score. This is a big help. In fact, encourage any player who is developing new physical skills to do this. It's much less threatening and allows for development without judgment. It's hard for anyone not to pay attention to how many pins are knocked down and then make a judgment as to whether the new skill is good or bad based on that.

Until a new skill is mastered, the "old style" will feel more comfortable and the youngster will have a tendency to return to it. By providing abundant feedback and encouragement, you can counter this tendency. Such coaching enthusiasm initially may be the only reason the youth doesn't go back to his or her original approach.

Psychological Skills

Learning psychological skill methods can contribute to a youth bowler's immediate development and sense of achievement as well as lay the foundation for a strong mental game. Goal setting, self-talk, routines, visualization, and relaxation skills are among the techniques which youngsters have effectively applied.

Just as with adults, it's best to set measurable goals. Good examples are converting three spares or hitting the head pin with six shots in a game. As the athlete matures, it's essential that he or she be taught goal-setting principles. Athlete and coach should set daily practice goals in addition to goals for competition. The coach then needs to monitor performance in relation to these goals and provide feedback (information and reinforcement) accordingly.

Use of positive self-talk is an important technique to instill early. It can contribute to confidence and increase the athlete's ability to cope with adversity. Continuously point young bowlers towards thinking about what they want to improve on the next shot instead of dwelling on what a bad shot they just made. This can make a world of difference.

Mental practice can be used by children to "see" performance strategies, cope with stress before and during competition, and better handle unexpected circumstances. Visualization has been successfully practiced by youths at home, at school, and while traveling to and from activities. If you teach mental practice, be sensitive to the capacities of the youngster regarding attention and motivation. When working with younger children especially, try to develop interesting scenarios and use a relatively brief amount of time.

Youth bowlers can learn relaxation techniques such as taking a deep, calming breath or imagining a peaceful setting. In order to create acceptance for a relaxation tool, provide an explanation for its use. Always use concise, straightforward language that brings to mind familiar, vivid images. For instance, one relaxation method for young children (developed by Terry Orlick) is called "Spaghetti Toes." The script directs children to imagine parts of their body becoming soft like cooked spaghetti. When completing a relaxation exercise with young bowlers, make sure they are fully alert.

In order to help young bowlers concentrate on the shot they face, have them develop a physical pre-shot routine. This is important because children are so easily distracted by friends while they're bowling. Something as simple as wiping the ball off with a towel three times before every shot or stepping onto the approach with the same foot each time may do the trick. When they get older, the routine can become a bit more detailed—but keep it simple to start.

A brief psychological pre-shot routine can have a calming effect at the same time that it increases confidence and primes the youngster to perform well. We recommend a simple two-method sequence: taking a deep breath and then visualizing a delivery with perfect form, resulting in a shot right on target. That's at the ball return. On the approach, before starting to move, another deep breath is followed by the bowler's picturing the target line to the pocket.

These same skills which make for a strong mental game on the lanes can be applied to life circumstances in general. As appropriate, point out to youngsters how they might apply a technique in their daily lives. For instance, using imagery to relax and positive self-talk to bolster confidence before a test in school.

Teaching children can be a two-way street. The following observation of Coach Edwards attests to that: "[W]hen polled about why they bowl, kids' overwhelming response was for the fun of it. So we adults can sometimes learn a lesson or two from the kids."[35]

Practice Hints

Beyond the "fun" and social aspects, youth bowlers derive motivation to continue participating in the sport through their display of competence. If you're coaching young bowlers, structure practices with the dual aims of increasing their skill and confidence. This can contribute to increased self-esteem and enjoyment.

Here are several strategies for making practices successful:

- Put variety in your drills. The effect will be heightened interest and better concentration.

- Match task difficulty to your bowler's capability. Tasks that are too easy provide insufficient challenge. Tasks that are too difficult result in frustration and potential discouragement.

- Allow the athlete to make some decisions concerning activities. This tends to raise involvement, advance independent functioning, and promote respect and cooperation.

- Regarding skills targeted for development, progress systematically from the simple to the more complex. The purpose is a step-by-step building of competence.

- Simulate events as the end of practice approaches. The two-fold effect will be to provide stimulation and to help ready the young athlete for specific competitive challenges.

Motivation Change

As young athletes grow older, motivation tends to change. When designing a training program, keep in mind these tendencies:

Before age ten, children gauge skills and success mostly by the feedback of parents and coaches. For this reason, it is of utmost importance to provide young bowlers with clear ways to improve and to let them know with conviction that you believe they can do so. Confidence and motivation can be all too readily eroded by excessive criticism, so be careful to avoid it. Going to the other extreme is also to be avoided. That is, excessive praising of easy skills may produce a sense that you doubt the bowler's ability.

Pointed in the right direction

After age ten, peers take on increasing significance to the young athlete. What results is a great reliance on comparisons to peers and how they are regarded by them. When there's a preoccupation with such comparisons, lapses in concentration can result (prior to age 15 especially). Therefore, take steps to transfer the attention of youth bowlers from peer comparison to self-comparison: One approach that can be exceedingly helpful here is individual goal setting.

Coaching Guidelines

The following are recommendations for coaching young athletes. These pointers are based on research in the field of youth sport.[36]

- Safety is the number one consideration. Take whatever steps are needed to guarantee this.

- Give priority to the teaching and practice of skills. Ensure the high quality of equipment, facilities, and, if applicable, staff.

- Provide reinforcement immediately. Reinforce your athletes' effort as much as you reinforce their results.

- After a mistake is made, give immediate encouragement. How to do it right should be emphasized, instead of what was wrong.

- Establish expectations that are straightforward and clear. Set realistic, challenging goals, for both individuals and the team.

- Place emphasis on your teacher's role. Offer instruction that's clear and brief and demonstrate as much as you can.

- At all times, be fully motivated. This conveys caring and interest and is a model for concentration and team cohesion.

- Consistently emphasize/reinforce team participation.

- Minimize your bowlers' fear of attempting new skills through a combination of empathy and encouragement.

- Be enthusiastic. Ample enthusiasm can produce a big impact.

- Keep the sport fun.

- Teach life skills. Do this by drawing lessons based on what the bowler has actually done or could do (such as displaying concentration, confidence, and determination in response to adversity) and by your own actions (for instance, acknowledging mistakes).

- Teach psychological skill methods (e.g., visualizing, breathing for relaxation, and routines) for improving performance and as life skills.

- Apply an approach which is consistently positive and develop/use effective listening skills.

- The development of a young athlete through participation in bowling is the appropriate guiding principle for those who coach. A solid framework in this respect is provided by the "Bill of Rights for Young Athletes."

BILL OF RIGHTS FOR YOUNG ATHLETES[37]

1. Right to participate in sports.

2. Right to participate at a level commensurate with each child's maturity and ability.

3. Right to have qualified adult leadership.

4. Right to play as a child and not as an adult.

5. Right of children to share in the leadership and decision-making of their sport participation.

6. Right to participate in safe and healthy environments.

7. Right to proper preparation in sport.

8. Right to an equal opportunity to strive for success.

9. Right to be treated with dignity.

10. Right to have fun in sports.

Adolescence: A Period of Personal Growth

The attitudes conveyed and actions taken by coaches and parents can assist greatly in the teenage bowler's mastery of skills for coping with challenges both inside and outside the center. Coaches, in fact, fill multiple roles for the young athlete—teacher, mentor, and parent figure. If you're a coach, remember that you're positioned to advance the youth's personal development while furthering his or her athletic growth.

Every life stage is characterized by specific developmental issues. A drive towards autonomy, formation of identity, impulse control, learning about intimacy/commitment, and acquiring a personal value system comprise the major developmental tasks of adolescence.

To help a teenage bowler better handle the intense anxieties and uncertainties of this time and increase skill mastery and self-worth, be aware of several coaching behaviors in particular. It is crucial to supply caring and empathy while at the same time providing firmness and consistency. Model essential skills. For example,

- Teach concentration by your own focus during competition and lessons;

- Teach self-acceptance by remaining calmly supportive when errors are committed;

- Teach confidence by your optimism in the face of a bowler's slow start, poor game, or slump;

- Teach sports dignity by displaying respect towards competitors; and

- Teach interpersonal skills by communicating clearly and constructively.

We strongly recommend providing relevant preventive information about high risk behaviors, including the use of performance-enhancing drugs. Know the signs of clinical conditions such as substance abuse, depression, and eating disorders. Exhibit great sensitivity when you communicate with the athlete, express your concerns to other involved adults, and, if needed, make referrals to a professional.

Undoubtedly, the responsibilities of coaching youths are considerable. Yet the rewards for a coach or parent can be immense. It is a profoundly meaningful activity to help young people fulfill their potential and, in the process, healthily mature.

In conjunction with personal growth, teens can develop an increasingly sophisticated mental game. They can work on a repertoire of skills drawing from the full range of techniques covered in the book. Motivation to learn is key, as it is at all ages. If they've been introduced to psychological skills earlier, the likelihood of their interest at this time increases. Inspiring them to strive in this area is a prime coaching goal. The message we can relate, and they can relate to, is simple: Ongoing mental game training is vital to becoming a great player.

When Seniors Bowl

Seniors represent a vibrant and growing segment of the bowling population. For many people, retiring means plenty of free time. Enter bowling. If a stranger to bowling walks into a center during the daytime hours, he or she will observe an active senior group having fun and getting great exercise. It is seniors who most enjoy open play as well as organized daytime programs. Newcomers to the sport are always welcome and bowlers of many years can always learn more.

For new and veteran bowlers alike, it helps to receive instruction. However, this input should be provided by an experienced coach who knows what's most relevant to the bowler's game. Because advice may be offered by many, it's essential that the senior bowler avoid receiving too much information, which can be as bad as no information. In particular, seniors can benefit from a Master Plan that takes into account the factors noted below. These factors, which involve honest and accurate self-assessment, are crucial for setting and reaching realistic goals. Skill development and motivation may well depend on giving them consideration.

Physical Game Considerations

For seniors who have bowled their entire life, sometimes it's extremely useful to step back and redefine their game and redefine success. If you're a senior, realize that physical games change over the years and recognize that you may bowl better if you help your body do the best job it can.

There are special considerations here, mainly strength and mobility. For instance, if you have trouble with your hips or knees, you'll want to start closer to the foul line to take some pressure off your legs. If you suffer from imbalance, starting a little closer to the foul line may help you keep your balance. Just because you've always started from a certain place, doesn't mean you'll always bowl your best from that spot. Be ready to pay attention to your body and help it help you.

Equipment Factors

Reason out your choices with respect to bowling ball selection. There are three main concerns here and each is important. First, determine the right weight of the ball. This is an area where many seniors struggle. Their minds won't let them drop in weight even though their bodies are ready to bowl with lighter equipment. It's better to throw a lighter weight ball with more speed and more consistency than to throw a heavier ball too slowly and inconsistently. It's a fallacy that you must use a 16 pound ball to score your best. If you feel tired after bowling or you throw the ball slower than you desire, then you may want to try a lighter ball. In most cases, it's the right decision.

Another area of importance is your grip. If you experience more than normal aches in your hand, see your pro shop operator. He or she may be able to drill the holes at a different angle and take the pressure off your hand.

Finally, choosing the right type of ball can make a big difference. The new reactive resin balls with a particle additive can hook more and can hook too soon if you throw the ball a little slowly. If the ball hooks too soon, it will reach the pins with little energy and won't hit that hard. Sometimes deciding to use a polished non-particle resin ball will be a better choice and enable you to score higher.

Mental Game Development

As far as the mental game is concerned, this is where seniors can shine. Calling upon their bowling experience and life experience, seniors often don't let anything rattle them. This combination of game savvy and life perspective can allow them to think out their moves, make them, and, if a move doesn't work, recognize that only one more may be required to solve the condition.

As a senior bowler, one of the most important things to keep in mind relates to pre-shot routine. Make the decision about what you're going to do before stepping onto the approach. Attitude is vital. When you step onto the approach, do so with confidence and make your shot boldly. It may work or it may not. But you understand there's always another shot, so give each one your best effort and watch your ball. It will tell you what to do.

From diaphragmatic breathing to thought stopping, seniors can master and apply all aspects of the mental game discussed throughout this book. We've simply called your attention to certain special considerations which can enhance development in this area.

Considerations for Women*

Bowling is a great sport for women. In many ways it allows them to fully compete at the same level as men. From youth leagues all the way to the professional level, there is a place for females. Special considerations in regard to the physical game, bowling equipment, lane play, and mental approach can be addressed.

Because women are generally smaller in stature than men, it's more difficult to generate ball speed. Often it helps to move at a more aggressive tempo even though many coaches urge you to slow down. Moving smoothly would be a better way of thinking about your motion. Women also hear that they don't hook the ball enough. Again, this information can be more detrimental than helpful. In the day of the big hook balls, the bottom line is that you can knock down all ten pins with a very heavy roll. So instead of trying so hard to hook a ball, work on developing great technique that allows repetition with a strong ball roll. Using a wrist support is often a "good thing." Many of the lady professional bowlers use them all of the time. This can improve your ability to repeat shots and should be thought of as a choice rather than a crutch.

When it comes to bowling balls, the most important consideration for women is weight. Especially with the newer balls, which are dynamically the same in the lower weights, it's an option to choose a lighter weight ball. So, heavier isn't always better if you sacrifice repeating shots all night long. You're not less of a bowler for throwing lighter equipment— you may just be smarter. It is also important to know your equipment and keep the fit snug. If your hand size changes, put tape in or take tape out of the holes. Customize the fit every time you play.

When playing lanes, women tend to stay in one place more than men. Mobility is a distinct advantage. So it is imperative for women to practice moving all over the lane and playing different angles in order to accustom themselves to looking at the lane with a big horizon instead of a constricted view. Buying into this expanded perspective requires testing it sufficiently in practice. To accomplish this, seek help from someone you trust who has patience.

With respect to the mental game, a challenge faced by all competitive bowlers is separating emotionally from the stressors of daily life and remaining keenly focused on the lanes (Chapter 11). We've observed any number of women bowlers struggling to let go of their outside

---

* The entire book addresses a vast range of considerations affecting bowlers of both genders. While the similarities between male and female bowlers are far greater than any differences, several factors concerning women are distinct enough to make their identification useful.

responsibilities. Unfortunately, if your mind is half in the center and half out of it, both performance and enjoyment will suffer. If "letting go" of thoughts of family or other commitments is an issue for you while bowling, consider the following:

1. It's healthy, psychologically and physically, to take a break from the stressful activities and thoughts of daily life.

2. It's healthy and rejuvenating to engage in an athletic activity such as bowling.

3. You'll have more to give others—family, friends, colleagues—if you're healthy and feel refreshed rather than stressed out.

4. You'll be more productive if you're healthy and energized.

5. You're *entitled* to have time to yourself for personal development and enjoyment.

Awareness of these various factors can help a woman realize her bowling potential, experience enhanced confidence, and derive maximum satisfaction from participating in the sport.

The Family that Plays Together, Stays Together

Of course, we can't guarantee that bowling will result in family harmony. However, the activity of bowling together can be an extremely positive experience where members of a family share a few hours of fun while supporting one another with encouragement and, possibly, advice. Some friendly competition can be enjoyable, although it's essential that this not be taken too seriously.

If Family Issues Emerge

Since family recreation doesn't exist in a void, conflicts and issues from everyday life could carry over to the lanes. Limited communication or cooperation, sarcasm or other forms of hostility, excessive competitiveness, or any other distancing behaviors deserve to be discussed—whether it's in the center and/or in the home. The occurrence of such behaviors opens a door to dealing with significant issues and can lead to a strengthening of family bonds and personal growth.

This potential strengthening applies to any relationship within the family, including the parents' relationship. In fact, the potential for conflict and the opportunity for resolution and growth apply to bowling couples regardless of whether or not they have children.[38]

The communication skills in Chapter 19 are as relevant to the team that is family as they are to any other teammates.

Tips for Parents

In addition to bearing in mind the applicable suggestions provided earlier in the chapter, parents stand to benefit from the following tips:

- Make clear your expectations regarding conduct (attitude and actions) and be firm, fair, and consistent when bringing about compliance.

- Emphasize sportsmanship, including encouraging and congratulating others and accepting disappointment with dignity, not dramatic displays.

- Ask older children to provide leadership in terms of taking responsibility for "chores" (e.g., making requested inquiries or getting a piece of equipment) and in how they behave.

- Provide a model of behavior—both in relating to family members and in reaction to your own performance.

- Direct attention to cooperative goals rather than competitive ones.

- Be honest, spontaneous, and level-headed.

- Demonstrate no favoritism in response to the performance of your children.

- If there's tension at home, try to resolve it before leaving for the center. If this isn't accomplished, ask that conflicts be "parked" outside the center and re-establish your definite expectations for conduct on the lanes.

- Praise your children for how they handled emotions and acted in terms of the family as well as in response to bowling situations.

The Family and Bowling's Future

Bowling's family dimension is highlighted in the following article of Dr. Lasser's which appeared in *USA Coach.*

FRED MEETS HUCK FINN

Blond, freckled, and fresh-faced, the kid resembled a young Huck Finn. Huck Finn with a bowling ball. Instead of the mighty Mississippi, his river of challenge was the sixty foot lane at Brunswick Circle Lanes in Colorado Springs. This river was much too narrow. Ball after ball found its way to the channel, generating a stream of frustration in its wake. His father looked on, offering support with seemingly no effect. He, too, appeared increasingly dismayed. Surrender loomed.

Spotting the forlorn twosome, I inquired and learned it was the boy's first time bowling. His dad, friendly despite frustration, admitted to his own novice status and a feeling of helplessness.

While this private drama unfolded at the deserted end of the center, at the other end all was aglitter as Team USA (1994) participated in a celebrity event. The event, covered by TV and print media alike, was a Team USA gift to the community serving as its host for the training week at the USOC Training Center. In the midst of all this was Head Coach Fred Borden.

Alerted to the youngster's plight, Borden immediately made his way to father and son. With the straightforward greeting, "Hello, I'm Fred Borden, Coach of Team USA," he volunteered to give some tips to the boy.

He then spent fifteen minutes teaching the basics, from grip and stance to approach and release. Again and again ball found channel. Yet Borden persisted with unstinting patience, continuous encouragement, and consistent direction. At last, some pins went down. The kid was elated; his father beamed. Borden provided information about programs to help the youngster develop, presented father and son with Team USA pins, shook hands, and returned to the bright lights, the river boat captain back on board.

The saga had not run its course. A half hour later, the kid made his first strike. Suddenly, Borden was there again—extending congratulations and introducing the Lanes' manager, Jerry Wilson, who explained more about the center's offerings. Privately, Borden said this was an opportunity to kindle a family's lifelong involvement in the sport.

Borden could give Nostradamus a run for his money. Not long after that first strike moment, Huck and dad were joined by two Finnettes whose pigtails flew when they released the ball. Laughter and youthful energy filled the air. The parent's pride was palpable. No one could doubt these were winners.

Also winning big on this day was the sport of bowling, which had enlisted a family into its ranks. And Fred Borden was responsible. The Coach had done his job.[39]

The potential for full family participation, from youth to senior, male and female, as individuals or together, is one of bowling's great assets and a key to its future. The sculpture seen below is situated in the National Bowling Stadium. It portrays the spirit of family and is a fitting tribute to the dynamism, scope, and vitality of our sport.

Sculptor: Gail Demarest Wilday

Exercises

1. As a coach of youth bowlers, what practice strategies do you already use? Are there any new ones you plan to implement?

2. Place a check next to guideline recommendations which now characterize how you coach. Double check those you will apply in the future.

3. Do you provide psychological skills training regularly as part of your coaching? If so, are there additional methods you can now teach? Develop a plan to begin or expand instruction in this area.

4. Describe three instances where kids you coach can clearly benefit from using one or more psychological tools.

5. Consider our other suggestions about the coaching of youth bowlers. Make a list of those recommendations you will start to apply.

6. As an athlete or a coach, what do you consider the four most important recommendations concerning seniors bowling?

7. If you're a senior, describe the pre-shot routine you've been using and, if different, the one you will use in the future. Include actions in the settee area, at the ball return, and the approach.

8. As an athlete or a coach, what do you consider the four most important recommendations concerning women bowling?

9. How readily can you "let go" of outside responsibilities when you bowl? (circle one)

   With Difficulty   Partly   Fairly Well   Easily

10. Indicate which of our five points is the most helpful in this regard.

11. If you bowl with a family member or members, how do you typically get along? (circle one)

    Poorly   Only Fair   Moderately Well   Very Well

12. If you're a parent, place a check next to the tips you already apply. Double check those suggestions you'll use in the future.

REVIEW

Bowling's universal appeal is reflected in the diversity of its participants. Its doors are open to all members of a family encompassing both genders and the full range of ages. In this chapter we consider factors specific to four categories of bowlers: youth, seniors, women, and families as a unit.

To develop trust and generate enthusiasm, allow young bowlers to combine their unique style with good fundamentals. A variety of psychological techniques can contribute to their game. Practice hints and coaching guidelines (including the "Bill of Rights for Young Athletes") are provided. There are special considerations to bear in mind when coaching adolescents.

Seniors who bowl can boost pincount by making various adaptations in their physical game and equipment choices. The competitive experience and life perspective of seniors can contribute to the strength of their mental game. Attention to pre-shot routine is vital for this group of bowlers.

Among the considerations for women bowlers to keep in mind are working on a strong roll, using the proper weight ball, and being mobile on the lanes. Putting aside thoughts of everyday responsibilities will contribute to excellence of performance.

Bowling can be a rewarding recreational activity for a family and lead to the strengthening of relationships. By following designated guidelines, parents can better enable family members to enjoy themselves and develop skills.

A key to bowling's future is the opportunity provided for full family participation.

EPILOGUE

GLORY IN HAVANA

Putting It All Together:
A Model for Bowling Success

I was strictly focused on my shots.
Patrick Healey Jr.

Through mental game training, Team USA athletes are geared to handle the pressures, distractions, and multiple other challenges encountered in elite competition.

We can think of no situation calling for more mental toughness than the final day of bowling in the 1991 Pan American Games in Cuba. What transpired in Havana on that occasion epitomized the value of psychological skills.

The setting was the state-of-the-art Ramon Fonst Bowlera, constructed expressly for these Games along with the national sports hall of fame in the same building. On this August day, a standing-room-only crowd jammed the new center in the Plaza de la Revolucion. They had come to witness the Games' top individual players vie for gold, silver, and bronze medals in the grand final. The leading men's qualifier entering this championship round was US bowler Patrick Healey Jr. of Niagara Falls, New York.

Healey takes pride in his mental game and has a full repertoire of psychological skills to draw upon. Throughout the week, he had regularly used visualization, relaxation techniques, and other methods in reaching the medal round. Yet not even this savvy athlete could have anticipated how essential his mental game would be on this particular day.

As Healey engaged in the warm-up round, he was suddenly informed that his towel and rosin bag couldn't be placed where he had put them the previous four days. In other words, Healey's physical routine would be interrupted. The US staff challenged this decision and ultimately the officials relented. In the meantime, Healey followed his regular pre-game routine. This included figuring out how to play the lanes (i.e., developing a game plan to bring home the gold). This adherence to the process of bowling and familiar routine contributed to his staying focused, emotionally steady, and primed to compete. (Earlier in the day, when the women's finals were delayed an hour, Healey seized the opportunity to similarly practice and consider strategy.)

Another change for these finals was the seating of Healey's teammates. The Team USA bowlers were told they had to move from directly behind the lanes where they had planned to root. The explanation offered was that TV and other media would need the area. This was essentially a pretext.

On hand for the event was none other than Premier Fidel Castro. The Cuban leader had entered the center quite unexpectedly with an entourage of some 15 people. He took a seat directly behind the bowlers, barely 20 feet from the lanes. Castro's entry jolted everyone on the US squad and his up-close presence potentially posed a major distraction for the competitors.

But Healey couldn't afford to be distracted or overly excited. As the men's finals got underway, Coach Borden instructed him to direct his attention solely to the lanes. Healey focused through mindset, diaphragmatic breathing, and his pre-shot routine. He strictly avoided looking at the stands.

Four bowlers faced off in the double elimination finals. Healey won back-to-back matches. This guaranteed silver and earned him a spot in the championship match against Venezuela's Louis Serfaty.

With gold on the line, the match was neck and neck for seven frames. In the eighth, Healey threw a strike and Serfaty opened. This gave the Team USA bowler a three pin lead entering the ninth frame.

At this point, the fans were on their feet, shouting, clapping, whistling. Healey stepped up to bowl his last two frames. The ball he threw in the ninth was executed as beautifully as any bowler could ever dream. Strike.

Turning to his coach, Healey then asked, "What do I need to win?" He was told that one more strike would shut out his adversary.

Healey used positive self-talk to ensure confidence, imagery to rivet his attention, and several deep breaths for composure. Stepping onto the approach, he set his stance and very calmly moved to the foul line in a fashion reserved for champions performing in the clutch.

The shot swung one to two boards out and hooked back to the pocket. Pins flew everywhere and the gold was won in front of Castro and the rest of the world. The final count was 237-201.

Afterwards, Healey commented that he "got a chill" when Castro walked in. Yet his play was unaffected: "But during bowling I was strictly focused on my shots."

The medal ceremony was something to behold. Healey stood atop the medal stand while our national anthem played and the Premier saluted the stars and stripes. The entire US team and contingent had tears in their eyes and were filled with immense pride. The history of Cuba and the US lent considerable poignancy to the moment. It was truly special to win the gold medal and have Castro himself drape it over Healey's head (see photo on the following page).

Healey's success as an elite amateur and professional* is attributable to the combination of physical ability and fitness, knowledge of equipment and lane adjustment, and a deep, versatile mental game. Having worked closely with him, we know how dedicated this remarkable athlete is to mastering and honing psychological skills. He has studied the range of methods covered in this book and applies these in standard routines and as called for by the competitive situation. From goal setting and mental rehearsal to thought stopping and self-affirmations, he is equipped to bowl his best.

You have the same opportunity to bowl your best and reach your potential as a bowling athlete.

Successful bowlers throughout the world, amateur and professional, know what Pat and other Team USA athletes know: Knocking down pins is a matter of both mind and body. Psychological skills are key to optimum performance and maximum enjoyment.

We hope you commit yourself to mastering mental game methods and get to experience their full benefits both on and off the lanes.

---

* Healey went on to earn US Amateur Bowler of the Year recognition three times and World Amateur Bowler of the Year honors twice. Today, he is one of the top players on the PBA tour.

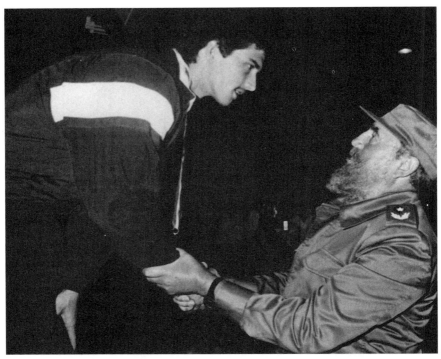

Red, white, blue, and gold: Patrick Healy Jr., receiving Pan Am Individual medal

Clockwise from top right: Mike Aulby, Danny Wiseman, Chris Barnes, Liz Johnson, Kelly Kulick, and Lisa Wagner. Lisa Wagner was the consensus Bowler of the Decade for the 1980s. Kelly Kulick, former US Amateur Champion and PWBA Rookie of the Year, won the 2003 Women's US Open. Achievements of the other bowlers were previously cited.

References

1. Material in this chapter is based mainly on information provided by FIQ Headquarters and Bowling Headquarters.
2. Lasser, E. (1995, August). Team USA meets challenge. *USA Coach,* p. 4.
3. Lasser, p. 5.
4. Wooden, J. R. (1991). Success is no secret—it's peace of mind in doing your best. *Kinney Cross Country Championships 1991,* pp. 2-3 [Program].
5. Vadakin, G. (2004). Personal Communication.
6. Both exercises adapted from Borden, F. (1991). *USA Bowling bronze level coaching manual.* Greendale, WI: USA Bowling, Ch. 3, pp. 9-10. [A revised manual will be issued by the USBC in 2006.]
7. Faces in the crowd (2003, 5 May). *Sports Illustrated, 98*(18), 30.
8. Borden, p. 3.
9. Lasser, E. (1997, September). Confidence. *Bowling This Month, 4*(9), 10.
10. Adapted from Murphy, S., & Raedeke, M. A. (1991, April). It's what you say to yourself that counts. *Olympic Coach, 1,* 5-6.
11. Edwards, J. (1995). Excerpt from *The Wisdom of Team USA Coaches* (CD)—series of interview highlights presented in *Sport Psychology for Coaches and Athletes* instructional programs (Instructor: E. Lasser, Sponsor: USA Bowling).
12. Adapted from Lenz, F. P. (1980). *Total relaxation: The complete program for overcoming stress, tension, worry, and fatigue.* New York: Bobbs-Merril, p. 204.
13. Adapted from Orlick, T. (2000). *In pursuit of excellence: How to win in sport and life through mental training* (3rd ed.). Champaign, IL: Human Kinetics, pp. 51-54.
14. Adapted from Rotella, R. J., & Lerner, J. D. (1993). Responding to competitive pressure. In R. N. Singer, M. Murphy, & L. K. Tennant (Eds.), *Handbook of research on sport psychology* (p. 529). New York: Macmillan.
15. Adapted from Peper, E., & Williams, E. A. (1981). *From the inside out: A self-teaching and laboratory manual for biofeedback.* New York: Plenum, pp. 10-12.
16. Martens, R. (1987). *Coaches guide to sport psychology.* Champaign, IL: Human Kinetics, p. 123.
17. Adapted from Lenz, F. P. (1980). *Total relaxation. The complete program for overcoming stress, tension, worry, and fatigue.* New York: Bobbs-Merrill, p. 201.
18. Lenz, p. 210.
19. Lasser, E. (1999, Winter). Team USA at the Team Cup: Psychological skills contribute to success. *USA Coach,* p. 4.
20. Benson, H. (1975). *The relaxation response.* New York: Morrow.
21. Sample suggestion and aspects of program description are drawn from Murphy, S. (1997). *The achievement zone: An 8-Step guide to peak performance in all arenas of life.* New York: Berkeley, pp. 128-130.
22. These techniques are based in part on Zaichkowsky, L., & Takenakea, K. (1993). Optimizing arousal levels. In R. N. Singer, M. Murphy & L. K. Tennant (Eds.), *Handbook of research on sport psychology* (pp. 511-527). New York: Macmillan; and Murphy, S., & Raedeke, M. A. (1991, April). It's what you say to yourself that counts. *Olympic Coach, 1,* 5-6.

23. Jackson, S. A., & Csikszentmihalyi, M. (1999). *Flow in sports: The keys to optimal experiences and performances.* Champaign, IL: Human Kinetics, pp. 15-31.
24. Lasser, E. (1998, April). Flow. *Bowling This Month, 5*(4), 15.
25. Jackson & Csikszentmihalyi.
26. Adapted from Nideffer, R. M. (1992). *Psyched to win.* Champaign, IL: Human Kinetics, p. 82.
27. The source for USOC recommendations regarding audiotapes is Fenker, R. M., & Durtschi, S. K. (1990). *Visualization training program: US Olympic Training Center* [Manual]. USOC: Colorado Springs, CO.
28. The discussion of prevention is partly drawn from Borden, F. (1993). *USA Bowling silver level coaching manual.* Greendale, WI: USA Bowling, Appendix B. [A revised manual will be issued by the USBC in 2006.]
29. The United States Anti-Doping Agency (2005). *I.O.C. prohibited classes of substances and prohibited methods of doping.* Colorado Springs, CO: US Anti-Doping Agency.
30. Edwards, J. (1998, December). I resolve . . . to bowl better in 1999. *Bowling Digest, 16*(5), 34.
31. Lasser, E. (1998, June). The emotional approach: An interview with Parker Bohn III, Part II. *Bowling This Month, 5*(6), 6.
32. Excerpted and adapted from Condron, B. (1994). Interview tips for athletes and coaches. In *USOC public relations handbook* (pp.42-43). Colorado Springs, CO: USOC Media and Public Relations Division.
33. List of limitations adapted from Martens, R. (1993). *Coaches guide to sport psychology.* Champaign, IL: Human Kinetics, p. 56. (The solutions are our own.)
34. United States Olympic Committee. (1998). *United States Olympic Committee Coaching Ethics Code.* Colorado Springs, CO: USOC.
35. Edwards. J. (1998, August). They hold the future in their hands. *Bowling Digest, 16*(3), 49.
36. In particular, the work of Ronald E. Smith & Frank L. Smoll and that of Maureen R. Weiss.
37. Youth Sport Task Force of the National Association of Sport and Physical Education (1979). *Bill of Rights for Young Athletes.*
38. See Lasser, E. (2003). How couples can survive and thrive bowling together. *American Bowler, 3*(4), 6. Examples of couples successfully bowling together are also provided in the issue.
39. Lasser, E. (1995, April). Fred meets Huck Finn. *USA Coach,* p. 8.

Photo/Illustration Credits

Page 16 photo of Carolyn Dorin-Ballard courtesy of H.H. Brown Media Lab. Reprinted with permission.

Page 252 photo of Anne Marie Duggan courtesy of Fred Borden. Reprinted with permission.

Page 288, 297, and 308 photos by Eric Lasser. Reprinted with permission.

Page 338 photo by Frank Haxton. Reprinted with permission.

Page 345 photo of Chris Barnes courtesy of Sleeping Dogs Communications. Photograph by Bill Vint. Reprinted with permission.

All other photos courtesy of United States Bowling Congress. Reprinted with permission.

Page 187 illustration by Maurice LaRochelle. Reprinted with permission.

All other illustrations by award-winning bowling cartoonist Walt Steinsiek. Reprinted with permission.

Index

Acknowledgments

We wish to credit and thank the following people for their meaningful contributions to this book:

The PBA, PWBA, FIQ, and USBC staffs, who so readily provided essential information.

These professional bowlers and elite coaches for kindly offering personal observations: Kim Adler, Chris Barnes, Lynda Barnes, Parker Bohn III, Pat Costello, Dave Davis, Carolyn Dorin-Ballard, Cathy Dorin-Lizzi, Ann Marie Dugan, Marshall Holman, Kelly Kulick, Mike Lastowski, Carol Norman, Johnny Petraglia, Kim Terrell, Tammy Turner, and Del Warren.

Walt Steinsiek and Maurice LaRochelle, for their fine illustrations.

Susan Shapiro. Her work on manuscript preparation went beyond the call of duty and was essential to the book. Kathy Tamalonis, Ginger Tully, and Patty Tsikos for their word processing skills.

Gordon Vadakin, Michael Sachs, Susie Reichley, and two other reviewers, for their detailed and expert feedback.

Chuck Pezzano, for verifying statistics, historical perspective, and insightful suggestions.

Mark Miller, who confirmed a range of facts, advised us on media-related matters, and provided photographs through the USBC offices.

Rod Ross, for his expertise concerning high-tech training tools.

Bill Spigner and Jon Eiss, for readily helping with our marketing research as well as welcomed input and support through the years. Bowlers across six states who volunteered to participate in that research.

Jim Mansfield, Jim Comedy, and Shelly Siegenthaler of Stonehedge in Akron, Ohio, who came through for us in countless ways.

Ken Yokobosky, for his unstinting support and overall assistance.

Andrew Gentile, whose encouragement and wisdom were a pillar. Peter Knobler—an accomplished author and editor, he flawlessly fielded key questions. Paul Coopersmith—the timely input of this wordsmith made a difference. Paul Jayson, a great coach and teacher, for his perspective on life skills. Tony Seymour, for his trusted legal counsel.

Saul Pavlin, whose knowledge of families remains unsurpassed. Stan and Diane Greenwald, for their expert advice concerning relaxation techniques and stress management in general. Larry Greene, for valued feedback when it mattered most and for being so generous with his time.

Cindy Slater, Kirsten Peterson, and Peggy Manter at the US Olympic Training Center, for assisting with references and other research.

John Kolvenbach and Henry Leyva, clutch performers on stage, screen, and the green, for their comments about specific mental game techniques. Eliza McLane of CPP, Inc., for facilitating our use of material concerning the MBTI® instrument. Bill Hoffman, Barry Schwartz, Ted Skeneky, and Katie Thomas, for their savvy marketing ideas.

The USBC's Barb Weitzer, Sue Jarvis, Dawn Emmrich, Jan Schmidt, Judy Santarius, Pat Winkels, and Kevin Hazaert, for essential assistance with photographs seen throughout the book. Bobby Dinkins of the PBA, for his recommendations concerning photographs.

Peter B. Wilday, architect of the National Bowling Stadium, the NBS's Catrina Barr, and staff of the Reno-Sparks Convention & Visitors Authority and the Nevada Museum of Art, for efforts to secure an image of "America Goes Bowling." Gail Demarest Wilday, for creating that dynamic and moving work of art. Frank Haxton, who photographed the sculpture, and Becky Murway, for her expertise in its digital processing. (Digiman Photography)

Michael Mullin, for providing diverse information on a timely basis. Steve Kloempkin, Michael Nyitray, Michael Slatky, Jose Zambrano, Robin Moyer, Robert Esposito, and Frank Bellinder—these outstanding bowlers contributed to key segments of the book.

USA Bowling officers who backed the educational programs in sport psychology and the inclusion of a sport psychologist on Team USA's coaching staff. Among these were Jerry Koenig (as FIQ President/USA Bowling's Executive Director) and Kevin Dornberger (now USBC General Counsel and Director of Team USA), who also assisted us with statistics.

Bob Maki, Cary Pon, and Tom Lemkuhl. As directors of the NGB's coaching program, they were instrumental to launching the basic and advanced (gold-level) training programs in sport psychology. They also facilitated the sport psychologist's involvement with Team USA. Janet Huss—her administrative talents were centrally important to the success of USA Bowling's coaching certification program (now the USBC program). Donna Partika, for coordinating the sport psychologist's activities during the annual training week at the US Olympic Training Center. Mention is also due those coaches who effectively promoted the *Sport Psychology for Coaches and Athletes* training program in their region.

Jim Goodwin, Bill Veint, Rorie Gillespie, and Bob Summerville. These publishers/editors have collaborated with us to advance sport psychology education for bowlers.

The following sport psychologists for the trails they've blazed and the kindnesses shown: Carole Oglesby, Ken Ravizza, Dan Gould, Sean McCann, Burt Giges, Bonnie Berger, Kate Hayes, Richard Suinn, Leonard Zaichkowsky, Anysley Smith, Robert Singer, Al Petipas, Andy Meyers, Steve Danish, Jerry May, Jim Taylor, Carol Cogan, Ed Etzel, Wayne Hurr, Judy Van Raalte, John Raglin, Steve Heyman, John Silva, Robin Vealey, Damon Burton, Rob Stainback, Jim Whelan, Rich Gordin, Betty Kelly, and Dave Yukelson.

Sue Borden, Nancy and Mike Federonich, Helen Jones, and John Borden; John and Marj Edwards and the Edwards clan, including Bryan Viator, Chip Zielke, and Denny Schreiner; Pauline Lasser, Karen Lasser, Josh Lasser-Freeman, and Jed Lasser. The best teammates three authors could have.

FIT's superlative staff: in particular, Andrew Ostrow for his publishing commitment; Corey Madsen for his copyediting prowess; and Joe Frontiera for his comprehensive marketing efforts.

Shane Murphy, for his vision and guidance, for his professionalism and knowledge, and for creating this opportunity.

The bowling athletes and coaches with whom it has been a privilege to work and who taught us so much. The bowling "family" around the globe—it has given us teammates, colleagues, friends, and inspiration. The sport of bowling which we cherish.

Author Biographies

Eric S. Lasser, Ph.D. has played a pioneering role in the application of sport psychology to bowling. Original contributions include serving as Team USA's team psychologist, as sport psychologist for the National Governing Body (NGB), and as sport psychology consultant to a pro staff (Brunswick). His training programs, workshops, and presentations for athletes and coaches, various columns, and the scope of his one-to-one consultations from youth to professional ranks have represented noteworthy educational steps for the sport.

Dr. Lasser received his doctorate in psychology from New York University. His experience as a clinical psychologist encompasses positions in federal, state, and private sector facilities in the roles of executive (three directorships), clinician, supervisor, and educator. He has been a member of NYU's graduate school faculty and holds a certificate in substance abuse treatment awarded by the College of Professional Psychology of the American Psychological Association (APA). Dr. Lasser has provided sport psychology services for over 20 years in over 20 sports to athletes and their families, coaches, teams, and organizations. His work in sport psychology has been seen on TV in the US and in Europe. Dr. Lasser has been his national team's psychologist for 12 years and a consultant to bowlers on all the pro tours. Under the auspices of the NGB, he developed the *Sport Psychology for Coaches and Athletes* program and has taught it across the country. He also has developed and taught an advanced course in sport psychology for coaches seeking the NGB's gold level coaching certification. His articles have been read by bowlers around the globe.

Professional affiliations include the Association for the Advancement of Applied Sport Psychology (Certified Consultant), the American College of Sports Medicine, and APA's Division of Exercise and Sport Psychology. He is a fellow of the American Orthopsychiatric Association and a member of the US Olympic Committee's Sport Psychology Registry. He serves on the Board of Directors of the Kindness Counts Foundation whose aim is "Helping adults help kids in youth sports and life."

Dr. Lasser's offices are located in Manhattan and Tenafly, New Jersey.

Fred Borden enjoys icon status in the world of bowling with good reason. For some 40 years, he has been the gold standard with respect to coaching accomplishments and overall contributions to the sport's development.

A gifted athlete (achievements include a 300 game at the 1990 ABC Championships), Coach Borden chose to dedicate his career to making others great. During his two tenures as Team USA Head Coach, he recorded a long series of successes on the world stage from the Pan Am Games to the World Championships to the World Team Challenge. He continuously provides consultation to the game's top stars and has been a consultant to multiple pro staffs and the PBA. He has published 14 books, created numerous instructional videos, and taught bowling in over 50 countries. He designed and wrote the National Governing Body's Original Coaching Certification Program and was its chief instructor for many years.

Coach Borden is the proprietor of Stonehedge Place, a 48-lane bowling center in Akron, Ohio, which several times hosted the PBA Touring Players Championship and the ABC Senior Masters. His innovations include various items of bowling equipment and invention of glow-in-the-dark Lunar Bowling. He has often provided color commentary during bowling telecasts and is regularly interviewed by the media. He is a partner in the recently formed Legends bowling ball company and the senior partner in the newly launched MyBowlingCoach.com, an educational website covering all aspects of bowling. Coach Borden has vigorously advocated for sport psychology education, reflected in his inviting a psychologist to work with Team USA and the NGB. He was twice selected the United States Olympic Committee's Coach of the Year for Bowling. He has served on the NGB's Board of Directors and been inducted into five Halls of Fame, including the USBC Hall of Fame.

Jeri Edwards made history in 2004 as the first female head coach of Team USA (comprised of men's and women's squads). Her first two years at the helm have been Bordenesque. Team USA performed strongly  at all international events with golds won at the Tenpin Team Cup, Women's World Championship, American Zone Championships, and Bowling World Cup.

Coach Edwards' appointment followed a highly successful tenure as a Team USA coach and the head coach of Junior Team USA. This gold certified coach (credentialed by the National Governing Body) first gained acclaim as a competitor. She was the Illinois State High School Champion, enjoyed an illustrious collegiate career at Penn State, was a WIBC National Team Champion, and won a professional title in her only full-time year on the tour.

Coach Edwards was a featured writer at *Bowling Digest* and then an editor there. She appears as the co-host in several series of educational videos and has co-authored two texts. She provides instruction throughout the US through the Borden/Edwards School of Bowling. For several years she was co-tournament director for two PBA events, is a former president of the Akron Bowling Proprietors Association, and has served on the ABC Board of Directors. She is also a partner in MyBowlingCoach.com.

Coach Borden describes Coach Edwards in these words: "She is one of the foremost coaches in the world, male or female. She has a unique combination of being able to listen and analyze and communicate back to students exactly what they need to do to improve regarding biomechanics, equipment, lane play adjustments, and the mental game. She has a great grasp of what coaches need to know to relate to athletes."